CONFESSION AND MISSION,
WORD AND SACRAMENT

CONFESSION AND MISSION, WORD AND SACRAMENT

THE ECCLESIAL THEOLOGY OF WILHELM LÖHE

DAVID C. RATKE

SAINT LOUIS

Copyright © 2001 David C. Ratke
Published by Concordia Publishing House
3558 S. Jefferson Avenue, St. Louis, MO 63118-3968
Manufactured in the United States of America

Library of Congress Cataloging-in-Publication Data

Ratke, David C.
    Confession and mission, Word and sacrament : the ecclesial theology of Wilhelm Lohe / David C. Ratke.
        p.   cm.
    Includes bibliographical references.
    ISBN 0-570-03319-5
    1. Church. 2. Lutheran Church—Doctrines. 3. Lohe, Wilhelm, 1808–1872. I. Title.
  BX8065.3 .R37 2001
  262'.041'092—dc21

00-011890

1   2   3   4   5   6   7   8   9   10   10   09   08   07   06   05   04   03   02   01

TO
NOELLE

CONTENTS

ABBREVIATIONS

AC   Augsburg Confession.

ACW   Ancient Christian Writers. 1946–.

Apol.   Apology of the Augsburg Confession

BC   *The Book of Concord: The Confessions of the Evangelical Lutheran Church.* Edited by Theodore Tappert. Philadelphia: Fortress, 1959.

CD   *Christian Dogmatics.* 2 vols. Edited by Carl E. Braaten and Robert W. Jenson. Philadelphia: Fortress, 1984.

Deinzer Johannes Deinzer, *Wilhelm Löhes Leben: Aus seinem schriftlichen Nachlaß zusammengestellt.* 3 vols. 4th ed. Neuendettelsau: Freimund-Verlag, 1935.

FC   Formula of Concord

GW   Wilhelm Löhe, *Gesammelte Werke.* Edited by Klaus Ganzert. 7 vols. Neuendettelsau: Freimund-Verlag, 1951–86.

GWE   Wilhelm Löhe, *Gesammelte Werke: Ergänzungsreihe.* Vol. 1, *Abendmahlspredigten (1866).* Neuendettelsau: Freimund-Verlag, 1991.

LC   Large Catechism. Quotations from the Large Catechism are from *The Book of Concord.* Edited by Theodore Tappert. Philadelphia: Fortress, 1959.

LW   Martin Luther. *Luther's Works.* American Edition. General editors Jaroslav Pelikan and Helmut T. Lehmann. 56 vols. St. Louis: Concordia, and Philadelphia: Fortress, 1955–86.

TRE   *Theologische Realenzyklopädie.* Edited by G. Krause and G. Müller. Berlin, 1977–.

RGG   *Religion in Geschichte und Gegenwart.* Edited by K. Galling. 7 vols. 3d ed. Tübingen, 1957–65.

SC   Small Catechism. Quotations from the Small Catechism are from *The Book of Concord.* Edited by Theodore Tappert. Philadelphia: Fortress, 1959.

PREFACE

As the third millennium dawns, Christendom is faced with a bewildering future. Among the issues that seem foremost on the church's agenda are those of mission and proclamation, of ecumenism and confessionalism, of tradition and contemporaneity. These are issues that particularly concerned Wilhelm Löhe. Although he lived 150 years ago, Löhe deserves to be heard on these issues. Despite his extensive writings on and consideration of these key topics, Löhe has often been overlooked or neglected on these—and, indeed, on other—issues.

Löhe literature is to be found in both English and German. The most striking thing about the secondary literature in English is the relative lack of it. James Schaaf's excellent dissertation on Löhe's relation to American Lutheranism is the first of six doctoral dissertations to appear in either German or English since the end of World War II.[1] The other three English dissertations are those of Erich Heintzen, Kenneth Korby, and Thomas Schattauer. Of these four dissertations, two are strictly historical in character and the other two are in the field of practical theology. No book-length study of Löhe has attempted to examine his theology or any dimension of it.[2] John Tietjen wrote an enthusiastic S.T.M. thesis on Löhe's ecclesiology, but it is handicapped by the unavailability of a critical edition of Löhe's works at that time.[3] The second historical dissertation, that of Erich Heintzen, explores the relationship between Löhe and the Missouri Synod.[4] The two dissertations by Korby and Schattauer deal respectively with Löhe's pastoral and liturgical theology.[5] These four dissertations and master's theses mark the extent of extended treatments of Löhe in English.

There are a number of smaller article-length treatments of specific aspects of Löhe, his theology, and his historical significance. Of particular notice is the work of Walter Conser Jr., which outlines the main themes of his useful doctoral dissertation. His dissertation is a study of conservative responses to the question of the relationship between church and state. Conser provides a fine historical treatment of Löhe and his involvement in the confessional struggles beginning in the 1840s.[6] Other articles include those by the authors of the dissertations mentioned above. One addition demands notice. Todd Nichol of Luther Seminary in St. Paul, Minnesota, has written an enlightening analysis of the influence of Löhe on the development of the ordained ministry in the Iowa Synod.[7] In general, relatively few articles about Löhe exist in English. The primary reason for this is likely that Löhe, while being important to the formation of at least three Lutheran bodies in the United States (not to mention Australia and Canada), was never a central player or the main character in the cast. He lost battles with the Ohio Synod over the direction of that body and its seminary and with the Missouri Synod over the nature of the ordained ministry and its relationship to the congregation. By the time of the formation of the Iowa Synod and Wartburg Seminary, he had withdrawn from active involvement in American missions and Lutheranism. So while his voice is always in the background of American Lutheranism, it is never a primary voice.

Löhe's overlooked and unnoticed contribution to American Lutheranism is perhaps best seen in the number of his works which have been translated into English. The single contemporary and critical translation of any of Löhe's voluminous works is that of Schaaf's 1969 translation of *Three Books about the Church* [*Drei Bücher von der Kirche*]. Löhe wrote two other books specifically for the American setting (in German) which were translated at the turn of the century under the direction of Edward Horn. These two books, *Liturgy for Christian Congregations of the Lutheran Faith* and *Questions and Answers to the Six Parts of the Small Catechism of Dr. Martin Luther*, have recently been reprinted by Repristination Press in Fort Wayne.[8] One other devotional book, *Seedgrains of Prayer*, which was translated by Horn, has not been reprinted.

The situation with respect to the literature in German is quite different. For primary literature, Löhe research has been greatly aided by the completion of the complete works of Löhe, edited by Klaus Ganzert.[9] I hesitate to be too negative about this project, but a few comments are necessary here. It has been published in the difficult-to-read Gothic typeface (*Frakturschrift*). Indeed, it has been noted by one commentator that on the basis of its importance and continuing relevance, *Drei Bücher von der Kirche* really ought to be reprinted in a study edition with commentary.[10] It contains numerous typographical errors[11] and no index to the works.[12] Moreover, no table of contents exists for the entire series. If one wants to find a specific essay or article by Löhe, one must search through the table of contents of each of the volumes. Finally, the editing is arbitrary. This is especially apparent in the first two volumes containing the diaries and letters of Löhe. The scholar interested in matters other than Löhe's ecclesiology and relationship to the Bavarian church and to the secular authorities encounters a number of difficulties in the *Gesammelte Werke*. Those interested, for example, in Löhe's missionary activity in North America will often be frustrated. Much of the material relating to Löhe's North American mission activity is omitted.[13] In fact, some of this material is to be found in the *Gesammelte Werke*, but one must search it out in the editorial notes which are to be found at the end of each volume. These drawbacks aside, the *Gesammelte Werke* mark a valuable and important contribution to Löhe studies, as well as to the study of the confessional movement in the nineteenth century, to missiology, ecclesiology, and all fields of practical theology.

An important work which does not strictly fall into the category of primary literature, but clearly is not secondary literature, is Johannes Deinzer's three-volume biography of Löhe.[14] This biography is an ordered collection of Löhe's journal entries and personal and professional correspondence interspersed with helpful commentary to clarify things where ambiguity and confusion threaten. Deinzer's opus is the only exhaustive account of the life of Löhe and as such is invaluable to Löhe research.

With three exceptions, no monographs have been dedicated entirely to Löhe since Hans Kreßel published the last of his biographical studies in 1960. In 1992, Werner Ost published a popular account of Löhe and his thought.[15] Löhe's understanding of the congregation is the subject of a second monograph: Gerhard Schoenauer's dissertation, which was submitted to the theological faculty in Erlangen.[16] A monograph which is now quite old but nonetheless valuable is Siegfried Hebart's 1939 study of Löhe's ecclesiology.[17] Christian Weber's dissertation, submitted to the theology faculty in Neuendettelsau, *Missionstheologie bei Wilhelm Löhe: Aufbruch zur Kirche der Zukunft*, is an outstanding contribution to Löhe studies. He has read all the published and unpublished works of Löhe, as well as having exhaustively researched the secondary literature. It is a gold mine. These monographs represent the most significant German language treatments of Löhe.

In contrast to the English literature, numerous shorter treatments of Löhe have been written in German. Unfortunately many of these are general, popular summaries of or introductions to Löhe and his thought, but some exceptions exist: Friedrich Kantzenbach, Rudolf Keller, Gerhard Müller, and Martin Wittenberg have each written a number of helpful and illuminating essays on selected aspects of Löhe's thought, as well as his historical and theological significance.

The German literature on Löhe is marked by the excellent availability of edited primary sources. But with respect to monographs, there is a yet even smaller number of works on Löhe. In comparison to English sources, a larger but still limited number of critical, scholarly articles have been written on selected aspects of Löhe and his theology. The field of Löhe studies in general can be characterized as a field that is largely unplowed, and it appears to be a rich and fertile field, promising a good harvest to the dedicated student. In general, the situation with respect to the research on Löhe in English might be summarized by saying that for the most part the best monographs on Löhe have been written in English with good support from a small number of articles.

Since the field of Löhe studies is relatively open, it is my intent to provide an overview of Löhe's theology from the vantage point of his ecclesiology. Clearly it will not be possible to provide a comprehensive overview of Löhe's theology. Like Luther, Löhe tended to address himself to specific situations as they arose.[18] Many gaps remain in his theology. For the most part, he does not address christological questions. He is generally not interested in questions of method or revelation, though he is on occasion, as will be seen. Nonetheless, it is possible to draw a picture of the main contours of his theology. His theology is a theology of the church, a theology oriented toward mission and ministry.[19] Moreover, Löhe's theology, or at least his ecclesiology, was essentially established by the time he completed his theological studies. That is to say that Löhe did not make any radical changes or adjustments to his theology later in life. The foundations were already in place in his earlier writings.[20] As noted above, the only monographs that are dedicated to Löhe are on Löhe's understanding of the congregation and some other historical treatments of Löhe's mission efforts in America. Siegfried Hebart's outstanding study of Löhe's ecclesiology is, as mentioned, more than fifty years old and is somewhat handicapped by the unavailability of a critical edition of Löhe's works. Historical treatments of Löhe, though in short supply, are available; up-to-date theological treatments of Löhe are nonexistent. My intention is to fill this gap by providing a general overview of Löhe's theology, especially as it relates to ecclesiology and, secondarily, mission and ministry.

Löhe was keenly interested in undergirding theological praxis and dedicated himself to working out the theological dimensions and implications of those problems that arose in the day-to-day activity of mission and ministry. It is my contention that Löhe is still of interest in the early years of the third millennium. Today, as yesterday, the church is concerned with ministry and mission. The church is particularly interested in ministry and mission in a pluralistic context, a context marked by a pluralism of language, culture, ethnicity, and denominational (or confessional, as Löhe might phrase it) adherence. Of course, Löhe's "world" was much smaller than ours; he addressed himself to a Western context. We can no longer ignore the thought and culture of the East, which seems so foreign and strange to us. This strangeness is what binds us to Löhe and Löhe to the contemporary context. How does the church proclaim its message in a world that is clearly not homogeneous, a world that is pluralistic? These are questions with which Löhe struggled and questions which will help determine Löhe's contribution to the church.

The preface to any work would be incomplete without acknowledging those who have contributed to its successful completion. First and foremost, I must express my grateful thanks to my wife. Noelle helped proofread the entire manuscript in its dissertation form. She is not a theologian and, as far as I know, does not aspire to be one. Her comments and questions were sometimes frustratingly difficult to answer but always necessary. Even more than her questions and proofreading, I am grateful for and humbled by the gift of her companionship. This book was originally submitted as a dissertation to the University of Regensburg. To my *Doktorvater*, Hans Schwarz, I must also express my gratitude. He first suggested Löhe as part of a different project. I rejected the project, but the project did suggest to me the possibility of doing something on Löhe. Professor Schwarz never gave up on me, even when my progress must have seemed aggravatingly slow. No work is completed in isolation. Martin Rothgangel encouraged me often and guided me through German academia. Thanks also to other doctoral students who worked under Hans Schwarz at that time. I hesitate to name them individually for fear that I might omit someone. My conversations with these classmates sharpened me and whetted my appetite for further theological reflection. Thanks finally to Ken Wagener, my editor at Concordia Publishing House. Ken believed in me and this project and without him this manuscript would not have seen the light of day.

NOTES

1   James L. Schaaf, "Wilhelm Löhe's Relation to the American Church: A Study in the History of Lutheran Mission" (D. Theol. diss., Heidelberg, 1961).

2   One exception is the Finnish study of Löhe's ecclesiology printed with a German summary at the end: Matti Sihvonen, *Jumalan Kaunein Kukka: Wilhelm Löhen*

kirkkokäsitys. Zusammenfassung: "Die schönste Blume Gottes: Wilhelm Löhes Auffassung von der Kirche" (Helsinki: n.p., 1980).

3   John H.Tietjen, "The Ecclesiology of Wilhelm Loehe" (S.T.M. thesis, Union Theological Seminary, New York, 1954).

4   Erich Hugo Heintzen, "Wilhelm Löhe and the Missouri Synod" (Ph.D. diss., University of Illinois at Urbana-Champaign, 1964).

5   Kenneth Korby, "The Theology of Pastoral Care in Wilhelm Loehe with Special Attention to the Function of the Liturgy and the Laity" (Th.D. diss., Lutheran School of Theology at Chicago, 1976); and Thomas Schattauer, "Announcement, Confession, and Lord's Supper in the Pastoral-Liturgical Work of Wilhelm Loehe: A Study of Worship and Life in the Lutheran Parish at Neuendettelsau, Bavaria, 1838–1872" (Ph.D. diss., University of Notre Dame, 1990).

6   Walter Conser Jr., *Church and Confession: Conservative Theologians in Germany, England, and America 1815–1866* (Macon, GA: Mercer University Press, 1984); and Walter Conser Jr., "A Conservative Critique of Church and State: The Case of the Tractarians and Neo-Lutherans," *Journal of Church and State* 25 (1983): 193–210.

7   Todd Nichol, "Wilhelm Löhe, the Iowa Synod and the Ordained Ministry," *Lutheran Quarterly* n.s. 4 (1990): 11–29.

8   Wilhelm Loehe, *Liturgy for Christian Congregations of the Lutheran Faith* (ed. J. Deinzer; trans. F. C. Longaker with an introduction by Edward T. Horn; Newport, KY: n.p., 1902; repr., Fort Wayne, IN: Repristination Press, 1995); and Wilhelm Loehe, *Questions and Answers to the Six Parts of the Small Catechism of Dr. Martin Luther* (2d ed.; trans. Edward T. Horn; Columbia, SC: W. J. Duffie, 1893; repr., Fort Wayne, IN: Repristination Press, 1993).

9   Wilhelm Löhe, *Gesammelte Werke* (ed. Klaus Ganzert; 7 vols.; Neuendettelsau: Freimund-Verlag, 1951–86).

10 Rudolf Keller, "Wilhelm Löhe im Spiegel seiner Briefe: Zum Abschluß von Löhes GW," *Zeitschrift für bayerische Kirchengeschichte* 56 (1987): 282. I would add that it should be printed in standard typeface.

11 C. F. W. Walther is repeatedly printed as K. F. W. Walther; see, for example, *GW* II: 42, 182.

12 Christian Weber helpfully provided both a chronological and an alphabetical table of contents in his study of Löhe's theology of mission: *Missionstheologie bei Wilhelm Löhe: Aufbruch zur Kirche der Zukunft* (Gütersloh: Gütersloher Verlagshaus, 1996), 444–63.

13 The content of omitted text is indicated by normal typeface and the text of the letters themselves are indicated by italic typeface, thus omitted text is quickly determined. For example, the "Brief an Friedrich Wucherer" (6 December 1842), *GW* I: 620, notes the omitted contents thus: "was in der NA-Sache getan hat, von kleinen Kreisen, die monatlich Beiträge für die Mission geben." Other examples of omitted text regarding mission activity in North America include: "Brief an Georg Güttler" (24 December 1842), *GW* I: 622; "Brief an Karl von Raumer" (29 January 1843), *GW* I: 625; "Brief an Karl von Raumer" (21 February 1843), *GW* I: 626; and "Brief an Friedrich Wucherer" (13 March 1843), *GW* I: 629–30.

14 Johannes Deinzer, *Wilhelm Löhes Leben: Aus seinem schriftlichen Nachlaß zusammengestellt* (3 vols.; 4th ed.; Neuendettelsau: Freimund-Verlag, 1935).

15 Werner Ost, *Wilhelm Löhe: Sein Leben und sein Ringen um eine apostolische Kirche* (Neuendettelsau: Freimund-Verlag, 1992).

16 Gerhard Schoenauer, *Kirche lebt vor Ort: Wilhelm Löhes Gemeindeprinzip als Widerspruch gegen kirchliche Großorganisation* (Stuttgart: Calver, 1990).

17 Siegfried Hebart, *Wilhelm Löhes Lehre von der Kirche, ihrem Amt und Regiment* (Neuendettelsau: Freimund-Verlag, 1939).

18 Löhe admitted that he was not a systematician and that his writings are oriented to situations as they arose: "Ich bin kein Mann der Wissenschaft, ich schreibe nicht systematisch; Briefe sind es, die Du bekommen sollst und die Folge derselben wird weit mehr von gelegentlichen Ursachen abhangen, als von der Disposition, die etwa eine Abhandlung hätte" ("Kirchliche Briefe," *GW* V/2: 844). Gerhard Rau, *Pastoraltheologie: Untersuchungen zur Geschichte und Struktur einer Gattung praktischer Theologie* (Munich: Christian Kaiser Verlag, 1970), 204, argues that "Löhe is a theologian in so far as theology includes intentional, conscious ecclesial actions, in so far as theology also encompasses the knowledge of the past and the present as well as the wisdom, knowledge, and breadth of life."

19 Hebart writes that the church is at the center of Löhe's thinking and ministry and that his ecclesiology cannot be easily separated from his activity (*Wilhelm Löhes Lehre*, 6–7).

20 See Hebart, *Wilhelm Löhes Lehre*, 39, who agrees, though the divisions in his book (organized chronologically) would suggest otherwise. See also Martin George, "In der Kirche leben: Eine Gegenüberstellung der Ekklesiologie Wilhelm Löhes und Aleksej Chomjakovs," *Kerygma und Dogma* 31 (1985): 216.

1

Biography and Historical Background

Birth and Family

On February 21, 1808, in the midst of the Napoleonic era, Johann Konrad Wilhelm Löhe was born in the city of Fürth near Nuremberg. He died nearly sixty-four years later in the farming village of Neuendettelsau on January 2, 1872. He lived the greatest part of his life—more than thirty-four years—in Franconia, in a small village of fewer than a thousand inhabitants.[1] Yet in this village, where he was removed from the large churches of Nuremberg and the sanctuaries of ecclesial power, Löhe had an impact upon liturgy, the Confessional movement, missions, and the relationship between church and state, not only in Bavaria, but in lands far-removed from Neuendettelsau.

Löhe grew up in the city of his birth, Fürth, an industrial and manufacturing center, in a middle-class home typical of the citizens of that city.[2] The faith and the piety of the Löhe family was not typical of their neighbors. The faith predominant in the first third of the nineteenth century in Bavaria was influenced to a large degree by the Enlightenment of the eighteenth century and its rationalistic and deistic elements. The Löhe family clung to a brand of faith more in keeping with an anachronistic and distant past than with the contemporary milieu. It was a faith influenced by sixteenth century Lutheran Orthodoxy, as well as seventeenth century Pietism.[3] The faith and piety of the Löhe family was noticeably out of step with that of their more enlightened neighbors. Pietism was also an important influence on Löhe, though its effects were more like that of an underground river which only later sprung forth from the depths of his faith and theology.[4] The faith of Löhe's childhood cannot be easily separated from the adult theology of the pastor and churchman in Neuendettelsau.

EDUCATION

Although the Löhe household was one where Pietism held sway, it was the Enlightenment with its rationalism that was dominant at school and at church. Rationalism was the first important influence on Löhe's formal religious instruction. At church and school the young pupil was introduced to deism with its emphasis on morality. As an adult Löhe decisively rejected the rationalist faith, but while he was still young, it exercised considerable influence upon him, especially in his prayer and devotional life.[5] But the Enlightenment was not able to retain its grip for long. Löhe attended the Melanchthon-*Gymnasium* in Nuremberg. The rector of the *gymnasium*, Karl Ludwig Roth, had an enduring influence on the pupil from Fürth.[6] Already as a young man, Löhe exhibited a conspicuous tendency to solitude which nonetheless did not prevent him from being sociable. His isolation often caused him to suffer at school and moved him to protest against societal conventions. Earnestness and seriousness were to be features of his personality throughout his life.[7]

Immediately after completing his studies at the gymnasium in Nuremberg, Löhe went to Erlangen, where he began theological studies in winter semester 1826–27. Löhe had wanted to be a pastor from the time he was a child. In Erlangen he came into contact with Christian Krafft and the writings of David Hollaz. Krafft, a Reformed professor, introduced Löhe to *Erweckungstheologie* (Theology of Awakening or Revival Theology). Löhe was not so much influenced by Krafft's thinking as by his intellect or spirit, as were Adolf von Hoffmann, J. C. K. Harless, and others.[8] Krafft inspired Löhe to read in dogmatic theology more deeply. His studies in dogmatic theology led him to the writings of David Hollaz, the last great dogmatician of Lutheran Orthodoxy. Hollaz, a professor of dogmatic theology in the eighteenth century, impressed upon the young theology student a deep appreciation for the Lutheran faith.[9] This faith was not necessarily that of Luther or even of the Confessions, but rather of Lutheran Orthodoxy.

In the summer semester of 1828, Löhe went to Berlin to hear lectures from the most prestigious theology faculty in Germany at that time. He heard lectures from Hegel as well as Schleiermacher. Hegel failed to impress him. In an entry in his journal (August 8), Löhe wrote that he attended a lecture of Hegel's in which he understood nothing and in which there was nothing to understand.[10] Schleiermacher, on the other hand, impressed him. Löhe was especially influenced by Schleiermacher's style of preaching.[11] As it was, Schleiermacher's preaching was not enough to overcome the strange and unfamiliar city with its incomprehensible philosophers and worldly students. Löhe returned to the familiarity of Franconia and its theology faculty at Erlangen.

Already during this period of studies at Erlangen, Löhe's shift away from rationalism can be readily detected. In a paper submitted to the faculty in 1829, he stated that pastors are God's stewards and co-workers whose task it is to proclaim God's honor and announce the resurrection of humanity.[12] Implicit in this understanding of the pastoral office is the rejection of the notion that God's honor is self-evident within creation; the glory of God must be actively and intentionally proclaimed. This task was neither light nor easy. It was not a task that once it was set in motion it would then run by force of its own inertia (*á la* the deistic prime mover theory) and be carried through to completion. The task of proclaiming the glory of God may not be light, but an important promise is attached to it— the promise of the Holy Spirit. Löhe had clearly and decisively left the Enlightenment behind.

Löhe completed his theological studies and passed his theological examinations in 1830. He was ordained on July 25, 1831, in Ansbach. In preparation for his ordination, he read the confessional writings, in particular the Augsburg Confession, several times. He decided that the Scriptures were properly understood in the Confessions.[13] He could, in good conscience, be ordained a pastor and teacher of the Lutheran church. Löhe's ordination was significant for another reason. Löhe always had a strong evangelical sense of mission. As a student at the university, he organized a mission society and distributed religious tracts.[14] On the day of his ordination, he prayed that he would receive a sign, a word, from the mouth of God. He opened his Bible and three times he was confronted with the commissioning text in Isa 6:8–10; the passage speaks of going out to the people with a message that they will not hear. Löhe responded, "Here I am, Lord, send me."[15] This sense of service in the work of mission and proclamation was a predominant motif in Löhe's own piety and in what he asked of others.

MINISTRY

In October 1831, Löhe began his internship in Kirchenlamitz (not far from the present border of the Czech Republic). Already he was an accomplished preacher who drew unusually large audiences, but his biblical and confessional radicalism also found enemies. From the beginning of his ministry, he urged for a stricter church discipline.[16] In 1834 he was recalled on account of his conflicts with more "sober" parishioners, colleagues, and overseers.[17] In its official letter of recall, the Consistory charged that Löhe "ruthlessly strived to win others over to his views by his one-sided theological direction."[18] Löhe was nearly universally beloved by his parishioners, but he managed to alienate a few with his attacks on the "social and religious evils he considered rampant in the community."[19] In particular he succeeded in alienating a prominent district judge in the village, who felt personally attacked and responded in kind. First, Löhe was merely reprimanded, but this did not satisfy the judge who wanted Löhe removed from office. Löhe was asked to appear before the *Dekanat* (deanery); he was here confronted with a variety of charges. Some were out-and-out fabrications; others were malicious distortion. Only one had substance: that he was a mystic. It was nearly inevitable that these more "sober" people, who were children of the Enlightenment, would be offended by Löhe who had rejected the Enlightenment in favor of a pietistic, revivalistic, and increasingly confessional agenda.

Regardless of whether Löhe had abused his authority and whether he had been unfairly accused by these sober people in the congregation with more of a rationalist or deist bent, he was unlikely to persuade the ecclesiastical authorities of his innocence. The church hierarchy and bureaucracy at that time was dominated by rationalists and unionists and would remain so for another decade until the Confessionalists (Löhe among them) gained the ascendancy in the Bavarian church. Löhe must have recognized that the force of his personality and the severity of his theology would always be a source of conflict. He wrote, "So it goes and so it will go with me. I am a knife and who gladly permits him or herself to be cut?"[20] These words of Löhe were prophetic. Because there were more pastors available at that time than congregations able to call them, Löhe had difficulty finding a parish and went from one temporary position to another before receiving and taking a call to Neuendettelsau.

The experience at Kirchelamitz was not all bad. One consequence was that Löhe was asked to write a report for the Upper Consistory in Munich. Then he was asked to personally appear there. The consequence of his report and appearance was that Löhe made such a favorable impression—especially upon Friedrich Roth, the president of the Consistory—that he was offered a temporary position at St. Egidien Church in Nuremberg.[21] This assignment was essentially a vindication of his actions in Kirchenlamitz. Löhe's residency in Nuremberg was successful on many counts. His skills as a preacher developed to their fullest extent, as did his effectiveness in the chancel as a liturgist. The sanctuary was often filled to overflowing when he preached. His preaching was powerful indeed. One time a group of *gymnasium* students came to hear one of his sermons in order to critique it, but they were so dumbstruck by it that they left the worship service without saying a word to one another.[22] Already at this early date, a few of Löhe's sermons were published. The most significant men in the city—Rector Roth, the mayor, and many others—participated in the young vicar's Bible study. Many people in the city were enamored of his charismatic personality and powerful presence, but Löhe made enemies too. He preached uncompromisingly against the evils and ills of urban life. He thus aroused the ire of the *Stadtmagistrat* (city magistrate), who took steps to have Löhe's call to the parish revoked. Many of the well-placed supporters of Löhe tried to plead his case, but it was to no avail. This scenario was to be repeated many times over: affection from the majority; opposition from a sometimes influential and almost always vocal minority.

Löhe's contract at St. Egidien's expired in March 1835. He wrote his second series of theological examinations later that year. Once again he attained the highest grade possible (*"sehr gut; dem Vorzüglichen nahe"*). A gifted student and gifted preacher such as Löhe should have had little difficulty finding a position, even in a time when positions were scarce, but he had little success. Friedrich Höfling, a professor in Erlangen, wanted a Lutheran preacher like Löhe at the university and even went so far as to request him, but it came to nothing. Finally, Löhe received and took a call to Neuendettelsau after a series of temporary assignments, beginning his ministry there on August 1, 1837. Little did he know that he would spend the rest of his life in this small farming village. Indeed, he tried repeatedly to obtain positions in larger cities but was rebuffed on each occasion. After 1848 he resigned himself to being a pastor in the country and did not seek positions elsewhere.

While he was in Nuremberg, Löhe met Helene Andreae, a confirmation student. Three years later, on the sixth anniversary of his ordination, one week before taking up his position in Neuendettelsau, he married his former student. They had four children. Six years after they were married, Löhe's wife died suddenly, leaving him to raise his children alone except for the assistance of his sister who came to live in the parsonage.[23]

NEUENDETTELSAU YEARS

In Neuendettelsau, Löhe did not retire to the life of a quiet, sedate, unassuming country pastor. That would have been easy, but it was not his way. Löhe was a gifted and dedicated pastor. He placed high value on preaching, instruction, and pastoral care. He put much energy into his sermons, writing them all out. Only later in his life did he resort to relying on outlines or preaching extemporaneously. Dedicating himself to an intensive study of liturgy, he slowly but certainly transformed worship life at Neuendettelsau.[24] He held pastoral care and visitation in high regard, and he prayed with and for his parishioners.[25]

In 1840 Löhe read an appeal by Friedrich Wyneken for help in North America. Wyneken was a German Lutheran pastor who had volunteered for missionary service in America and had returned to Germany to raise financial support and recruit volunteers for mission in the New World. The Lutheran church there was in desperate need of pastors and others willing to serve its German community. Almost immediately Löhe wrote an article titled "Die lutherischen Auswanderer in Nordamerika: Eine Ansprache an die Leser des Sonntagsblattes" [The Lutheran Emigrants in North America: An Address to the Readers of the *Sonntagsblatt*] for the *Sonntagsblatt*, edited by his friend and collaborator, Pastor Johann Friedrich Wucherer. Löhe quoted directly and often from the pamphlet written by Wyneken and concluded with an appeal of his own for help for the German brothers and sisters who were wilting without the benefit of spiritual leaders to nourish them with Word and Sacrament in their native tongue.[26] Löhe's article generated a missionary enthusiasm which he had not foreseen. Wucherer and Löhe were flooded with donations. This was the beginning of Löhe's missionary activity.

ACTIVITY IN NORTH AMERICA

At first Löhe and Wucherer did not know what to do with the money that was sent to the *Sonntagsblatt* for the "German mission in North America." The problem was soon solved, though, by the appearance of a volunteer. Adam Ernst was a journeyman shoemaker who had not had the benefit of a *gymnasium* education, which would have prepared him for theological studies at the university. Ernst had been moved by Löhe's appeal and sought ways to serve. After being rebuffed by a mission organization in Dresden, he finally came to Wucherer. Since Ernst was not theologically trained, Wucherer was unsure what to do with this unsolicited volunteer.

Soon he sent Ernst on to Löhe, who decided to instruct Ernst. His idea was to sufficiently instruct Ernst so he could become a schoolteacher in North America, as he did not think that Ernst was sufficiently qualified to be a minister. Soon after, Ernst was joined in his instruction by another volunteer, Georg Burger. These two men were instructed and in 1842 were commissioned for missionary service in North America.

When Ernst and Burger arrived in New York, they were introduced to Friedrich Winkler, who had just accepted a call to become professor at the Evangelical Lutheran Theological Seminary in Columbus, Ohio. The two missionaries were encouraged to go to Columbus and study further to prepare for the ordained ministry since the likelihood of them finding positions as schoolteachers was remote and ordained clergy were urgently needed on the frontier.

This began Löhe's association with the Ohio Synod and its seminary in Columbus. The timing was propitious. The seminary was undergoing difficult times, having trouble finding teachers, and experiencing financial difficulties caused by an ambitious building campaign. Löhe was pleased that Ernst and Burger had found their way to Columbus and were enrolled. He wrote Winkler at the seminary and asked if they would be willing to accept more students like Ernst and Burger (Löhe would cover their costs), as well as books and other necessary materials (Löhe would cover purchases and shipping expenses).[27] In his letter, Löhe also enclosed a request for a statement of faith; he wanted to know if the seminary was confessional. The seminary's response satisfied Löhe that the Ohio Synod and its seminary was sufficiently confessional to justify cooperative efforts; it also gratefully—even eagerly—accepted Löhe's offer of students and books.[28] When the Columbus seminary accepted this offer of students and books, a fruitful, though ultimately painful, relationship between Löhe and the Ohio Synod was established. This became the pattern of Löhe's missionary activity. He trained men, sent them to the United States with instructions to present themselves to an appropriate church, and then supported these men in their studies. He also advocated establishing and funding seminaries. Unfortunately, the relationship between Löhe and the Ohio Synod came to an end in 1845 over questions of confessional integrity. Löhe looked farther west to form another relationship.

Löhe had foreseen the end of the relationship with the Ohio Synod and had made appropriate alternate plans. He instructed his men—Sendlinge or Nothelfer ("sendlings" or "emergency workers")—to approach the Missouri group of whom he had became aware in the time since Ernst and Burger had first arrived in the United States.[29] Löhe's men met in Cleveland and formed a committee to lay plans for the formation of a genuinely Lutheran synod. This committee was charged with the task of going to St. Louis and meeting with C. F. W. Walther to explore the possibility of uniting with the Saxon Lutherans there. At the time of the organizing convention of the "German Evangelical Lutheran Synod of Missouri, Ohio and Other States" in 1847, Löhe's *Sendlinge* comprised more than half of the charter pastors.[30] Löhe became as enthusiastic a supporter of the Missourians as he had been of the Ohioans. He sent men; founded and financially supported the seminary in Fort Wayne; and organized colonies of German Lutheran immigrants in Michigan. His contribution to the growth and development of the Missouri Synod cannot be lightly overlooked: "Löhe's contributions of manpower, money, institutions, and missionary spirit must be reckoned among the infant Synod's most valuable material and spiritual assets."[31] The relationship with the Missouri Synod (like that with the Ohio Synod) was destined to be short-lived. The seeds for its unfortunate end were already present in the beginning at the constituting convention. Löhe was concerned about the congregational polity of the Missouri Synod.[32] This difference in polity would be the cause for the dissolution of the relationship after only seven years.

Once again, Löhe was forced to start anew in North America. Those loyal to Löhe went to Iowa to start again. Most of these were in Michigan and were attached to either the Saginaw Seminary that Löhe had founded or the colonies in that area. The plan was the same. They went to Dubuque, Iowa, to establish a seminary that would be a base for missionary activity among the American Indians in the region, as well as for training pastors for the German immigrants.[33] The one difference in strategy in Iowa was that because it was as yet unclaimed territory among German Lutherans, the Neuendettelsau missionaries formed their own synod. This synod proved to be the independent, moderating voice between the Buffalo and Missouri Synods that Löhe hoped it would be in the dispute over the ordained ministry.[34] The Iowa Synod also proved to be independent of Löhe as well. Löhe never exercised the same influence on that synod, and especially its pastors and seminaries, as he did in the Ohio and Missouri Synods. In part the Iowa Synod chose to act independently of Löhe, and in part he turned to other interests.

CHURCH-STATE STRUGGLES

Löhe was not, however, simply an organizer, supporter, and booster of foreign missionary activity. He was a gifted preacher and published many sermons. He wrote extensively: devotion books, prayer books, instructional books, as well as books on the practice of ministry. The topics of these books on pastoral theology ranged from liturgics to pastoral care to church discipline and order. Löhe was deeply concerned about and involved in the question of the identity of the church in Germany.[35] What was its confessional identity? What should its relationship be to the state? to other confessions? Löhe was a man of deep faith and convictions; it was his faith that had led him to respond to Wyneken's appeal for help in the American mission field. His convictions also led him into a bitter struggle with church authorities.

Although Löhe was deeply influenced by the Pietism of the preceding century, he was not one to conceal his deeply felt Lutheran confessionalism. His abiding principle was to make "the invisible church as visible as possible."[36] He had hoped that with the Revolution of 1848 there might be change in the church, that it might return to its apostolic roots. But these hopes were dashed; everything remained as it was. Löhe even permitted himself to stand as a candidate for the Frankfurt Parliament in 1848; to his relief he was not elected.[37] More important, he wrote almost unceasingly on this issue. In 1845 Löhe published *Drei Bücher von der Kirche* [*Three Books about the Church*] to a warm reception. In it he argued that the Reformation is "complete in doctrine but it is incomplete in the consequences of doctrine."[38] The kneeling controversy (1838–45) was at its height at the time of the writing of *Three Books about the Church*. Ludwig I, king of Bavaria, had been impressed by the French practice whereby soldiers had knelt at Mass and at Corpus Christi processions when the host passed.[39] Ludwig ordered his soldiers to do likewise. Lutherans in Bavaria were outraged, and the nascent confessional movement in Bavaria was spurred to quick response. Protestant soldiers were punished for refusing to kneel, and one pastor was removed from his parish and sentenced to a year in prison for advocating open defiance of the king's order. The controversy threatened to topple the monarch; it was not until 1845 that the king finally heeded the advice of more pragmatic advisors and the crisis passed. Löhe nowhere mentions or alludes to this controversy, but it must have been at the back of his mind as he formulated his arguments for the superiority of the Lutheran church over other confessions.

In *Entwurf eines Katechismus des apostolischen Lebens*, published in 1848, Löhe began to move away from the center of the mainstream of the church (not that he ever was particularly close to the center). He wrote that "confession without discipline has not accomplished what it ought."[40] This year was a fruitful year in terms of Löhe presenting his ecclesiology; he also published "Aphorismen über die neutestamentlichen Ämter und ihr Verhältnis zur Gemeinde." These publications signaled the beginning of his difficulties with the state church.

Löhe was uneasy about the close relationship between the church and the state, calling the relationship between throne and altar an "unhappy mismarriage" which ought to be annulled and that "what God has not joined, goes in opposite directions."[41] He petitioned the Bavarian state church several times in the years following the Revolution of 1848, protesting the union of the Lutheran church with the Reformed church. He even toyed with the idea of leaving the church and joining forces with the burgeoning Lutheran free churches.[42] After visiting a free church, though, he decided that these churches were no more apostolic than what could be attained within the state church.[43] Indeed, if Adolf von Harless had not been named as head of the Bavarian Lutheran Church, Löhe might well have left the *Landeskirche*.[44]

In 1849 Löhe spearheaded a press and letter-writing campaign which succeeded in presenting a petition with more than 330 signatures to the General Synod that year. This petition contained a series of demands, which gave it more the character of an ultimatum than an attempt at reform. The confessionalists were not successful on this front, but they did not lose hope and abandon the campaign. They turned their attention to the Upper Consistory, but again to little or no effect. Now they focused on a complete separation between the Lutheran and Reformed congregations on matters of church and communion fellowship. At this point the Upper Consistory threatened to suspend Löhe and eight other leaders. Popular pressure mounted, and the Upper Consistory was forced to backpedal. After a vote of the Upper Consistory, the official in charge of the case had to reluctantly drop the charges. The threat of a suspension for Löhe and the other confessionalists only served to galvanize the Confessional forces. A suspension would have moved the *Landeskirche* to the brink of a complete rupture. The overreaction of the Upper Consistory was an embarrassing situation for the pastors who were not necessarily close to or sympathetic to Löhe and his ideals. A rupture was avoided and a resolution was effected when King Ludwig I, sensing the threat of a separation, acted quickly and named Adolf von Harless president of the Upper Consistory.

Harless was an excellent choice. He was respected and trusted by both parties—most notably the Löhe party. Immediately the tensions began to subside. A relaxation of the association between the Lutheran and Reformed confessions effectively dissolved the laws enforcing congregational life and the duties of pastors (*Parochialordnung*). An independent Lutheran church body and an independent Reformed church body were created. Other ecclesial reforms were set into motion and gradually carried out. This immediate action, combined with the universal trust in and respect for Harless, served to calm the storm. In 1853 the Bavarian church was renamed the Evangelical Lutheran Church of Bavaria [*Evangelisch-Lutherische Kirche in Bayern*]. With this settlement, Löhe turned his attention to other matters.

A brief but unfortunately sharp and bitter conflict occurred between Löhe and the church authorities over the practice of church discipline, which caused Löhe a two-month suspension in 1860. He had refused to marry a member of his congregation who he felt had unjustly abandoned his wife and divorced her.[45] The member had received the legal right to remarry, but Löhe felt that as an advocate for the poor and defenseless he was obligated, by virtue of his office as pastor, to take a stand. Unfortunately, two demands of this office came into conflict. At that time pastors were the only officials authorized to conduct marriages. This put pastors in the uncomfortable and unenviable position of being legally obligated as officials of the state to conduct marriages. On the other hand, pastors had a divine, or at minimum an ecclesial, obligation to conduct marriages in accordance with Christian teaching. Pastors like Löhe who took their call to the pastoral office more seriously than their duties as officials of the state were bound to run into conflict. And so it happened. Löhe refused to conduct the wedding. The state demanded that he conduct the marriage or be suspended. Löhe refused again and was suspended. The suspension deeply hurt Löhe and signaled the end of his battles with the church authorities and the state.

THE FINAL YEARS—
DIACONAL SERVICE AND INNER MISSION

Löhe focused his attention on a quiet reformation and renewal of the church and dedicated the last decade of his life to realizing his goals within the framework of establishing diaconal orders or associations. In 1849 he was instrumental in the founding of a missionary society, the *Gesellschaft für innere Mission im Sinne der Lutherischen Kirche*. Four years later he founded a female diaconate, the *Lutherischer Verein für weibliche Diakonie*, which consecrated its motherhouse a year later in 1854 in Neuendettelsau. These two societies had the aim of quietly (and sometimes not so quietly) reforming and renewing the Lutheran church in Bavaria.[46] Löhe and the others who formed the *Gesellschaft für innere Mission im Sinne der Lutherischen Kirche* were clear about their unhappiness with the state of the Bavarian church. In 1855 an unsigned article appeared in the *Correspondenzblatt der Gesellschaft für innere Mission nach dem Sinne der lutherischen Kirche*. The author spoke of the "wretched condition of the Bavarian church" and stated that the goals of recalling the Bavarian church to its Lutheran roots had not been realized.[47]

This women's diaconate had a twofold aim. Its more specific aim was for the awakening and formation of a sense of service to those who were suffering among the Lutheran population in Bavaria, particularly among women.[48] Its second and broader aim—and one might say its more subversive aim—was the continuing formation of the "apostolic-episcopal church."[49] Its life was organized around service and worship, specifically Lutheran worship. This emphasis on Lutheran worship pointed to one of the reasons, if not the primary reason, that Löhe formed yet another diaconal association. He felt that the associations active at that time (such as that established by Wichern in Hamburg) were not sufficiently confessional and, therefore, were given to unionistic tendencies. The basic idea of the diaconate was to provide education to young women in difficult social circumstances and then to place them into settings where they might help others in need. The order was not restricted to those who desired to enter the diaconate; no young woman who was in need was turned away. Nonetheless, this order was not the fulfillment of Löhe's vision; it was merely a model of what the local church should look like. Despite his earnest efforts to develop such communities, most notably the communities in Michigan, Löhe did not succeed. He died in 1872 a disappointed man who felt his goals for the Bavarian church had not been adequately realized.

INFLUENCES

Löhe and his theology have often been characterized as a mere reception of Lutheran orthodoxy. This assessement might be true if one examines only his theology in terms of his expression of the classical loci of theology (e.g., Christology and soteriology). However, this assessment is short of the mark when one begins to examine his ecclesiology, especially as it is presented in his occasional writings. His suggestion in *Vorschlag zu einem Lutherischen Verein für apostolisches Leben* for the formation of core groups which would model authentic Christian (apostolic) life recalls the *ecclesiola* ("little churches") of the Pietists.[50] To be sure, Lutheran orthodoxy was probably primary in the formation of Löhe's theology, but it is most certainly not the only influence. Pietism played an important role as well. Hebart rightly concludes that Löhe is "one of the most original thinkers in Lutheranism."[51] Löhe's theology was not simply a mere reception and repristination of Lutheran Orthodoxy or of Pietism or, indeed, of any other theological school. He combined and borrowed what was necessary and useful for the building up of the church. This mixing was always creative and always fresh.

Löhe was influenced by the Pietism which was transmitted through his mother more than through his reading of Pietist theologians such as Spener, Nicolai, Francke, and Zinzendorf. His family was closely related to Pietists active in the greater Nuremberg area. It would be a mistake to discount the influence of Pietism on Löhe.[52] The devotional writings of the Pietists were read daily in the Löhe household during his youth. As Hebart writes, "his thinking is always Lutheran, the Orthodox element is the dominant, but the Pietistic always makes itself apparent and the one is not to be thought without the other."[53] Löhe's instincts tended to Lutheran Orthodoxy, but his pastoral sense recognized the value of Pietism. His vision of mission was not unlike that of Zinzendorf. Indeed, Löhe was familiar enough and fond enough of him that he told members of his congregation about Zinzendorf's life.[54] Perhaps the central difference between the confessional theology of Löhe and the theology of the Pietists was that Löhe "insisted that the church was the vehicle through which the gospel message of salvation was transmitted."[55] Salvation, in the Pietist view, tended to be a personal matter. In any case, it is fair to say that in Löhe's view the faith of the Pietists was a vibrant alternative to the dead, moralistic faith of the Rationalists.

Romanticism ought to be named as an influence upon Löhe as well. Nothing indicates that he was influenced by the theologians one normally associates with Romanticism (Schleiermacher, for example, or in philosophy Hegel), yet the influence is there. Löhe read Johann Gottfried von Herder, who influenced his understanding of Scripture and history.[56] Furthermore, as a student in Erlangen, Löhe named Jean Paul as his favorite author.[57] As Wolfgang Trillhaas points out, Löhe "was a romantic Lutheran, that is, not a Lutheran of contradictions, but rather a man of synthesis insofar as it concerned the church."[58] His ecclesiology is an attempt to synthesize the ecclesiologies of the Lutheran confessions and the New Testament. His interest in history and his desire to respect the heritage of Lutheran theology and the apostolic tradition as represented in the New Testament and the writings of the early church also hint at his Romantic inclinations.[59] These two characteristics, synthetic thinking and historical perspective, suggest Romantic influences.

Löhe's language at times reflects the animate, organic imagery favored by Romantics. His comparison of the church in *Three Books about the Church* with a stream and a flower (and even the moon!) reflects his affinity to Romanticism.[60] At the same time, Löhe was not a man given over to excessive enthusiasm in the same way that many other Romantic thinkers were.[61] This difference aside, sufficient evidence exists to say that Löhe was influenced and shaped by Romanticism even while he was not limited to its influence.

Yet another influence on Löhe was that of the "Awakening," especially as it was mediated by Christian Krafft. Löhe incorporated the biblicism of Krafft and the Awakening.[62] Throughout his life and his theology, Löhe turned to the Bible over and over again as the fount which fed and nourished his thought. He looked to the practices of the early church as recorded in the New Testament for guidance in his own ecclesiological thinking. These are traits of his thinking which are held in common with "Awakening Theology."

The confessionalism of neo-Lutheranism exerted its influence upon Löhe also. Perhaps because Löhe is often mentioned in the same breath as other representatives of neo-Lutheranism (e.g., Hoffmann, Harless, and Thomasius), one tends to overlook the influence of his contemporaries on him. Yet the similarities are clearly there. Like Hoffmann, Harless, and Thomasius, Löhe returned to the Lutheran tradition for theological insight.[63] In this return to the Lutheran theological tradition, Löhe built upon its foundations and contributed to its growth. In fact, one could say that Löhe's program was one of providing a confessional basis to the Pietist and Awakening impulses that influenced him.

Although one can point to traces of Romanticism, Pietism, or Lutheran Orthodoxy in Löhe's thinking, it is difficult to say that any of these are primary. Georg Merz rightly remarks that Löhe "followed his own path beyond Idealism, Pietism, Rationalism."[64] His path, though not one that followed any particular school, drew upon the strengths of many streams flowing in nineteenth-century theological thinking.[65] Löhe was clearly an independent thinker who, while appreciating the strengths of many different theological streams, schools, and traditions, did not consider himself a representative of any one of these influences. Even the most common of the labels applied to him—neo-Lutheranism or sometimes Lutheran Orthodoxy—shows his difference from the Erlangen faculty as the events of 1849 and following highlight. Löhe's theology was shaped not by reasoned reflection, but by his reflection on what it means to be a pastor and what it means to proclaim the Gospel.

NOTES

[1] Wolfhart Schlichting, "Löhe, Johann Konrad Wilhelm (1808–1872)" in *TRE* 21: 421. In addition to Schlichting, introductions to the life and work of Löhe include Friedrich Wilhelm Kantzenbach, "Wilhelm Löhe, Frankens Grosser Lutheraner," in *Evangelischer Geist und Glaube im neuzeitlichen Bayern* (Munich: C. H. Beck'sche Verlagsbuchhandlung, 1980), 158–98; and Gerhard Ottersberg, "Wilhelm Loehe," *Lutheran Quarterly* 4 (1952): 170–90; as well as the other sources cited.

[2] For a detailed account of Löhe's life until he went to Neuendettelsau, see Adolf Schwammberger, "Der junge Löhe," in *Wilhelm Löhe—Anstöße für die Zeit* (ed. Friedrich Wilhelm Kantzenbach; Neuendettelsau: Freimund-Verlag, 1972), 13–36.

[3] Hans Kreßel, *Wilhelm Löhe, der lutherische Christenmensch: ein Charakterbild* (Berlin: Lutherisches Verlagshaus, 1960), 15, reports that Löhe's maternal grandfather, Gürtler Walthelm, was active in a Moravian [*Herrnhuter Brüdergemeinde*] congregation in Fürth. Friedrich Wilhelm Kantzenbach, "Wilhelm Löhe (1808–1872)," in *Klassiker der Theologie* (ed. Heinrich Fries and Georg Kretschmar; vol. 2; Munich: Verlag C. H. Beck, 1983), 176, notes that Löhe's parents were pious people who read Lutheran devotional literature and for whom Sunday worship attendance was a given. Löhe himself reports in Deinzer, I: 7–8, that he and his siblings went to church and received the Sacrament regularly; daily prayer and readings from the Bible, Luther's writings, and other devotional sources were also an integral part of their spiritual life.

[4] Wilhelm Maurer, "Wilhelm Löhe und der römische Katholizismus" in *Wilhelm Löhe—Anstöße für die Zeit*, 80.

[5] Martin Schmidt, *Wort Gottes und Fremdlingschaft: Die Kirche vor dem Auswanderungsproblem des neunzehnten Jahrhunderts* (Erlangen: Martin Luther Verlag, 1953), 48; see also Gerhard Müller, "Wilhelm Löhe" in *Die neueste Zeit II* (vol. 9 of *Gestalten der Kirchengeschichte*; ed. Martin Greschat; Stuttgart: Verlag W. Kohlhammer, 1985), 72. Müller, in something of a minority viewpoint, asserts that it was not so much the pietistic tradition that shaped the young Löhe as the Enlightenment tradition. Furthermore, the Enlightenment, even into Löhe's adult life, was not without effect, though the adult Löhe clearly distanced himself from rationalism and deism. Siegfried Hebart, *Wilhelm Löhes Lehre von der Kirche*, 13, claims that Orthodoxy and Pietism exerted the biggest influences on the young

Löhe, though the Enlightenment is not without its effects (16).

6 Rector Roth may well have been the first to expose Löhe to Revival Theology. For more, see Müller, "Wilhelm Löhe," 72–73.

7 Concerning Löhe's penchant for solitude and how it moved him to respond to his cultural, social, and spiritual environment, see Hans Kreßel, *Wilhelm Löhe*, 20.

8 K. G. Steck, "Krafft, Christian" in *RGG* 4: 30; see also Deinzer, I: 266; and "Brief an Dorothea Schröder" (14 November 1827), *GW* I: 261; as well as Deinzer, I: 58; and "Brief an E. Huschke" (6 December 1836), *GW* I: 480. Krafft's influence extended not only to Löhe. Georg Merz, *Das bayerische Luthertum* (Munich: Verlag des Evangelischen Pressever-bandes für Bayern, 1955), 20 and 22, names Krafft as "the leader of the young generation" in Erlangen.

9 Hans Kressel, *Wilhelm Löhe als Prediger* (Gütersloh: C. Bertelsmann Verlag, 1929), 25; and Hans Kressel, *Wilhelm Löhe: Ein Lebensbild* (Erlangen: Martin Luther-Verlag, 1954), 13.

10 Deinzer, I: 71.

11 See Deinzer, I: 74–76, 80. Löhe stated that Schleiermacher controlled himself when he preached; he was a great man and, therefore, a great preacher. That Schleiermacher was a powerful preacher is not an opinion unique to Löhe. Schleiermacher was not afraid to comment on social and political issues (a quality shared by Löhe, as seen in his struggles against the state in the 1840s and 1850s). Robert M. Bigler, *The Politics of German Protestantism: The Rise of the Protestant Church Elite in Prussia, 1815–1848* (Berkeley: University of California Press, 1972), 31, notes that "toward the end of the [Napoleanic] war Schleiermacher became so bold that some of his sermons were indictments of the social system of inequality and of aristocratic arrogance." Apparently Schleiermacher was not afraid to speak against the prevailing government policies. See Bigler, *Politics of German Protestantism*, 29–32.

12 Gerhard Müller, "Der Student Wilhelm Löhe und das Amt: Eine Äußerung aus dem Jahr 1829," *Jahrbuch für fränkische Landesforschung* 34–35 (1975): 595. Löhe's paper is included in its entirety as an appendix to Müller's essay.

13 Deinzer, I: 103–04. See also Müller, "Wilhelm Löhe," 75.

14 Wilhelm Löhe, *Three Books about the Church* (trans., ed., and with an introduction by James L. Schaaf; Philadelphia: Fortress, 1969), 5, n. 13.

15 Deinzer, I: 109.

16 Schlichting, "Löhe," 421.

17 In its report, the Consistorium said that Löhe was a captivating man, but his understanding of worldly matters, his social skills, were lacking (Deinzer, I: 154).

18 Deinzer, I: 180–82. The language of the letter is strong, with phrases such as "ruthlessly strove," "forced" or "compelled," and acted "without knowing and observing the boundaries of pastoral power."

19 Schaaf, introduction to *Three Books*, 8.

20 Deinzer, I: 177.

21 Müller, "Wilhelm Löhe," 77; and Schaaf, introduction to *Three Books*, 11–12. Friedrich Roth, the brother of Löhe's beloved rector at Melanchthon-*Gymnasium*, was a lawyer with a distinguished record of service to the state, including serving as the president of the consistorium from 1828 until 1848.

22   Adolf Stählin, "Löhe, Wilhelm," in *Realenzyclopädie für protestantische Theologie und Kirche*, 11: 577.

23   The impact of the death of Löhe's beloved Helene cannot be underestimated. Her death spurred Löhe to write *Three Books about the Church*. As late as 1859, he published a book of prayers (*Hausbedarf christlicher Gebete*) which included this "Prayer of a Father Whose Wife Died in Childbirth": "O living God and Comforter of those who mourn, I have lost my dearest treasure on earth in childbirth. You have torn a rib and a piece of my heart from me. It is, however, your good will, Lord my God. You gave her to me and let her be with me for a short time and now she has been taken out of this misery back to you, because she knew and called upon your Son. Comfort me, a sad, miserable widower and help carry this pain and raise my children and send a holy glimpse that I and my children can come together before you in a new joy and eternal love, which you plant in all marital love and can make all suffering eternal joy and goodwill. We praise you in eternity. Amen." See *Hausbedarf christlicher Gebete, GW* VII/2: 103.

24   For a description of Löhe's ministry in Neuendettelsau, see Kenneth Frederick Korby, "The Theology of Pastoral Care in Wilhelm Löhe with Special Attention to the Function of the Liturgy and the Laity" (Th.D. diss., Lutheran School of Theology at Chicago, 1976), 132–45, esp. 132–36.

25   Hans Kressel, *Wilhelm Löhe als Katechet und als Seelsorger* (Neuendettelsau: Freimund-Verlag, 1955), 79, states that Löhe had an extraordinary charismatic gift of healing through prayer and the laying on of hands. Accounts of such healing are in Deinzer, II: 201–13. Eduard Thurneysen, *Die Lehre von der Seelsorge* (Munich: Christian Kaiser Verlag, 1948), 299, nearly a century after the publication of Löhe's opus on pastoral care, *Der evangelische Geistliche*, asserted that it is "to be considered still a standard work."

26   Both Löhe's and Wyneken's appeals were as much directed to Germans' sense of patriotism as they were to their evangelical spirit. See James L. Schaaf, "Wilhelm Löhe's Relation to the American Church: A Study in the History of Lutheran Mission" (D. Theol. diss., Heidelberg, 1961), 10–14, for a more extended account of this entire episode.

27   Wilhelm Löhe, "Brief an Prof. Winkler" (4 December 1842), *GW* I: 619–20.

28   James L. Schaaf, "Wilhelm Loehe and the Ohio Synod," *Essays and Reports of the Lutheran Historical Conference* 5 (1974): 88. Schaaf reports that "within six months more than one thousand books had been collected and dispatched to America" (89).

29   Löhe wrote in a letter to Ernst that he and the other missionaries should seek to ally themselves with a German Lutheran body which adheres to the Confessions. If that should not be feasible, then they should form their own independent synod. See Wilhelm Löhe, "Brief an Adam Ernst" (2 February 1845), *GW* I: 688.

30   Schaaf reports that 22 of the 42 original clergymen and ministerial students came from the Neuendettelsau mission seminary. By the time Löhe ended his association with the Missouri Synod, 84 of his men had entered the ministry of the Missouri Synod. James L. Schaaf, "Wilhelm Loehe and the Missouri Synod," *Concordia Historical Institute Quarterly* 45 (1972): 59, 64.

31   Erich Hugo Heintzen, "Wilhelm Loehe and the Missouri Synod, 1841–1853" (Ph.D. diss., University of Illinois, Urbana, Ill., 1964), 155. Much of the missionary zeal of The Lutheran Church—Missouri Synod can be attributed to Löhe and his men. For example, Adam Ernst, Löhe's first missionary, was instrumental in

organizing congregations in southern Ontario. Ernst eventually became the first
president of the Ontario District of the LCMS. See Norman J. Threinen, *Like a
Mustard Seed: A Centennial History of the Ontario District of Lutheran Church—
Canada* (Kitchener, Ontario: Ontario District, 1989), 5–20, esp. 6–7, 10–11. On
Ernst's election as the first president of the district, see p. 25. Löhe was rightly
proud of his role in the founding of the synod and its expansion; see Löhe, "Die
Gesellschaft für innere Mission im Sinne der lutherischen Kirche und ihre
Verhältnisse zu Nordamerika," *Kirchliche Mittheilungen aus und über Nord-Amerika*
17 (1859): 59.

32 Schaaf, "Löhe and Missouri Synod," 59–60. Löhe expresses his misgivings explicitly in *Rechenschaftsbericht der Redaktoren der kirchlichen Mitteilungen aus und über
Nordamerika über das, was seit 1841 geschehen ist, samt Angabe dessen, was sofort
geschehen sollte, GW* IV: 135. In the *Kirchliche Mittheilungen*, there was concern
expressed about the "democratic, independent and congregationalist principles"
that the Missouri Synod mixed into its constitution ("An den Präses der deutschen
evangelisch-lutherischen Synode von Missouri, Ohio und andern Staaten, Herrn
Karl Ferdinand Wilhelm Walther zu St. Louis, Mo.," *Kirchliche Mittheilungen aus
und über Nord-Amerik*a 6 [1848]: no. 6, col. 44). Having said all that, Löhe grieved
the separation and lack of contact with the Missouri Synod; see Löhe, "Die
Gesellschaft für innere Mission im Sinne der lutherischen Kirche und ihre
Verhältnisse zu Nordamerika," *Kirchliche Mittheilungen aus und über Nord-Amerika*
17 (1859): 59. Hermann Sasse, "Zur Frage nach dem Verhältnis von Amt und
Gemeinde," in *In statu confessionis: Gesammelte Aufsätze* (ed. by Friedrich Wilhelm
Hopf; Berlin: Lutherisches Verlagshaus, 1966), 128, says that Löhe's misgivings
were misplaced. The Missouri constitution had nothing to do with the democratic
inclinations of the Americans.

33 Wilhelm Löhe, "Brief an G. M. Großmann und J. Deindörfer" (August 1853),
GW II: 208. See also Schaaf, "Löhe's Relation to the American Church," 170–74.

34 For a fine analysis of the Iowa Synod's contribution to the debate on the ordained
ministry in the United States, see Todd Nichol, "Wilhelm Löhe, the Iowa Synod
and the Ordained Ministry," *Lutheran Quarterly* 4 (1990): 11–29. On the mediat-
ing position of Löhe and the Iowa Synod, see especially 15–18.

35 These questions of identity were raised in part by the union of Reformed and
Lutheran churches in Prussia imposed by King Friedrich Wilhelm III beginning
in 1817. For an account, see Walter H. Conser Jr., *Church and Confession:
Conservative Theologians in Germany, England, and America 1815–1866* (Macon,
GA: Mercer University Press, 1984), 13–27; and Bigler, *Politics of German
Protestantism*, 37–38. Conser, "A Conservative Critique of Church and State: The
Case of the Tractarians and Neo-Lutherans," *Journal of Church and State* 25
(1983): 332, states that "the theology of Wilhelm Löhe was influenced by the situation in Silesia [a center of resistance to the Prussian union]." This assertion is
simplistic. It would be more accurate to say that the Silesian situation provoked
Löhe to action in Bavaria during the *Kniebeugungstreit* in 1838 and the confessional struggles at the end of the 1840s.

36 Hebart, *Wilhelm Löhes Lehre von der Kirche*, 125.

37 Deinzer, II: 247. For an account of Löhe's political sympathies and activities, see
Friedrich Wilhelm Kantzenbach, *Gestalten und Typen des Neuluthertums: Beiträge
zur Erforschung des Neokonfessionalismus im 19. Jahrhundert* (Gütersloh: Gütersloher
Verlagshaus Gerd Mohn, 1968), 227–33.

38 James L. Schaaf has done a fine translation of *Drei Bücher*. The quote is from

Three Books, 152.

39 For more on the kneeling controversy, see Schaaf, introduction to *Three Books*, 35–36; as well as Conser, "Tractarians and Neo-Lutherans," 333–34; and Conser, *Church and Confession*, 51–52.

40 "Vorschlag zu einem Lutherischen Verein für apostolisches Leben samt Entwurf eines Katechismus des apostolischen Lebens" in *GW* V/1: 213–52. The quote is from 226; hereafter, "Vorschlag."

41 "Aphorismen über die neutestamentlichen Ämter und ihr Verhältnis zur Gemeinde," *GW* V/1: 320; hereafter, "Aphorismen."

42 Gerhard Müller, "Die Erlanger Theologische Fakultät und Wilhelm Löhe im Jahr 1849," in *Dem Wort Gehorsam: Landesbischof D. Hermann Dietzfelbinger DD. zum 65. Geburtstag* (ed. Wilhelm Andersen et al; München: Claudius Verlag, 1973), 242–54, esp. 247, 254, provides a helpful account of the role of the theology faculty at Erlangen (especially Johann Christian Konrad Hoffman and Gottfried Thomasius) when, in 1849, Löhe was threatening to leave the *Landeskirche*. Friedrich Wilhelm Kantzenbach, "Die 'befreundeten Gegner': Ekklesiologische Konzepte rund um Wilhelm Löhe," *Zeitschrift für bayerische Kirchengeschichte* 44 (1975): 114–42, provides a detailed examination of the events and especially the personalities involved in this church-state struggle in these years.

43 Müller, "Wilhelm Löhe," 82. In 1852, as the confessional struggle reached its peak, Löhe wrote that leaving the *Landeskirche* would be a step of last resort for him and his friends; they were inclined to remain in the Bavarian church. He wrote that the question of altar fellowship (inter-Lutheran communion) was "the last resort for those who wanted to remain in the Bavarian Church." See "Einige Worte über Herrn Prof. Delitzsch's neueste Schrift betreffend die 'bayerische Abendmahlsgemeinschaftsfrage,' " *GW* V/1: 634. He repeated this in his lecture, "Das Verhältnis der Gesellschaft für innere Mission im Sinne der lutherischen Kirche zum Zentralmissionsverein in Bayern." In this lecture, Löhe said that he felt it was important for him to stay within the *Landeskirche* so as to continue to struggle for confessional renewal; see *GW* V/2: 695; hereafter, "Das Verhältnis."

44 Herbert Krimm, "Wilhelm Löhe und Johann Hinrich Wichern: Vergleichende Betrachtung anläßlich der 150. Wiederkehr ihrer Geburtstage," in *Diakonie der Kirche* (Herbert Krimm, Walter Künneth, and B. Dyroff; Nürnberg: Landesverband der inneren Mission in Bayern, 1958), 18. Wolfgang Trillhaas, "Wilhelm Löhe—ein unbürgerlicher Christ," *Zeitwende* (Hamburg) 25 (1954): 379, states that Löhe forced the ouster of Harless's predecessor, thus paving the way for the appointment of Harless and guaranteeing that Harless had the freedom to institute much-needed reforms in the Bavarian church.

45 See Stählin, "Löhe, Wilhelm," 582, for a fuller description of the conflict between Löhe and the state over his refusal to conduct this wedding.

46 Anne Stempel-de Fallois argues persuasively that the impulses for Löhe's interest in diaconal service stem from his early association with the Awakening movement (above all through Christian Krafft) and Pietism. On the impact of the Awakening movement and its theology, see Anne Stempel-de Fallois, "Die Anfänge von Wilhelm Löhes missionarisch-diakonischem Wirken im Bannkreis von Erweckungsbewegung und Konfessionalisierung (1826–1837)," *Pietismus und Neuzeit* 23 (1997): 40–45. On the impact of Pietism on Löhe through his reading of Spener's *Pia desideria*, see Stempel-de Fallois, 47–48.

47 "Die Gesellschaft für innere Mission im Sinne der lutherischen Kirche am Anfang des Jahres 1855," *Correspondenzblatt* 6 (1855): 2, 3.

48 Stählin, "Löhe, Wilhelm," 583.

49 Deinzer, III: 327.

50 Sihvonen, "Wer sein will, der muß werden," *Homiletisch-Liturgisches Korrespondenzblatt* n.s. 13 (1995–96): 455; also Kantzenbach, "Die 'befreundeten Gegner,' " 142.

51 Hebart, *Wilhelm Löhes Lehre von der Kirche*, 8.

52 Theodor Schober, "Die Gemeindediakonie," in *Wilhelm Löhe—Anstöße für die Zeit*, 111, rightly notes that Löhe's understanding of "community" is incomprehensible seen apart from Pietism and Romanticism.

53 Hebart, *Wilhelm Löhes Lehre von der Kirche*, 13; see also 32 (as well as 294) where Hebart writes that Löhe took the best of both traditions.

54 Löhe, "Brief an Karl von Raumer (23 November 1837)," *GW* I: 517; also cited in Deinzer, II: 104.

55 Conser, *Church and Confession*, 321; see also Friedrich Wilhelm Kantzenbach, "Wilhelm Löhes Stellung in der Frömmigkeitsgeschichte," *Zeitschrift für bayerische Kirchengeschichte* 41 (1972): 56.

56 Löhe reports that he read Herder's religious writings regularly while in university; see Deinzer, I: 55; see also *GW* II: 557, 590–91, 620. Regarding the influence of Herder, see Hebart, *Wilhelm Löhes Lehre von der Kirche*, 22.

57 Deinzer, I: 37–38. In this same passage, Deinzer also mentions that Löhe read "Klopstock, Herder, Goethe, Schiller, Jacobi, and Matthisson." That Löhe enjoyed Jean Paul is confirmed by a cursory reading of his diaries. See, for example, *GW* II: 565, 567, 568, 570, 582, 583, 584, 589. That Löhe read Schiller is confirmed by at least one passage in the same diary; see *GW* II: 575.

58 Trillhaas, "Wilhelm Löhe—ein unbürgerlicher Christ," 383.

59 Löhe wrote, for example, a history of the Reformation in Franconia: "Erinnerungen aus der Reformationsgeschichte von Franken, insonderheit der Stadt und dem Burggraftum Nürnberg ober und unterhalb des Gebirgs," *GW* III/2: 523–681. On the Romantic (and Idealistic) organicism of Löhe, see Martin George, "In der Kirche leben," 214.

60 *Three Books*, 55–57.

61 Gerhard Müller, "Wilhelm Löhes missionarisch-diakonisches Denken und Werken," in *Sichtbare Kirche: Für Heinrich Laag zu seinem 80. Geburtstag* (ed. Ulrich Fabricius and Rainer Volp; Gütersloh: Verlagshaus Gerd Mohn, 1973), 47.

62 On the influence of the Awakening and Krafft, see Martin Wittenberg, "Wilhelm Löhe und die lutherische Kirche," *Lutherische Kirche in der Welt* 19 (1972): 11, 13; see also Gerhard Müller, "Wilhelm Löhes Theologie zwischen Erweckungsbewegung und Konfessionalismus," *Neue Zeitschrift für systematische Theologie* 15 (1973): 1–7.

63 Müller, "Löhes Theologie zwischen Erweckungsbewegung und Konfessionalismus," 36.

64 Merz, *Das bayerische Luthertum*, 24.

65 Müller, "Löhes Theologie zwischen Erweckungsbewegung und Konfessionalismus," 8.

2

ECCLESIOLOGY

Löhe held a catholic view of the church. For all his confessionalism and adherence to Luther, he reached back beyond Luther and the confessions to the church fathers and sought to establish a church that was, in many respects, more akin to that of Rome or Constantinople than the Lutheran confessions. Löhe envisioned and sought to establish a church that, while small, would be more effective in performing its important role in educating and instructing the human race concerning eternal life. The church leads people into God's reign of grace in its activity of mission and ministry. In and of itself, the church is not holy; only in its Spirit-driven activity is it holy. The Spirit has given the church its gifts of apostolic teaching, which give grace and life; the church's holiness is found in the use of apostolic teaching.

If the church were not dynamic, if the Spirit were not dynamically at work in the church, it would stagnate and rot and eventually die away. As it is, the Spirit is constantly at work within the church, strengthening, renewing, and purifying those who dwell within it, preparing and outfitting them for the task of ministry. Because the church is dynamic and not constant, but always in a state of motion, certain parts of the truth are now better understood than previously. Löhe believed that the special gift of grace given to his period in history was a better understanding of those questions of eschatology that previously had not been understood.[1] This gift of grace was proof that the Holy Spirit was at work in the life of the church.

As Löhe grew older, he developed a more chiliastic or eschatological view of the church. He understood the church as progressing toward a fullness or completeness or perfection. So while the true, authentic church was apostolic in the sense that it grew out of the apostolic teaching, it also continued to grow into perfection. Indeed, of necessity it must grow. The church cannot be content to rest on the work begun in the apostolic age, but it must continue to strive for perfection, to grow into fullness.[2] This striving for perfection and completion in the church was not compatible with the reality of the state church system then in effect.

Much of the conflict between Löhe and the state and the church authorities had its basis in the conflict Löhe saw around him and felt within himself. His life was dedicated to reconciling the ideal and reality. Better stated, Löhe was dedicated to realizing the ideal. He yearned for a genuine, authentic church which more closely matched the ideal portrayed and posited in the New Testament. He yearned for a true community of believers; he wished for a church that would not be merely an article of faith, but one that would enter and appear in a person's life.[3] The element of faith is central to Löhe's concept of the church. Perhaps it would be more accurate to say that the element of an active faith apparent in love and service is central to Löhe's concept of the church. Faith bound and binds a community of believers together. Löhe, in a yearly report to the *Gesellschaft für innere Mission nach dem Sinne der lutherischen Kirche* [Society for Inner Mission in the Sense of the Lutheran Church], wrote that "the church is a visible, an external, community of the children of God who are bound together through faith and confession."[4] These concepts—faith and confession—were centered in or focused on the central marks of the church: Word and Sacrament.

THEOLOGICAL MARKS OF THE CHURCH

Most things have distinguishing marks. These marks define that thing apart from everything else. A cow has certain marks that define it and set it apart from horses, pigs, chickens, and the other animals in the farmyard. In like manner, groups have marks which distinguish them from other groups. Service organizations such as the Shriners or the Rotary Club have marks that distinguish them from each other, and service organizations in general have marks which set them apart from sports clubs.

Every thing, every group in the world, has marks. More than that, they have marks that distinguish or set them apart from other things and other groups. The question then arises, What exactly is a mark? Löhe answers, "The distinguishing marks of something must be things which it possesses exclusively and perpetually."[5] The church, too, has its own distinguishing marks, which it alone possesses.

Theologians and pastors have quarreled about the marks of the church for centuries as the church has sought to distinguish itself from false teachers and their doctrines. As Avery Dulles states, "Efforts have been made in every generation to establish criteria for determining the truth of Christianity."[6] Löhe seeks to make his own contribution, particularly in light of the kneeling controversy (*Kniebeugungstreit*) and of his involvement in American missions.

Until the Reformation, the marks of the church (*notae ecclesiae*) were those named in the Nicene Creed: one, holy, catholic, and apostolic. At times during the life of the church one or another of these marks were emphasized over the others, but since at least the time of Augustine, if not earlier, this definition was the operative definition. Luther, in his treatise *On the Councils and the Church*, named seven marks (the Word, Baptism, the Lord's Supper, the keys, the ministry, worship, and suffering for the sake of the cross).[7] Calvin named two marks, Word and Sacrament, to which later Reformed theologians added discipline.[8] In the twentieth century there seems to be something of a return to the classical *notae ecclesiae*. Vatican II reiterated them, ecumenically aware theologians have argued for these marks, and at least one evangelical theologian claims them as genuine marks of the church.[9] Christendom seems relatively clear in its insistence to recognize unity, holiness, catholicity, and apostolicity as marks of the church. Löhe, for all of his reliance on the church fathers, rejects these as decisive marks of the church. Why?

The sixteenth century was a period of ferment in ecclesiology. Luther had his seven marks, Calvin had his two, and later Reformed theologians had three. Melanchthon proposed two marks. These two marks were declared in the Augsburg Confession and elsewhere in the confessional writings. The two marks? Word and Sacrament. Melanchthon writes that the outward marks of the church are "the pure teaching of the Gospel and the administration of the Sacraments in harmony with the Gospel of Christ."[10] Confessional Lutheran theologians since then have followed this lead.[11] Löhe, following the lead of the reformers, also names Word and Sacrament as the marks of the church.

Word and Sacrament are not just marks of the church. That is, they do not serve merely to distinguish the church from other groups and organizations. Word and Sacrament are also the means of grace. As the means of grace they give expression to the invisible church; they make the invisible church visible. The Word, Baptism, and Holy Communion are the lifeblood of the church; they are the axis around which the church gathers.[12] Word and Sacrament establish, identify, and nourish the church.

THE APOSTOLIC WORD

The Word stands at the center of Löhe's understanding of the church, more so than the sacraments or any other concept. Since ecclesiology is never far from the center of Löhe's theology, the Word also occupies a central position in his theology. There is an intimate relationship between the church and the Word. The Word is at the heart of the church; the church gathers around the Word.[13] The Word defines the mission and ministry and the life of the church.

Löhe does not have just any word in mind. When Löhe speaks of the "Word," he has the apostolic Word in mind. This Word is truth. This Word unites. From this Word all else flows. Löhe's understanding of "apostolic" is crucial for understanding why the Word is at the center of the church, why the life, mission, and ministry of the church have their source in this Word. He defines "apostolic," at least in this context, as that which is "founded on the apostles' teaching."[14] Thus a church can be apostolic even if no apostle has ever entered its territory; conversely, a church is not necessarily apostolic even if it can trace its lineage to an apostle.[15] The apostolic Word is that Word contained in the Scriptures; it contains everything "necessary and more besides."[16] The apostolic, that is the scriptural, Word is sufficient and as such is the center of the church. It is the Word that the apostles proclaimed.

Apostolic succession or apostolic unity then has nothing to do with church order and organization. It has everything to do with the Word, a succession, in concrete terms, of doctrine. Doctrine arises out of the writings, the theological reflections, of the early church in the first century following the death and resurrection of Christ. In the development of the Lutheran confessions, the reformers declared their adherence to the Scriptures in the principle of *sola scriptura*.[17] They demonstrated their adherence to the doctrine enunciated by the early church. The theologians of the early church in turn submitted to the authority of the apostles, whose Word is contained in the Scriptures.[18] To unite with the apostles is to unite with the doctrine, the Word, of the apostles. To stand in apostolic succession is to adhere to the doctrine and the Word of the apostles. This apostolic succession and unity, Löhe states, is the succession and unity for which the church strives.

> There is a succession, not of places and persons, but of doctrine. Doctrine never dies, and wherever it goes there are the true church, the true bishops, and the true priests. Where it is not present any other kind of succession is an empty grave of the prophets, an empty vessel, a vessel filled with mould and rottenness.[19]

To be sure, the church's exposition of the apostolic Word has not remained static since the first centuries of the church. The church has not lived in a vacuum. Löhe asserted that there is "a development and inter-pretation of apostolic doctrine in the course of history and an understand-ing that in the course of history and an understanding that in the course of time the one Word had revealed its treasures ever more richly."[20] Nonetheless, the intent is not to add anything to the apostolic Word, to doctrine, but to preserve it and retain continuity with the past.

This apostolic Word has a power of its own. It has a power apart from any human mediation. It gives birth to the congregation and is powerful even when proclaimed from the mouths of those unworthy to speak it: "Nobody can doubt that the Word gives birth to the congregation and that the Word has power with those who speaking it, are ordained, and with those who speaking it, are not ordained."[21] The Word alone gives birth to the church and preserves it.

The apostolic Word as the center of the church offers hope. From the Word flows the confession, the life, and the ministry and mission of the church. The Word which the apostles proclaimed is the same Word to which the bishops and theologians of the early church bound themselves. This Word is also the same Word to which the reformers and their fol-lowers adhere. As long as there are members of the church who adhere to the apostolic Word, there the church is found. Löhe writes: "Hope is with-out limit as long as the Word and doctrine hold sway; it is the source of all good things and the death of all vanities."[22] The Word by itself and in itself is the fount of all that is good, of all that flows from the church.

The Word is accessible to all and does not need intermediaries. It is, for example, independent of tradition; one does not need tradition to explain or clarify or amplify the apostolic Word. Christians do not depend on tradition, but on the apostolic Word. Likewise, "the church lives not by tradition but by every word which proceeds from the mouth of God, just as the church once lived with the incarnate Word."[23] Nor does one need another person with exclusive access to or even better knowledge of tradi-tion to interpret the Word.[24] Löhe rejected the notion of a magisterium that determines the content of the common faith: "It is ludicrous that a man who is just as human and no better than anyone else is supposed to be the repository of all the wisdom of the apostles."[25] The Scriptures them-selves are clear. Even the theologians of the early church cannot be relied upon in the same manner. Of course, a consensus reigns among them: The *consensus patrum* is the most reasonable understanding of tradition, but it is not a tradition which interprets the Scriptures. The theologians of the early church "themselves refer to the Holy Scriptures and make the

Scriptures themselves the basis for understanding the Scriptures, rather than turning things around and making their own intellect the key to interpreting the Scriptures."[26] But how is one to establish such a consensus? And even if one does, why bother when the clear Word of God is contained in the Scriptures? One could direct the layperson to read this gospel or that epistle without fear of contradiction, but this is not so with Augustine or Tertullian. They even contradict themselves on certain points! As Löhe pointedly states, to direct somebody to the writings of the early church

> would mean, apart from everything else, that the homesick child who is only a few miles from home would have to journey all the corners of the world to get there. God forbid that we should lead our people into such a wilderness when we could lead them into green pastures beside the still waters![27]

Tradition, no matter what its guise, is of little benefit to the church. If it adds to the apostolic Word, it ought to be condemned. If it adds nothing, it is superfluous. Tradition can only confirm what is already clear in the Scriptures.[28] There is no compelling reason to rely on tradition to clarify, explain, or amplify the apostolic Word.

The Word stands alone like a beacon on a hill. It is clear and bright. It is intelligible to all who have eyes to see and ears to hear: "the Scriptures are clear and understandable to all."[29] Indeed, this is the most important doctrine of all. Everything is lost if this doctrine is not true. An unintelligible Word is of no use to the church and to the members of that church who attempt to understand for themselves the meaning and force of the content of this Word which gives eternal life. Such an unintelligible Word could not unite the church. The New Testament stands on its own; it needs nothing other than itself to be comprehensible. Read alongside the Old Testament, the gospels and epistles of the New Testament are that much more comprehensible since Christ is the fulfillment of the prophecies contained within the Old Testament. What of those parts of the Old Testament where that is not obvious? those parts which are not easy to understand? Löhe answers that it is true that the Old Testament needs to be interpreted and much of it is not understandable without an interpretation. But there is an interpretation. The New Testament is the interpretation of the Old, and inasmuch as it reveals the fulfillment of all prophecies in Christ Jesus, it sheds an irresistible light on every dark and obscure passage.[30]

There might even be some obscure and obtuse passages in the New Testament, but these are fewer than one might think.[31] Furthermore, these passages are not of sufficient importance to conceal the general meaning of the Scriptures and the doctrines contained within them. The Scriptures are clear enough, unambiguous enough, and intelligible enough that it is possible for one to come to eternal life just by reading and taking the Word therein to heart.

Indeed, reading Scripture and taking it to heart—confessing and repenting of one's sin—is the point of Scripture. God's Word calls humankind. The apostolic Word calls humans from darkness to light, from Satan to God. Löhe rejected any inclination of universalism.[32] Why proclaim the Word to those who are already saved? Löhe states that because the Word is for all nations, for all people, Christians are called to preach and proclaim the apostolic Word all the more fervently.[33] Löhe holds to the Lutheran doctrine of universal grace, of a *vocatio catholica*. God's gift of grace goes out to all of humanity. This is why it is important to proclaim this Word. Humans are inclined to reject this gift. Only by appropriating God's gift of grace through Word and Sacrament can one live in the power of this gift. Some people resist this gift of grace; those people who "wantonly and maliciously" oppose the Word are lost.[34] Nobody is condemned merely on account of their own sins or of original sin—only those who refuse God's gift of grace.

Humans are not called merely to turn from the world. They are called to dwell in the fellowship of the Word and the Sacraments. They are called out of the world; they are called to the church. The church is the place where the Word is proclaimed and the sacraments administered. It is an invitation which comes to each person, calling them out of the world into the church. One's attitude or stance toward the church is determined by the degree to which one heeds this call:

> Those who do not obey [the call] at all, although they hear the call, belong to the world. Those who outwardly turn from the world and confess Christ and his church before all men are honored with the title of the "called," for they do not hear that call in vain but obediently come to the marriage feast of the eternal King. But those who (not merely outwardly before the eyes of men but inwardly according to the judgment of the Lord himself) have turned from the world and joined his church, those whom the Lord will declare publicly at the end of time to be his own, are the ones who are called the "chosen."[35]

One's membership in the church, or rather one's membership as demonstrated by one's participation in the church, determines one's place at the feast in paradise.

This passage hints at another important aspect of Löhe's theology: his understanding of the distinction (or perhaps nondistinction) between the visible and invisible church. There exists both an invisible church and a visible church.[36] These two "churches" correspond more or less to the classical definitions. The visible church is the institutional church; the invisible church is the church of those who are saved. The visible church includes those who visibly hold fast to God's Word and Sacrament before everyone's eyes and confess Christ and his kingdom before everyone's ears. The invisible church embraces those who are not only called but also enlightened, converted, justified, sanctified, preserved, and perfected by the Word of the living God.[37]

But, Löhe goes on to say, the chosen members of the invisible church are, properly speaking, not only its ranking members, but also its only members. For all intents and purposes, "the visible and invisible church are identical" and ought to be regarded as one and the same, just as body and soul make one person.[38] One might protest, "What of the hypocrites in the visible church?" Löhe has already foreseen this objection and replies that the visible church is not to be despised because of the hypocrites in it.[39] The visible church is the place where the Word is proclaimed and the sacraments administered; it is the tabernacle of God. And outside this tabernacle there is no salvation. The visible is the invisible made manifest.[40] The invisible church may be precious, but it is of little consequence and little use without the outward form, without the public confession of humans in word and deed. In the visible is the invisible church, and though the visible may be a mere image of the invisible, though it may be full of all sorts of hypocrisies and lies and false doctrines and loose discipline, this church contains the roots of the apostolic Word. The apostolic Word sustains and preserves the visible church, despite its shortcomings, for the sake of the invisible church.

The love that arises out of right confession (right doctrine) is the basis for Löhe's assertion that there is no essential difference between the visible and invisible church. He acknowledges that there is an invisible church in which only God can definitively know who belongs and who does not belong.[41] Christian love, which arises out of a right confession, out of a right faith in the apostolic Word, is also apparent to those who have eyes to see and ears to hear. Löhe further states that the aim is to make the visible church—which is admittedly tainted or corrupted by unfaithful elements—more like that community envisioned by Christ.[42] (This fellowship of the apostolic Word is a community which is revealed in "the holiest human love.")[43] If, as Löhe phrased it, "the invisible church embraces those who are . . . enlightened, converted, justified, sanctified, preserved, and perfected by the Word of the living God," then this church will be visible by virtue of the purity of the light that shines forth from it.[44] There may be tares in the wheat, but the wheat is recognizable for what it is. The wheat still clearly stands in a field that is wheat. The church is the church despite the corrupt and immoral elements that may seek to shake human faith and confidence in God's perennially blooming flower—the church.

The church is inclusive of all peoples of all times and of all places. Once it was centered in Israel, now it is universal.[45] Löhe notes that Jesus' ministry focused on the Jews, but the apostles' ministry was universal. The universality of the apostles' mission is demonstrated in that after the disciples fled from Jerusalem, some of them went to Samaria though it was despised by the Jews (cf. Acts 8:4–5, 14, 25).[46] The Word of the apostles goes out to all people in every place and every time. It is a Word that seeks to gather all people into "the universal—the truly catholic—church which flows through all time and into which all people pour."[47] In an allusion to the different gifts and ministries given to all and that they are all equally essential to the body of Christ, Löhe asserts that all Christians should strive to overcome the external inequalities among them.[48] In this way they might demonstrate their oneness in Christ. Through mutual love, through love for the other, can the spiritual kinship of Christians be apparent to the world.

Although the church is inclusive and seeks to unite, that is, though it is catholic, this does not necessarily mean that it has a large membership. The number of people who can claim membership in this church is in the hands of God. The church is wherever people cling to the apostolic Word. If there are only two people in a location who cling to the Word, then the church is present and it is large enough.[49] The location of the church has less to do with a physical building than it does with people who cling in faith to the Word. This Word draws all people, all nations, to it. This is the meaning of the Lutheran doctrine of universal grace. The Word calls all people and all nations. The Word seeks ever more people for the church: "The apostolic Word is clear, and the church which revolves around the Word as its center is a host drawn from all nations and all generations."[50] All are called, but only a few answer.

The church is eternal as the Word is eternal. The church is one as the Word is one. Löhe says that the Word heard at the first Pentecost is the same Word at the center of the church today.[51] Those who were present at the first Pentecost do not belong to a different church than those who have been present at every outpouring of the Spirit since then. The faithful who have died and the faithful who live are not separated. They dwell on the same mountain; they dwell in the same church. The whole church already dwells on Mount Zion—the heavenly city. Some members of the church are near the gate at the summit, other members are at the foot,

> yet all belong to the city on the mount, the heavenly Jerusalem. The entire goal of the church on its pilgrimage is there. Here it is hastening on; there is its resting-place. It knows that its lot is the same as the lot of those who have overcome; with them it is one eternal host.[52]

Those who have died and those who yet live are one church before God and according to their own consciousness.[53] The church is one and remains one into eternity.

That the church is eternal and one means it is so not only for the infinite extension of linear time into the future. That the church is one and eternal also means that it is one in the fullness of the present. It is an assembly that extends beyond itself in a particular time and location by means of prayer. The congregation that gathers together to pray, hear, and proclaim God's Word joins itself to the church in every time and in every place.

The apostolic Word will sustain and preserve the church. This is the basis of the hope of the church. As it has been sustained and preserved, so it will be. The Word is eternal and sustains and preserves the church eternally. The Word that was let loose and heard at the first Pentecost is the same Word at work in the church today.[54] The apostolic Word is a Word of promise and of hope; it will preserve and sustain God's church. This is the promise to which the church clings. The church that adheres to the apostolic Word in a pure confession will be preserved and sustained.[55] The Word is everything; without it the church is lost. Without the Word, the church is deprived of the source of its life.

THE SACRAMENTS

The sacraments—Baptism and Eucharist—are the other marks of the church. The Word stands at the center of Löhe's ecclesiology while the sacraments are central to his liturgical theology.[56] They alone are unique to the church. No other human body or organization possesses these marks. As marks of the church, distinctive to the church alone, Löhe sought to restore Baptism and Eucharist to their rightful place of honor. During the Enlightenment, the sacraments had been devalued and their significance in the life of the church and of the individual undermined. They became mere signs or remembrances.[57] Löhe was determined to re-establish them in their proper place at the center of faith, especially in its communal manifestation.

Eucharist plays an important role in the formation and sustenance of the church. It preserves community and fellowship. In the Eucharist, the congregation brings the fruit of the earth—the bread and wine—to the Table. In these elements, the faithful receive the body and blood of Christ for the forgiveness of sins and life. The celebration of the Eucharist is not unlike a marriage. In the Eucharist, a marriage between heaven and earth, divinity and humanity, Christ and his bride, takes place.[58] The Eucharist thus effects a fellowship between humanity and God, but it also effects a real relationship between each member. This relationship is one that extends to the ends of the earth.[59] They come as equals. They have con-fessed their sins and received absolution for these sins. Each person is sin-ner; each is saint. They are equal before Christ and, therefore, before one another.

When Löhe speaks of community or fellowship, he means an empha-sis on or a faith life centered and grounded in the Sacrament of the Altar. The Eucharist is not merely a doctrine; it is the source, the wellspring, by which believers are nourished and strengthened for the journey. Justification by grace alone and its visible expression in the Sacrament of the Altar are central to the association Löhe has in mind. Löhe wrote in *Vorschlag zu einem Lutherischen Verein* [*Proposal for a Lutheran Association*] that

> above all we adhere to the doctrine of salvation by grace alone, to jus-tification by faith alone. And we daringly name all those lives false which do not stem from this correct belief. The Sacrament of the Altar is more than a mere doctrine to us. The conflict over it, in our eyes, is not a mere struggle of opinion; it is about the greatest act of God, which meets us in life, it is about the unification of the transfig-ured body and costly blood of Jesus with bread and wine. And in par-taking of this sacrament we stand upon the peak of temporal Christian life, where divinity and humanity encounter each other in Christ. His real body, his costly blood make us participants in his life and impresses upon our lives the seal of the resurrection.[60]

The sacraments and the Reformation principle of *sola gratia* (grace alone) are central to the Lutheran identity and, therefore, to the Christian identity.

FALSE MARKS

Löhe is clear about what are not the marks of the church. He has, in general, determined this on the basis of what other denominations claim are the marks of the church. Some churches claim that universality is a mark of the church or holiness is a mark. Löhe rejects these claims. His reasons for doing so are worth exploring.

Antiquity and Duration. Antiquity and duration are not marks of the church. Duration is rejected as a mark because it includes the future. We cannot know what the future holds for the church; it is yet undecided. Löhe states: "No form of the visible church has an eternal continuation, not even to the end of the day. A life blooms and brings fruit, but then it withers again."[61] Antiquity is rejected because marks are perpetual. Antiquity encompasses all of time in the past. Time once had a beginning, a beginning so far in the past that one could not speak of age, much less antiquity. It is impossible to assert that the church has always existed; "antiquity cannot be a mark of the church because it applies not only to the church but also to the world and to the sects."[62] Antiquity is hardly unique to the church.

Wide Extension. That the church is everywhere, that it is to be found in the four corners of the world, is not a mark. Wide extension is not a mark of the church. The church has not always been found throughout the world. Indeed, as Löhe noted, "it is obvious that at the beginning, on the first Pentecost in Jerusalem, the true church was in existence before it was widely extended."[63] In fact, the size of the church has nothing to do with its authenticity. The authenticity of the church has more to do with its unique distinguishing marks. Wide extension or "catholicity" of the church has less to do with numbers. Rather, it has more to do with "the doctrine of the universal grace of God which wants to see true doctrine and the true church spread as widely as possible."[64] Löhe even goes so far as to suggest that the church might more properly be small than large.[65] Quantity is unimportant in determining the location of the church.[66] A large membership is a gift of God; a small membership is the world's misfortune. Both are in God's hands.

Unity and Succession. Löhe rejects unity and succession as marks of the church, at least as they are often understood in Roman Catholic or

Anglican circles. He does not deny that unity is an attribute of the church; there is absolutely no question of this.[67] But Löhe has unity of a different kind in mind.[68] A unity based on apostolic (episcopal) succession is a unity that Löhe cannot accept. An episcopate that claims authority on the basis of apostolic succession is suspect at best and a corrupt play for empty power at worst. He asks rhetorically:

> Where was this unity at the beginning and for at least six hundred years after that? Where was it when the church had no papal head or when several heads towered above its shoulders? Where was it when, as has often happened, the pope was condemned by his own followers as a heretic or when he obtained his see by force, fraud, simony, etc.?[69]

On the one hand the episcopate has not existed in perpetuity; and, on the other hand, it has been corrupt. Popes and bishops have claimed power by immoral means and without support and recognition of genuine believers. Furthermore, such a succession is founded upon order. For the sake of maintaining peace is such a succession and unity founded. It is not grounded in the true marks of the church or the authentic calling of the church.

Holiness of Life. Neither are good works and holiness of life marks of the church. They are not limited or unique to the church. Muslims, Hindus, Jews, and other nonbelievers can just as easily do good works and live lives that are apparently holy; even the "Antichrist does not mind affecting a certain sort of piety."[70] True sanctification is possible only by the miracle of "simple love to Christ."[71] Good works and holiness of life are related to one's vocation, one's calling. Löhe follows Luther closely here: "all works of one's calling should be works of love, good works."[72] The craftsworker, to use Luther's famous example, does good quality work out of Christian love in obedience to the Golden Rule.[73] One loves one's neighbors, and out of this love one does good works. Thus Löhe argues in a manner reminiscent of Matt 6:2 that Christians do their good works in secret. Even so these good works are noticed: "The dwelling place of the head of the family, the nursery of the mother, the workshop of the mechanic, the field of the farmer, the kitchen and barn of the servant are all transfigured by the lovely doctrine of the calling and the goodness of works done in such a calling."[74] These dwelling places and places of work are set apart in a way perhaps not so very different than the sanctuary of a church. After all, all those called into the reign of God share only one type of holiness.

Miracles and Prophecies. Nor are miracles and prophecies marks of the church. They are not limited to the church. There are fewer miracles and prophecies today than previously because the truth and the church have proven themselves to the world. Prophecies and miracles are no longer needed to contribute to the broadcast of the Gospel.[75] At one time miracles and prophecies helped pave the way for the proclamation and reception of the Gospel, but that time is past. Furthermore, the example of Balaam and his ass (Num 22:22–40) illustrates that a prophecy or miracle proves nothing about the person from whom it came. The fact is that "miracles and prophecies do not give a clear testimony."[76] As a mark they do not indicate the character or essence of the thing or group to which they belong. They are ambiguous.

For Löhe, then, antiquity and duration, wide extension, unity and succession, holiness of life and good works, miracles and prophecies are *not* marks of the church. Only the possession of the Word and the Sacraments may be counted as marks of the church.[77] Only the Word and the Sacraments make the church unique among all other groups in the world; only these two treasures set the church apart. The Word and the Sacraments "are clearly defined, easily observed, and complete in themselves."[78] That which "distinguishes the church from all other groups in the world is its possession of the pure Word and Sacraments."[79] The church "has been and will continue to be established, gathered, nourished, and preserved through Word and Sacrament."[80] For this reason they are marks of the church. They are the norm and the rule of the church. The church is bound to Word and Sacraments in such a way that without them it is not the church. The church alone possesses Word and Sacrament; no other group can lay claim to these treasures.

Judging a Church:
Confessional Purity and Apostolic Faithfulness

If Word and Sacrament are the marks of the church in general, what is it that sets denominations apart from one another? Löhe answers that it is the denominations' confessions. "There is no doubt that a denomination is separated, gathered, nourished, and preserved from the other denominations through its understanding of the Word and its use of the Sacraments or, to put it briefly, through its confession. Its confession must therefore be its distinguishing mark."[81] A denomination's confessions lay out how that denomination understands the Word and how it administers and interprets the sacraments. The church in general is defined by its *possession* of Word and Sacrament; a denomination (the church in particular) is defined by its *understanding* of Word and Sacrament. A denomination is set apart from other denominations by its own confession of what Word and Sacrament is. If people want to become acquainted with a denomination, to get to know it, they must direct their attention to its confessions.

That which defines denominations is its confessions. One could also say that doctrine distinguishes denominations from one another. Doctrine is a denomination's expression of the truth, of what it understands to be true about the Word and Sacraments. Clearly, not all denominations can possess the truth in fullness, in purity, and in clarity. If they did, the barriers between them would have fallen long ago. That leaves only two possibilities: "either none has the complete truth or only one of them has it."[82] For a person to claim that none has the truth is to presume that he or she alone possesses the truth or the ability to decide.[83] Löhe argues otherwise: "Whoever claims that one denomination is right must believe that someone beside himself can judge properly and therefore that he is not alone in holding the truth."[84] One denomination has a lock on truth. Which denomination is it? He argues that one church must stand out among the others. The Lutheran church has precedence over all the others as being the purest, the most faithful, to the Word and Sacraments.[85] The Lutheran church stands out among all denominations as that church that has pure doctrine, whose confessions are truest to the apostolic Word.

In the absence of the confessions of a church, one could still measure a church. How? One can measure a church using doctrine and sacrament as standards. In the foreword to his *Agende*, Löhe writes:

> With the yardstick of pure doctrine, of pure Sacrament in hand, we may go through the subordinate fields of constitution and liturgy in other ecclesial fellowships examining everything and preserving all that is good. Constitution and liturgy are subordinate fields. But if the talk is about them, but if, for and through constitution and liturgy something can and should happen, then it is right to gather everything good that is found elsewhere and not to neglect everything that is praiseworthy for the church.[86]

All this, however, does not contradict Löhe's point about the integrity of a church's confessions. Liturgy is the expression of a church's confessions. *"Lex orandi, lex credendi"* ("the law of praying is the law of believing") is the ancient formula. A congregation confesses its faith in its Sunday worship. Indeed, it might be said that it is only in Sunday worship that a church's faith may be measured for its truth.

Can the truth be tested? This question is important. For if the truth can be tested, if it can be determined, then one can discover which denomination possesses the truth. One could alternatively frame the question thus: What is the mark of the denomination that stands out among the others in its possession of the truth, in its understanding of Word and Sacrament? Löhe responds to this without missing a beat:

> To this we answer without fear of contradiction that faithfulness of its confession to the Scriptures is the mark of the denomination which has the most truth or the complete truth, the denomination which for this reason may be called the church *par excellence*, the one which enjoys all the promises the Lord gave to his church.[87]

How can one test the truth? How can a person determine which church is the purest in its doctrine, the most faithful to the Word? How does a believer establish which church stands out among the crowded cacophony of confessions? A Christian can determine which denomination possesses the truth by comparing a church's confession with Scripture because truth is God's Word, the word of the apostles.[88] This is the most important thing because "no confession can do anything more than agree with the clear Word."[89] Thus it is possible, Löhe argues, for one to test the truth.[90] Even the humblest and simplest of people can determine a denomination's claim to priority, to the truth. Everyone who has eyes to see *can* see which denomination stands out among the others as being the possessor of the truth, which denomination is worthy to be named as the church *par excellence*. To know and recognize this church *par excellence* is to know and confess the Word.

> A church which knows and confesses the Word is truly a church. That is to say that a church which knows and confesses the Word is a community in the fullest sense of the word. A church which has right doctrine will have a clearer understanding and experience of the Gospel. It is easier for a community to achieve authentic community when its sees the Gospel in its purity and fullness than if it is tainted and tarnished by false doctrine.[91]

Right doctrine is necessary if true community is to be experienced.

THE CHURCH AS COMMUNITY

It must not be overlooked or forgotten that Löhe served in a congregation all of his adult life. As a child, too, he had looked forward to serving as the pastor of a congregation. Löhe's entire thought and perspective and life revolved around the axis that is the congregation. It is here that the apostolic Word comes to life; it is in the congregation that the church finds expression. Löhe did not emphasize praxis at the expense of dogma.[92] To be sure, doctrine was the pillar of fire which guided the church during the dark nights of apostasy and the pillar of cloud during the days when everything seemed lost. But the impulse for Löhe's reflections was always the congregation and its life.

COMMUNITY

The congregation is the locus of the church. It is that location where the Word is proclaimed and the sacraments celebrated. A number of key questions, therefore, must be raised: What is a congregation? What is its role in the larger church? Is it the basis for the church? Is renewal of the church necessary for renewal in congregations? Or must congregations experience renewal before the church can experience renewal? To both of these last questions, Löhe answers in the affirmative. Both those who say that a renewal of the congregation is necessary for the renewal of the church and those who say that a renewal of the church is necessary before congregations can experience a renewal are correct. It is, Löhe says, certainly true that the church is to be not merely a *gathering*, but also a *gatherer* of saints. Its tasks in this time are not only to seek its own perfection, but also to recover lost sheep, to influence the rebellious, to educate the entire human race into eternal life and into a gathering of holy and sanctified essence.[93]

The church is not a passive organization, a mail-order club; rather, it is an active body that makes demands upon its members.

This active body that is the church cannot go about its business as long as it is not one body but merely a collection of members. As long as it is a collection of members who understand themselves as individuals who gather occasionally, then the church cannot be the decisive and influential force in society and the world that it is called to be. The church must be united, a community of individuals who, while retaining their individuality, also submit themselves to the community. One cannot be a Christian apart from the church.[94] The local congregation is the concrete and visible manifestation of the church. This is not to say that it is somehow enclosed or that the church is limited and restricted and, therefore, comprehensible or objectifiable. To say that the church is concretized in the local congregation is merely to say that it is in the congregation where the church finds expression, where it lives.[95] The congregation is where the church is realized: "As living stones of the great house of God the individual congregation bears the name of the wide, the large, of the entire church which is willed by God, and bears the name *ecclesia*, church."[96] The church is the congregation, and the congregation is the church.

The church is not the building or the institution. Rather, it is the location where the work of God is carried out. The church is the gathering of the people of God, as is the congregation the gathering of God's people. The church is the people; the people are the church.[97] For it is the people who are active in creating community (*koinonia*), in proclaiming the Gospel, in gathering around Word and Sacrament (worship), and in various ministries of mercy and compassion (*diakonia*); the church as an inanimate institution cannot carry out these ministries. The church is those people who are disciples of Jesus and who regularly gather for the mutual uplifting of the community (Rom 15:2; 1 Cor 14:26).

All those who cling to Christ are necessary for the work of the church. To every disciple is "given the manifestation of the Spirit for the common good" (1 Cor 12:7). Everyone has something to contribute. Furthermore, Christ's grace is sufficient for all; each member of the church has been "given grace according to the measure of Christ's gift" (Eph 4:7). Individually every follower of Christ is a member of the church; corporately they are the body of Christ. Different members of the body of Christ serve and fulfill different needs in the church. Some are called to be prophets, some apostles, and some teachers (cf. 1 Cor 12:27–28). All are necessary for the mission and ministry of the church. This and the precedent set by the early church demand that nobody be severed from Christ (that is, the body of Christ) on the basis of works or the Law.[98] The first council in Jerusalem (described in Acts 15:1–35) established that God "made no distinction" between the Gentiles and the Jews. All are called to the ministry of the church and all "are God's servants, working together" (1 Cor 3:9). The church is one and none of its members are to be lightly cast away.

The disciples of Christ constitute the members of his body, the church. The sinew of this body, that which binds the members of this body together, is Word and Sacrament. Löhe writes, "Word and Sacrament of the Lord binds them as members to one whole, to one body."[99] The church is, in and of itself, a collective whole. It is not a gathering of individuals who go about their business unaware and unconcerned about others; it is, rather, a gathering of the people of God who are one in their celebration and proclamation of Word and Sacrament.

That Löhe values the contribution of each individual is readily apparent. No member of the church is to be lightly cast away. And while Löhe holds an exalted view of the office of the holy ministry, he also considers the contribution and participation of every disciple of Christ in the church to be of the utmost importance. The church ought to be structured such that it contains a democratic element so as to allow—even encourage—the lively participation of the congregation and its individual members in the church. At the same time there ought to be an aristocratic element contained within the church structure as well.[100] God is a God of order, and the Spirit is a Spirit of differentiation. In God's kingdom there is a union of large and small, powerful and weak, of democracy and aristocracy, of monarchs and peasants. All are subsumed into the kingdom; all are subsumed into the body of Christ—the church.

Since God is a God of order and the Holy Spirit is a Spirit of differentiation, different offices exist in the church. To be sure all are equal; in Christ there is "no longer Jew or Greek . . . no longer slave or free no longer male or female" (Gal 3:28). The whole of the New Testament bears witness to the radical equality in Christ, but it is also true that there is a recognition and differentiation of the gifts and ministries. The Acts of the Apostles and parts of the Pauline corpus witness to the differentiation and ordering of the various charisms and ministries. Some of the ministers stand over others though all are equal in Christ. In keeping with this understanding of the ecclesiology of the New Testament church, Löhe asserts that those who are learned in doctrine ought to stand over other presbyters to prevent them from unintentionally falling into error. The assumption is that those who are theologically trained and learned may often be from outside the congregation, whereas the presbyters within a congregation may well—and ought to—come from the congregation itself.[101] A dynamic relationship is at work here between the local congregation and the catholic church. The local congregation is actively involved in the day-to-day demands of mission and ministry in its midst, but it also receives a pastor who oversees this ministry especially with respect to doctrine.

The pastor, in many respects, represents the catholic church. This pastor will often be an outsider overseeing the ministry of the local congregation. This pastor oversees, not in the sense of directing the particular ministry of that congregation, but in interpreting the apostolic doctrine for the congregation as it endeavors to put this apostolic Word into practice. The congregation is also part of a synod. In this way it is bound to the larger church, the church catholic. The congregation is bound to the decisions of the synod. Not to obey the decisions of the synod is to leave the diocese.[102] Such disobedience would effectively remove the congregation from "the holy catholic church, the communion of saints."[103] A unity of doctrine exists within the church catholic, even if a congregation does not always agree with the decisions of the synod.

The synods are comprised of the presbyterate. The presbyterate is, in brief, the ordained pastors.[104] Actually it is not quite true that synods are comprised of the presbyterate. In fact the presbyterate represents only the nucleus of the synod. Synods are public; anybody may attend—deputations are, of course, invited as well. But the synods are in large part comprised of pastors; congregations do not send any other representatives (at least no other representatives with voting privileges).[105] Congregations do not have any need to send representatives other than the pastor. The pastors represent the apostolic tradition in their locations and represent their congregations in the catholic church. The synods are not about congregations and their own particular needs; rather, they are about uniting around a common vision of mission and ministry. Synods are about the kindred coming together and expressing their unity.[106] "How very good and pleasant it is when kindred live together in unity," the psalmist writes (Ps 133:1). Synods are an expression of this unity and the goodness that is experienced in it.

Löhe endeavored throughout his theology to unite paradoxical elements. This is nowhere more apparent than in his understanding of the congregation, especially as it relates to its pastor and to the catholic church. Löhe attempted to unite free movement and staticism, established order and strength, the whole and the individual. This attempt has its basis in the long history of the Christian church.[107] It finds its roots in the church described in Acts. The apostles, from an early date, had to struggle with a viable and dynamic polity which would serve the needs of the apostolic Word, which would let the disciples of the risen Christ go about the task of proclaiming the Gospel in word and in deed.

Discipline. Discipline is central to Löhe's understanding of congregational life. It is essential for the confession of right belief or doctrine, which is essential for sanctification. Clearly Löhe has a special definition of discipline in mind when he speaks of it as being integral for the cultivation of right belief and confession, of right faith. Discipline cultivates the heart and the mind. The heart believes and the tongue confesses. Through the intentional, conscientious exercise of discipline, Löhe seeks to foster faith that is confirmed by a right confession.

Faith and sanctification go together. It is God's will that we be believers, just as it is God's will that we be sanctified. Without faith, sanctification is not possible; without sanctification, an authentic faith does not exist.[108] Yet sanctification and faith are closely related to discipline.

To train the heart and mind to act together in harmony and discipline is necessary. If the heart believes, then it naturally follows that the lips will confess the faith of the heart. For this reason discipline is not only necessary, it is desired.[109] The true believer wants to confess the faith of the heart. The true believer wants to live the faith of her or his heart. Clearly faith and confession belong together and sanctification and discipline belong together. The believer confesses the faith of the heart. The heart and the mind are disciplined into right thought and right deed. The faithful heart will make a right confession of what it believes. A false heart makes a false confession that gives rise to a false life.[110] Discipline, then, educates the heart and the mind to make one confession. Some believers believe only with their hearts; they declare or confess a different faith with their tongues. Löhe cannot accept this discrepancy between faith and confession. Discipline is his response to the discrepancy that he sees everywhere in the church. With the responsible and loving exercise of discipline, Löhe seeks to form believers who have the same faith in their hearts and on their lips. Discipline perhaps cannot change the heart, but it can effect a change of confession or doctrine. This recognition of right confession, of right doctrine, may be able to effect a change in the heart.

Right doctrine or right confession is crucially important. It has been noted elsewhere that the Lutheran church is not destined to irrelevancy or to apostasy. The Lutheran confessions function as a guiding beacon.[111] Of all the confessions in existence, the Lutheran confessions adhere most closely to the apostolic Word. The confessions of the Lutheran church are the basis of its hope for renewal and reawakening. They ensure a right heart out of which right practice will arise. Right doctrine "plus" right practice add up to sanctification. Whoever believes correctly in the heart, will confess correctly with the lips and will desire to live in holiness.[112] More than that, such believers will also desire discipline so as to keep themselves honest and upright. Discipline provides the believer with the parameters within which he or she is to live and believe. These parameters keep them within the fold of God, members of the Shepherd's flock.

This is the will of God. God wills that all believers be holy. God wills that humanity be sanctified. Discipline is a way by which people might be made holy. Discipline is not a human statute instituted so people can live more peaceably with one another and more harmoniously. Certainly the exercise of discipline may—and often does—lead to such peace and harmony among those who exercise it. Nonetheless, it is not a human device. Discipline is a holy law given to us by God and the apostles. Humans have not devised discipline; therefore, they are not authorized to dissolve it. Discipline is the commandment of God and can, therefore, only be dissolved by God.

God has given discipline so his people might live together in the church. In this sense it is a gift. This command or gift of discipline enables believers to live together harmoniously and peaceably. The church is the active instrument of this command to discipline. As such, every member of the church has the responsibility, the obligation, to exercise discipline in the congregation's life.[113] Sanctification is about salvation; the church is about both of these. Discipline must be exercised so what is to be saved will be saved. If souls are to be saved, then discipline must be exercised so these souls can know the bliss of sanctification. Furthermore, a congregation risks its own destruction if it continues to neglect discipline as an integral part of its life in Christ. For the sake of the congregation, each and every member of that congregation has the duty of praying for the spirit of sanctification and discipline and that the commandment of discipline is recognized and exercised as often as possible in both word and deed.

What is discipline? What exactly does Löhe have in mind when he speaks of discipline? Discipline admittedly has some rather negative connotations and associations. One thinks of corporal punishment in schools, or of the severe—even excessive—discipline exercised in the military, or the discipline of the police in controlling criminal activity. None of these and all of these are what Löhe has in mind. Löhe does not have in mind the humiliating practices of the Middle Ages, which were intended to be punitive. He writes:

> the name "discipline," like the biblical name "disciplinarian," points rather at educating a person to her/his station, it points to sanctification. And because the significance of the word "education" is the same as discipline, the repulsive nature of the expression disappears.[114]

Sometimes a mentor will employ extreme measures when training a student, or a master an apprentice, but the overall character of discipline in this sense is of closely supervised training. It is a training or an education which is more than the mere acquisition of a skill or body of knowledge. An entire ethic is part of this education, this discipline. For this reason, discipline is more about being trained into not only a way of thinking, nor even a way of doing, but rather a way of being. Discipline is about being brought up into an ethos that encompasses all aspects of life.

This type of discipline may be harsh, but it has a compassionate goal as its end. Just as mentors discipline students into a particular field, masters discipline apprentices into a skill or trade, parents discipline children into family life and values, so discipline in the church has a similar aim. The discipline exercised by Christians among one another has the goal of socializing believers into the fellowship. Christian discipline has the aim of bringing people into community with one another. Discipline thus functions to foster Christian fellowship and community. Believers are socialized into a way of life, an ethos that encompasses all of life. Discipline provides the foundation by which people know how to interact with one another. It provides the basis by which believers can rely on a shared set of values, a shared ethos, that directs their interaction with one another.

Education and Faith Formation. Discipline is not the only means by which people are socialized into the church. Education (or faith formation, as it might be called) is equally, if not more, important. The church is infected with unfaithful elements, but some of those who are unfaithful seek to bind themselves to the apostolic Word. In Löhe's mind, it went without saying that those who adhere to the apostolic Word will work to gather the weak and simple into an authentic faith. This work consists of educating people in the confessions and gathering all those who accept the confessions and understand them in like manner. Paramount in this task is not merely gathering those who claim to accept the confessions, but gathering those who know and understand the confessions.[115] Löhe had in mind those who were convinced of the validity and the reliability of the Lutheran confessions.

What of those who do not accept the confessions or the Word? Should they really be left to the wolves? The answer, quite simply, is no, they should not merely be forgotten and cast away as if they were unredeemable sinners since, of course, all people are sinners. The church must continue to hope and pray that these people will receive a spirit of questioning, learning, recognizing, believing, and confessing—a spirit which they did not formerly possess.[116] They should be cared for as if they were confessing believers in the apostolic Word. Meanwhile, those who have united around the entire *Book of Concord* will act as salt, as yeast in the loaf, which will awaken in others the desire to seek and know the truth as it is revealed in the apostolic Word.

The knowledge of this apostolic truth will impel the believer forward into greater knowledge and greater zeal for the Word and the responsibility such knowledge imposes upon us. This knowledge of the confessions, of the apostolic Word, should move believers into a more committed and active role in the church. These believers, in turn, would draw others into their midst.

WORSHIP

The Word finds expression in the church. And the place where the Word finds expression in the church is in its worship, in its preaching, and in its prayers. Worship and prayer are two of the chief functions of the church. If, as Löhe asserts, the church is the only fellowship on earth which can satisfy the human thirst for community, then this community is a community of like-minded individuals who come together to acknowledge the truth and power of the apostolic Word.[117] What does it mean to be a fellowship dedicated to worship? to prayer?

Worship is the means by which the church expresses its fellowship with God and with one another. In worship the called come together to sing God's praises, to ask God's favor, and to confess to God before one another their own sense of sinfulness. If the Word is the wellspring of the church, then its liturgy is the place in which the Word finds expression. The church is a fellowship that prays, a fellowship that prays corporately and privately. It is an assembly that "prays not only as individual members in their closets but also together as large gatherings in its houses of assembly. It worships as it speaks and as it sings, and the Lord dwells among its songs of praise with his sacraments."[118] The church does not just express itself in worship as it wants. It is not a worship subject to the whim of its participants.

There are certain forms to worship which, by and large, are not obligatory. Few of them are commanded and demanded by Scripture. Yet these forms—which are called the liturgy—ought not to be arbitrarily altered. If the church is one through the centuries, then it should have a worship that is recognizably one. The church has historically developed certain forms that fulfill its needs. These forms allow the people to approach God and then retreat in patient waiting upon God's word of forgiveness and absolution. These forms have been tried and tested since the first Pentecost. For this reason, the church will avoid the new and the innovative. Older forms of liturgy are preferred, at least until they are well-known, then after one is competent, new forms may be created: "Once a man has first learned from the old he can profitably use the developments of recent times (in language and methods of speech) for the benefit of the liturgy."[119] Löhe, as with everything else, is cautious about unnecessarily changing the liturgy. If it has served the church well, one ought not to be too quick to change it.

The liturgy, the pattern of the church's approach to God and God's approach to the people, fulfills the task of allowing the worshiping community to respectfully and reverently approach God and then to retreat and receive the divine Word that saves. The church has chosen certain forms that express its unity in time and place. The church has freedom to be sure, but it has chosen to bind itself to liturgies that express its relationship to God:

> From its very beginning the church has been pleased to select certain forms. A holy variety of singing and praying has grown up and a lovely pattern of approach to and withdrawal from the Lord of lords has been established. Just as the stars revolve around the sun, so does the congregation in its services, full of loveliness and dignity, revolve around its Lord. In holy, childlike innocence which only a child's innocent heart understands properly, the multitude of redeemed, sanctified children of God dances in worship around the universal Father and the Lamb, and the Spirit of the Lord of lords guides their steps.[120]

The liturgy is like a holy dance that changes according to the orchestra and the dancers in a given time and place, but the dance is recognizably the same dance that gives honor and praise to God.

Preaching occupies the first position in the church's means of reaching lost souls. It is more important than the sacraments in this respect, and it is more important than the liturgy itself.[121] Preaching occupies this position at the head because "it is the means for calling those who are far off and for confirming the call and election of those who have been called and have drawn near."[122] Preaching is the proclamation of the Word. The goal of the effective preacher is not to clarify that which is obscure; the preacher's aim and intention is "not primarily explaining obscurities but confirming and maintaining what is clear."[123] In doing so, effective preachers of the apostolic Word do not draw attention to themselves but simply witness to the Word. Löhe writes that the preacher is a simple, faithful witness to the Word, and the Word witnesses to him—he and the Word appear as one.

> All his preaching is based on holy calm. . . . [The preacher] will use neither human eloquence, nor stimulation of the emotions, nor the impure means of exciting nerves to win friends for the Lord Jesus. What he desires is not the excitement of an awakening but the turning of men's thoughts to God. Just as calling proceeds to enlightenment and every advance in the inner life is conditioned by an advance in knowledge, so he seeks above all to have the holy ideas of the divine Word rightly understood and to have them brought very close to the memory, contemplation, will, and inmost being of his hearers.[124]

Clearly the Word is central to the ministry of the church. It is central to that most important task of calling souls to accept God's grace.

The highest calling might well be that of preaching to the heathen. Mission was the center of Löhe's ministry; it was his passion. He desired that all people might be drawn into the community of the apostolic Word. To this end there was no call nobler than that of proclaiming the Word to those who had not yet heard it. The preacher to the heathen, Löhe wrote, must recognize by the authority of God's Word (for example, Mark 16) that he is indebted to each and every creature he can reach. He is a stranger and will, in a certain sense, remain a stranger. Yet he strives to make the message of the Gospel sweet and delightful to young and old, to men and women, and to the greatest and the least.[125]

> The call to preach to the heathen is noble; at the same time it is demanding. It is not a light burden and demands much effort and dedication.

Preaching is important enough that Löhe wants others to get it right. He supplies much advice. He encourages pastors to "resort" to simple, faithful witness to the Word and not to zeal and excitement. The preacher ought not to speak, but to allow the Lord to speak through the apostolic Word. The preacher should give the people enough of what they need but not too much, that is, to preach sparingly! As Löhe says, people will sooner open their hearts to the truth when it is gladly but sparingly imparted than when they hear its voice speaking constantly. The Word itself understands how to give people enough of its means but not too much.[126]

If souls are to be saved, if people are to respond to the call of the Lord, then everything depends on the Word. And the Word is most effectively proclaimed in the context of preaching. Indeed, Löhe says that he would rather give up liturgy than pure doctrine.[127] Nothing else matters but the proclamation of the apostolic Word in its purity and beauty.

CONCLUSION

Certain themes or motifs in Löhe's theology are distinct and unique to him; some may not be easily transported into the milieu that surrounds the church and its theology at the beginning of the twenty-first century. Other themes and motifs may anticipate emphases in the church and its theology today. One of these is Löhe's emphasis on the church as the people of God.

He often speaks of the church as the chosen people of God, of those individuals who adhere to the Word, particularly when he speaks about the church as community. Seen apart from his qualifying adjectives of "chosen" or of "adherence to the Word," the notion of the people of God has endured in classical and contemporary theology. Löhe's specific understanding of the church as the people of God who gather to worship, to hear the Word, to receive the sacraments, to simply be with one another, offers fresh insights into this important concept.[128]

The word "people" is used frequently in the Scriptures to signify a particular ethnic community. In the Septuagint, *laos* usually identifies the Israelites as the people of God. In the New Testament, *laos* undergoes a further development in Luke-Acts and particularly in the Pauline corpus. The former definition of *laos* is "now broadened to denote the Christian community."[129] The old ethnic boundaries are swept aside, "there is no longer Jew or Greek" (Gal 3:28). Paul especially transformed the meaning of *laos*: "*Laos* is now the people of God whom God has called and who confess his Son as Lord."[130] The people of God are those who have been adopted by God and who confess Christ as Lord.

While the definition of the people of God has been broadened, it has not lost its sense of peculiarity. The national, ethnic, and political connotations that the people of God had in the Old Testament are never entirely abandoned. They are expanded: "Paul broadens it [the image of the people of God] to universal dimensions without losing sight of the fact that it specifies a temporal, historical reality. The *ecclesia* is a people without national boundaries or a common language and ethnic identity—a peculiar sort of people indeed."[131] The trend in twentieth-century theology has been to note that the people of God is an inclusive term intended to point the church beyond its own ethnic and geographic (and, in part, theological) particularity.

Loyal to his confessional heritage, Löhe did not think of the church as the people of God in this way. In the Augsburg Confession, the church is defined as "the assembly of saints and true believers" (AC 8).[132] John Gerhard (1582–1637), the great Lutheran Orthodox dogmatician, clearly distinguished the church (as saints and believers) over against those who have not yet believed the Gospel of Christ.[133] The tradition that Löhe received was one which set "us" against "them." Some are saved and some are damned. Some are Christians and some are infidels. Some belong to the church and some do not. Some adhere to the right faith and some do not. A line is drawn and the individual takes up a position on one side or the other. Löhe does not in any way cast this tradition aside. He is faithful to it. Löhe's innovation is to take up the Lutheran Orthodoxy definition and apply the name "the people of God" to it as opposed to simply using "church."

What is important here is not so much the definition Löhe assigns to church as the people of God because he reiterates the Lutheran Orthodoxy line. Rather, the significance lies in the fact that he *uses* the phrase "the people of God." To be sure, he does not explore the scriptural connotations or even the theological dimensions, but he introduces the phrase and that opens up other possibilities previously unforeseen. In practice, what happens is that Löhe emphasizes the community of believers even while the black-and-white definition—believer or unbeliever—hovers in the background. He becomes less concerned with determining who is "in" and who is "out" and more concerned with what it means to be "in." Löhe's emphasis on the church as the people of God necessarily forces him to think about what it means to be the people of God. Unconsciously he changes the question. Gerhard asked, "Who is the church? How can we determine who is in the church and who is not?" Löhe's questions are primarily of another variety. He asks, "What is the church? And what does it mean to be the church?" To ask the question about the nature of the church is to ask the same question that many contemporary theologians have been asking.

Löhe's questions arise because of a shift in his primary language. Because of their high regard for the confessions, the theologians of Lutheran Orthodoxy often drew on the language of the confessions in their writings. Löhe, too, affirmed the value of the confessions, but he sought to begin with the Scriptures. Löhe never backtracked from an unwavering confessionalism. He was keenly aware of the close relationship between the confessions and Scripture. The confessions, he was convinced, are inerrant and incontestable. Löhe boldly states that "no one has yet been able to prove that our confessions are in error on one single point. The Augsburg Confession may be refuted by the writings of the fathers, which do not always agree, but it can never be refuted by God's Word."[134] Yet Löhe did not stop at the confessions; he examined the apostolic witness.

Löhe's study of the biblical and apostolic witness led him to some of the same conclusions as contemporary Roman Catholic theologians. Löhe began to notice the communitarian elements of the New Testament church; or, to state it in language Löhe might have used, he began to notice the communitarian elements in the apostolic understanding of the church.[135] Löhe began to develop his concept of the church as a community gathered around the altar.

To think of the church merely as those who rightly believe or confess is not enough in Löhe's view. More important was the union or fellowship that Christians enjoyed with one another and with Christ in Holy Communion. In this emphasis of a mystical union with Christ and of a sacramental fellowship with other Christians, Löhe approaches many of the features of contemporary liturgical theology and ecclesiology.

This understanding of the church as communion or as the people of God occurs over and over again in twentieth-century theology.[136] In the *Handbook of Catholic Theology*, the church is defined as "the communion of those who believe in the gospel, have been incorporated into the 'body of Christ' by Baptism, come together at the table of the Eucharist, and give expression to their faith in witness and service."[137] In this definition one can easily see Löhe's favorite themes: "the body of Christ," the celebration of the Eucharist, and one's own ministry in the world.

The theological writings of Karl Rahner, perhaps the most pivotal figure in twentieth-century Roman Catholic theology, also demonstrate similarities between the ecclesiologies of contemporary Roman Catholicism and of Löhe. *Foundations of Christian Faith* is Rahner's systematic presentation of his theology. Rahner defines the church as "the historical continuation of Christ in and through the community of those who believe in him, and who recognize him explicitly as the mediator of salvation in a profession of faith."[138] In Rahner's view, Christ continues to tangibly (historically) dwell in and with those who confess him as Lord and Savior and do so in community. Christ dwells in and with the community of those who confess that he is "the way, and the truth, and the life" (John 14:6). Already one notices two elements common to both Löhe and Rahner: the emphasis on community and the emphasis on the community's confession.[139]

This common ground is particularly noticeable when one considers the question of community. Rahner states that the human being is a social being; he, therefore, speaks about the church as being the people of God, a people who are necessarily communal in their orientation.[140] The Sacrament of the Altar is an expression of this community. More than that, it manifests divine interpersonal love. At the altar the Christian experiences community with Christ.[141] In this sense the Eucharist is the highest expression of the confession of the church. The church confesses God's love in Christ. This love is evident in Holy Communion where the Christian experiences community with Christ and with other members of the church. The central emphases of Rahner's ecclesiology are twofold. The first is the communal nature of the church where members of the church share fellowship with one another, as well as, most important, with Christ himself. The second is that the Eucharist is the highest expression of this community in both its forms.

These emphases are most apparent in Löhe's theology. His understanding of the church as the people of God leads him almost by necessity to the question of how the people of God distinguish themselves. How does the church differentiate itself from other communities? What are the marks of the church? The answer, Löhe asserts, is Word and Sacrament. This question of how the church can be distinguished from other groups or communities indicates that Löhe did not cast aside this heritage of Lutheran Orthodoxy. He focuses on Word and Sacrament as marks (as do Lutheran Orthodox theologians) and carefully considers what it means for the church to be a community of Word and Sacrament.

Löhe's arguments for Word and Sacrament as the defining marks of the church are still tenable. Word and Sacrament are unique to the church. No other organization, no other association, no other club, no other community can lay claim to the possession of the Word and Sacraments. Yet Löhe's rejection of the classical marks have more to do with his confessionalism than with actual theological arguments. Indeed, Löhe often does speak of the unity, the holiness, the catholicity, and the apostolicity of the church.[142] The issue is twofold. On the one hand, Löhe is not prepared to reject the confessions. On the other hand, the classical marks are useful in describing the church. Indeed, the classical marks appear often in his theology and play a much greater role than he admits. Löhe is faced with a real dilemma.

In a helpful study, Philip Hefner calls the classical marks "adjectives." That the church is one, holy, catholic, and apostolic is an eschatological statement about the church.[143] The church is not yet on earth fully one, holy, catholic, and apostolic. Only in the eschatological reign of God can the church completely be so described. In the interim other marks will have to suffice. We must use other marks to describe the church as it is now.

Löhe's confessionalism led him to demand doctrinal unity before altar fellowship. Is it possible, as Löhe attempted, to harmonize a confessional stance with a commitment to the ecumenical church? If we take seriously Jesus' prayer that the church be one (John 17:11, 21–22), we must faithfully and earnestly seek paths which express this unity. At the same time we must take care not to be misled by those who seek to confuse and who "want to pervert the gospel of Christ" (Gal 1:7).

An examination and consideration of Article VII of the Augsburg Confession is important. It is the marks of the church as given in the Augsburg Confession, which ultimately constitute the identity and the unity of the church. The text of Article VII declares that "it is sufficient for the true unity of the Christian church that the Gospel be preached in conformity with a pure understanding of it and that the sacraments be administered in accordance with the divine Word."[144] The Augsburg Confession has a twofold purpose. It was presented to Emperor Charles V by the reformers to briefly outline their faith. Second, they wanted to demonstrate that the Reformation faith stood in the tradition of the historic apostolic faith. On the one hand, the reformers wanted to distinguish between themselves and the abuses that characterized the Roman Catholic Church. On the other hand, they wanted to demonstrate that they are not in opposition to the received faith of the church.[145] In this sense, the Augsburg Confession is an ecumenical proposal. The reformers are saying, in effect, that the church does not need to be uniform in its practice and organization, but that it does need to proclaim the Gospel of Christ.[146] The church in Word and in its sacraments must proclaim the message that one is justified by grace through faith.

Löhe certainly knew and understood that the Word could be experienced as Law or Gospel. Nonetheless, he does not seem to recognize that the same Word is manifested in different guises to different people. Indeed, there is a sense in which he tended to equate Word with Law and Sacrament with grace. This is more apparent in his liturgical theology, where he speaks of the word of confession and the preached Word, which prepares one for the Sacrament. This dynamic, in one sense, is similar to

Paul's conception of the Law as the preparation for the Gospel (Rom 3:15–6; 5:18–21).

Where Löhe really stands out is in his emphasis on the Sacrament. He is one of the few Lutherans since the Reformation to recognize the centrality of the sacraments, especially the Lord's Supper, in the life of the church. He anticipates much of modern ecclesial theology in this respect. In asserting that the Lord's Supper is the sustaining and forming principle of the church, he parallels the thinking of many contemporary theologians.[147] The twentieth century was, in some respects, the century that rediscovered the Sacrament of the Altar. Löhe discovered it a century earlier.

NOTES

[1] Matti Sihvonen, "Die schönste Blume Gottes," 142.

[2] Löhe, "Kirchliche Briefe," *GW* V/2: 858, said that the church must not rest on the laurels of its history, but continue to grow.

[3] Stählin, "Löhe, Wilhelm," in *Realenzyclopädie für protestantische Theologie und Kirche*, 11: 578; see also "Vorschlag," *GW* V/1: 221–23.

[4] Löhe, *Correspondenzblatt der Gesellschaft für innere Mission nach dem Sinne der lutherischen Kirche* 4 (1853): 112.

[5] *Three Books*, 106.

[6] Avery Dulles, *Models of the Church* (Garden City, NY: Doubleday, 1974), 116.

[7] LW 41: 148–66.

[8] For Calvin's marks, see *Institutes of the Christian Religion*, IV.1.9. Wendel helpfully points out that Calvin, as his career progressed and his thinking developed, added a third mark—discipline. See François Wendel, *Calvin: The Origins and Development of His Religious Thought* (trans. Philip Mairet; London: William Collins & Sons, 1963; Fontana Library Edition, 1965), 297–301. The Belgic Confession (Art. 29) and the First Scottish Confession (Art. 18) are two early confessional writings of the Reformed church that included discipline as a mark. For more on the marks of the church within the Reformed tradition, see John T. McNeill, "The Church in Sixteenth-Century Reformed Theology," *Journal of Religion* 22 (1942): 251–69, esp. 261–62; also reprinted in Donald K. McKim, ed., *Major Themes in the Reformed Tradition* (Grand Rapids: Eerdmans, 1992), 169–79.

[9] Wolfhart Pannenberg, Peter C. Hodgson, and Ted Peters name unity, holiness, catholicity, and apostolicity as marks of the church. See Wolfhart Pannenberg, *The Apostles' Creed in Light of Today's Questions* (trans. by Margaret Kohl; Philadelphia: Westminster Press, 1972), 145–48; Peter C. Hodgson, *Winds of the Spirit: A Constructive Christian Theology* (Louisville, KY: Westminster John Knox, 1994), 298; and Ted Peters, *God—The World's Future: Systematic Theology for a Postmodern Era* (Minneapolis: Fortress, 1992), 292. At least one evangelical systematician uses these four marks as well. James Garrett writes: "For centuries the Roman Catholic Church has utilized these marks for polemical or apologetic purposes, but it is possible to give to these marks or alternate interpretations." See James Leo Garrett Jr., *Systematic Theology: Biblical, Historical, and Evangelical*, 2 vols. (Grand

Rapids: Eerdmans, 1990–95), 2: 478. Philip Hefner also uses these four marks but does not name them "marks." Rather, he asserts that in these four "adjectives" is contained the church's self-understanding which is already-but-not-yet realized. See Philip Hefner, "The Church," in *CD*, 2: 203.

10   Apol. 7 and 8. See also AC 7. Luther, in the Smalcald Articles, tips his hat to Melanchthon's assertion. Luther speaks of the "pure Word and the right use of the Sacraments" in practice in Lutheran churches (Smalcald Art., Pref.). Quote is from *BC*, 169.

11   See, for example, Helmut Thielicke, *The Evangelical Faith*, 3 vols. (trans. and ed. Geoffrey W. Bromiley; Grand Rapids: Eerdmans, 1974–82), 3: 210–13; and Francis Pieper, *Christian Dogmatics*, 3 vols. (St. Louis: Concordia, 1950–53), 3: 409. Hans Schwarz also follows this line, see *The Christian Church: Biblical Origin, Historical Transformation, and Potential for the Future* (Minneapolis: Augsburg, 1982), 181.

12   Wilhelm Löhe, "Kirche und Amt: Neue Aphorismen," *GW* V/1: 536.

13   *Three Books*, 63–64.

14   *Three Books*, 63.

15   Löhe finds even this claim of lineage to an apostle to be dubious in the case of the Roman Catholic Church and suggests that the Lutheran Church in certain territories has a claim just as strong as that of the Romans in the Roman sense of apostolic succession and unity. He writes: "Where is a primacy of Rome in the presently fashionable sense to be found?" (*Three Books*, 134). Concerning the equally valid Lutheran claim to an apostolic succession of the episcopate, Löhe writes in an apparent reference to the Church of Sweden: "There are even Lutheran lands in which, if one considered it important, one could easily demonstrate a succession with no more gaps in a way that perhaps no other church which values its succession so highly does" (*Three Books*, 136). For more on this, see *Three Books*, 131–40 passim, esp. 132–34.

16   *Three Books*, 76. Kreßel, *Löhe als Prediger*, 107, asserts that Löhe did not always distinguish between the content and the vessel of Scripture as the Word of God.

17   Löhe stated that the Reformation was not about going forward, but about returning the church to its roots: "namely the Word." See Löhe, "Predigt über Jer. 3,12, D.D.p.Trin. XXIII. 1834. Reformationsfest (2 Nov.)" *GW* VI/1: 179–80; and *Three Books*, 150.

18   *Three Books*, 78. In "Der Tod zu Dettelsau," it was emphasized that the Neuendettelsauers "pursued their eternal goal in accordance with the Scriptures" (*GW* IV: 440).

19   *Three Books*, 139.

20   *Three Books*, 150. Yet Löhe tended to overlook the historical dimensions of Scripture and the nature of historical settings.

21   "Kirche und Amt: Neue Aphorismen," *GW* V/1: 547.

22   *Three Books*, 139–40.

23   *Three Books*, 80.

24   Löhe writes: "All parts of the church have access" to the Word of the apostles (*Three Books*, 64).

25   *Three Books*, 77.

26 *Three Books*, 78.

27 *Three Books*, 79.

28 *Three Books*, 75.

29 *Three Books*, 65. In "Kirchliche Briefe," *GW* V/2: 859, Löhe compares the Scriptures to the word of humans: "The Scriptures are more illuminating and clearer than the word of humans."

30 *Three Books*, 66.

31 *Three Books*, 68.

32 *Three Books*, 84.

33 *Three Books*, 85.

34 *Three Books*, 82.

35 *Three Books*, 87.

36 Apparently the question of whether the church was visible or not was a matter of some discussion in the mid-nineteenth century. See Holsten Fagerberg, *Bekenntnis, Kirche und Amt in der deutschen konfessionellen Theologie des 19. Jahrhunderts* (Uppsala: Almqvist & Wiksells Boktryckeri, 1952), 5–7. For an overview of the discussion of ecclesiology in America in the nineteenth century (in which Löhe was an important participant), see the helpful essay by E. Clifford Nelson, "The Doctrine of the Church among American Lutherans in the Nineteenth Century," in *Ich glaube eine heilige Kirche: Festschrift für D. Hans Asmussen zum 65. Geburtstag am 21. August 1963* (ed. Walter Bauer et al; Stuttgart: Evangelisches Verlagswerk, 1963), 202–11.

37 *Three Books*, 88.

38 "Kirche und Amt: Neue Aphorismen," *GW* V/1: 527.

39 *Three Books*, 90; see also "Kirche und Amt: Neue Aphorismen," *GW* V/1: 529. Löhe argues that those who are pious or holy trust the visible church even in the midst of its failures and shortcomings. This is so because the community (*koinonia*) is experienced in our existential lives, not in some metaphysical heavenly realm. The fellowship of the invisible church is experienced, felt, and known in the fellowship of the visible church. The visible church "is a pure mirror of the invisible church" ("Kirche und Amt: Neue Aphorismen," *GW* V/1: 528).

40 Löhe, "Zur Amtsfrage," *Kirchliche Mitteilungen* 11 no. 7 (1853): 55, wrote that the visible church is to be a manifestation of the invisible church in the world through which the saved are called and gathered (see also no. 8: 57–58).

41 In the outline of a manuscript which was never published, "Kirche und Mission," Löhe writes that the church is apparent to God in terms of the number and gloriousness of its members, but it is invisible to humans. The outline of "Kirche und Mission" is in Klaus Ganzert, "Erläuterungen," *GW* IV: 626.

42 Wilhelm Löhe, "Unsere kirchliche Lage," *GW* V/1: 376; hereafter "Unsere Lage." For more on how good works done out of love are apparent to all, see *Three Books*, 144–45.

43 *Three Books*, 164.

44 *Three Books*, 88.

45 *Three Books*, 57. In "Von der Barmherzigkeit: Sechs Kapitel für jedermann, zuletzt ein siebentes für Dienerinnen der Barmherzigkeit," *GW* IV: 473 (hereafter "Von der Barmherzigkeit"), Löhe says that Israel is the bearer of God's mercy and righ-

teousness and that it is through the people of God that all nations are blessed.

46 "Aphorismen," *GW* V/1: 273.

47 *Three Books*, 59.

48 "Vorschlag," *GW* V/1: 245.

49 *Three Books*, 124.

50 *Three Books*, 80.

51 *Three Books*, 74. Elsewhere Löhe compares the church to God's presence in the world and to truth in the world. The church will shine and illuminate the way through all darkness ("Kirche und Mission" in Ganzert, "Erläuterungen," *GW* IV: 627).

52 *Three Books*, 53.

53 *Three Books*, 52.

54 *Three Books*, 74.

55 Löhe goes even further; he asserts that "anywhere on earth where the church grew and flourished, it either had the apostolic order or approached it" ("Unsere Lage," *GW* V/1: 466; also *Three Books*, 121).

56 For this reason, the sacraments will be discussed in more detail in a following chapter, "Liturgy and Worship."

57 Löhe's adamancy or fervor on the sacraments was at the root of his quarrels with the Ohio Synod and to a lesser degree with the state church. The Ohio Synod had unwittingly introduced in its German liturgy a phrase that already had been used by Friedrich Wilhelm III in Prussia to forcibly effect a union on the Lutheran and Reformed churches. The referring formula forced upon the Lutherans in Prussia and the similar formula adopted by the Ohio Synod obscured the doctrine of the real presence. For more on this quarrel, see Schaaf, *Löhe's Relation to the American Church*, 55.

58 "Vorschlag," *GW* V/I: 251.

59 One of the impulses for mission was to maintain eucharistic fellowship with brothers and sisters overseas; see Löhe, "Aus der von Pfarrer Löhe am Jubiläum der amerikanischen Mission gehaltenen Festpredigt," *Correspondenzblatt* 17 (1866): 41.

60 "Vorschlag," *GW* V/1: 220.

61 "Kirche und Amt: Neue Aphorismen," *GW* V/1: 535. At the same time, though, Löhe states that "the church possesses the future." See also "Unsere Lage," *GW* V/1: 453.

62 *Three Books*, 116.

63 *Three Books*, 122.

64 *Three Books*, 124.

65 *Three Books*, 122. Löhe writes: "We may also claim that sometimes the Scriptures themselves ascribe just the opposite of wide extension to the church, comparing it, for example, with a narrow way found only by a few [Matt 7:14 KJV, also NRSV] or with a little flock [Luke 12:32]." See also the brief discussion above regarding Löhe's vision of a small but effective church. An important idea or reason running throughout Löhe's "Vorschlag" was that of an association which would be the kernel of a truly apostolic, confessional church in the midst of the state church. Such an association would act as yeast, a focal point, for the renewal of the church ("Vorschlag," *GW* V/1: 220).

66 *Three Books*, 124.

67 Indeed, Löhe often talked about the unity that exists among congregations separated by vast distances. For example, in the opening of the *Zuruf aus der Heimat an die deutsch-lutherische Kirche Nordamerikas*, he noted that though those in North America had left Germany, the bonds which bound them were not broken (*GW* IV: 68).

68 Interestingly, though Löhe is often remembered as a strict confessionalist separatist, he was the same man who wrote during the heat of the confessionalist battles in 1848–51 that "one must try every means in order to be able to avoid what one would rather avoid [separation]." See "Unsere Lage," *GW* V/1: 452. For the unity that Löhe does have in mind, see the discussion beginning on page 40.

69 *Three Books*, 132.

70 *Three Books*, 141.

71 *Three Books*, 143.

72 *Three Books*, 144. For more on Luther's understanding of vocation, see Philip Watson's informative essay, "Luther's Doctrine of Vocation," *Scottish Journal of Theology* 2 (1949): 364–77; also Gustav Wingren, *Luther on Vocation* (trans. Carl C. Rasmussen; Philadelphia: Muhlenberg, 1959); Marc Kolden, "Luther on Vocation," *Word and World* 3 (1983): 382–90; and Hans Schwarz, *True Faith in the True God: An Introduction to Luther's Life and Thought* (Minneapolis: Augsburg, 1996), 134–41, esp. 137–40. Luther's explanation of the Fourth Commandment in the Large Catechism outlines the main features of his thought (*BC*, 379–89).

73 LW 21: 237–39.

74 *Three Books*, 144–45.

75 *Three Books*, 145–46.

76 *Three Books*, 147.

77 In Löhe's regard for the ordained (preaching) ministry, he comes very near to naming it as a mark of the church. He calls the ordained ministry "an external sign" of the church because "on it appears the other signs: the pure Word and Sacrament" ("Kirche und Amt: Neue Aphorismen," *GW* V/1: 564).

78 *Three Books*, 116.

79 *Three Books*, 106. Interestingly, Bruce D. Marshall arrives at a conclusion not entirely unlike Löhe's in "Why Bother with the Church?" *Christian Century* 113 (24 January 1996): 74–76. He argues that the church is not so much about justice, personal healing, reconciliation, etc., as it is about a people gathered around the sacraments.

80 *Three Books*, 106.

81 *Three Books*, 106.

82 *Three Books*, 102.

83 Löhe states "that none among all the denominations possess the truth is a claim to which a humble and sensible man can never subscribe" (*Three Books*, 103). He goes further in his polemic: "whoever claims that no group is right claims all truth for himself and insults everyone else—even God" (*Three Books*, 102).

84 *Three Books*, 102.

85 In "Warum bekenne ich mich zur lutherischen Kirche?" *GW* IV: 223, Löhe

referred to the Lutheran church's pure confessions and its accordingly pure doctrine. See also "Brief an H. W. E. Reichold" (15 June 1828), *GW* I: 270.

86 Löhe, *Agende für christliche Gemeinden des lutherischen Bekenntnisses*, *GW* VII/1: 11–12; hereafter *Agende*.

87 *Three Books*, 107.

88 *Three Books*, 61–62.

89 *Three Books*, 109.

90 *Three Books*, 103.

91 Löhe, "Die Mission unter den Heiden," *GW* IV: 55. Löhe maintains that the better one's knowledge of the Gospel, the fuller one's life is and will be. In a letter to Adam Ernst, the first missionary to North America, Löhe reminded Ernst that the Neuendettelsau missionaries were committed to realizing a Lutheran church; see"Brief an Adam Ernst" (3 December 1842), *GW* I: 616.

92 See the discussion on holiness of life beginning on page 49, as well as those on the importance of doctrine beginning on page 51 and that on the relationship between dogma and praxis beginning on page 53.

93 "Aphorismen," *GW* V/1: 258. This is an apparent change of mind. Within a year of his arrival in Neuendettelsau, Löhe wrote that "the congregation regenerates itself always—even yet today—from within to without." See "Brief an das Königliche Dekanat" (16 May 1838), *GW* V/1: 61.

94 Löhe, "Kirche und Amt: Neue Aphorismen," *GW* V/1: 528, writes that "whoever is not Christ's certainly does not belong to those who are Christ's." He reiterated this assertion in the *Zuruf aus der Heimat an die deutsch-lutherische Kirche Nordamerikas*, saying that anybody in whom the thought of the one holy Christian church is alive would belong to a congregation (*GW* IV: 74–75). Martin Wittenberg, "Geistliches Leben nach Martin Luther und Wilhelm Löhe," *Lutherische Kirche in der Welt* 24 (1977): 41, rightly notes that for Luther there is no "personal" or "individual" Christendom; one must always speak of the *communio sanctorum* at the center of which are Word and Sacrament.

95 It is here that Löhe's above statement regarding the regeneration of congregations becomes comprehensible. The congregation is the local expression of the church. When a congregation is renewed, then the catholic church in that place is also renewed.

96 "Aphorismen," *GW* V/1: 259. For more on the congregation as the concretization (or manifestation or expression) of the church, see "Aphorismen," *GW* V/1: 257. Löhe states that *ecclesia* in the New Testament means the local congregation, it is the congregation that is at work among the heathens and in the world.

97 Löhe likens the church to a human: "like the human, so is the church" ("Kirche und Amt: Neue Aphorismen," *GW* V/1: 527). For this reason, the church is as diverse as the human community. See also "Aphorismen," *GW* V/1: 257.

98 "Aphorismen," *GW* V/1: 317.

99 "Aphorismen," *GW* V/1: 328. Perhaps for this reason, Löhe was loath to look kindly upon and accept United States-style congregationalism, though he recognized its broad base. He wrote ("Brief an Adam Ernst" [4 August 1845], *GW* I: 704) that "the entire synodical structure is saturated with democratic-Reformed elements." He was deeply suspicious of congregationalism. It placed too much power in the masses and threatened the authority of the office of holy ministry

that was the bearer of the apostolic Word. Truth is not found in the will of the majority, but in the Word. See "Aphorismen," *GW* V/1: 328; and "Brief an William Sihler" (12 October 1846), *GW* I: 761, for more on congregational polity.

100 Ultimately, the constitution (structure) of a church is a matter of Christian freedom; see "Brief an William Sihler" (12 October 1846), *GW* I: 760. At the same time, a constitution is decisive for the form a relationship takes between the pastor and congregation and between congregation and church (see "Das Verhältnis," *GW* V/2: 698–99). On these grounds, it could be said that a "constitution was a dogmatic adiaphora but not a practical adiaphora" ("An den Präses," *Kirchliche Mittheilungen* 6 [1848]: no. 6, col. 44). Regarding the democratic and aristocratic elements in the church, see "Aphorismen," *GW* V/1: 326. Interestingly, Herman Sasse ("Zur Frage," 123) remarks that the nineteenth-century debates on the nature of the church within Lutheranism are the result of the questions and problems facing other denominations.

101 "Aphorismen," *GW* V/1: 327. Löhe is here arguing for a truly dynamic polity whereby consecrated presbyters (literally "elders") carry out much of the active day-to-day ministry in a congregation under the supervision of a learned presbyter who would stand above them only in matters of doctrine.

102 "Aphorismen," *GW* V/1: 320.

103 "Apostles' Creed," Third Article.

104 See "Aphorismen," *GW* V/1: 326, where Löhe points out the other names of presbyters ("elders," "bishop," "supervisor," or "shepherd's office"), or "Aphorismen," *GW* V/1: 302, where he calls the presbyterate the "holy aristocracy." For a fuller description of the office, tasks, and responsibilities of presbyters, see "Aphorismen," *GW* V/1: 283–98 passim.

105 "Aphorismen," *GW* V/1: 319. Because synodical assemblies are public, anybody has the right to be heard. This is the rationale for permitting deputations—even deputations from outside the synod.

106 Löhe states that without doctrinal unity, there cannot be unity and, therefore, community; see "Unsere Lage," *GW* V/1: 391.

107 "Aphorismen," *GW* V/1: 330.

108 "Vorschlag," *GW* V/1: 226.

109 "Vorschlag," *GW* V/1: 226.

110 "Vorschlag," *GW* V/1: 234. Indeed, Löhe goes further and says that the worst part is that false doctrine inverts the will so it, in the words of Paul, does not do what it wants to do.

111 Löhe, "Die Mission unter den Heiden," *GW* IV: 55, speaks about the doctrine of the Lutheran church as its treasure.

112 "Vorschlag," *GW* V/1: 226. For a fuller discussion of the relationship between private confession and discipline, see Joachim Heubach, "Das Verständnis des Schlüsselamtes bei Löhe, Kliefoth, und Vilmar," in *Bekenntnis zur Kirche: Festgabe für Ernst Sommerlath zum 70. Geburtstag* (ed. Ernst-Heinz Amberg and Ulrich Kühn; Berlin: Evangelische Verlagsanstalt, 1960), 313–17.

113 "Vorschlag," *GW* V/1: 227. Löhe acknowledges that some sincere souls may be afraid of such "extreme" measures.

114 "Vorschlag," *GW* V/1: 228.

115 Löhe was even prepared to lose the undecided. He felt that for the sake of a *Book of Concord* which is merely named and not known, not taught, not recognized, and not believed, undecided souls would be left behind ("Vorschlag," *GW* V/1: 217).

116 "Vorschlag," *GW* V/1: 218.

117 For more on Löhe's assertion that only the church satisfies human longing for community, see *Three Books*, 50.

118 *Three Books*, 176. This is not to say that Löhe neglected individual prayer. He published numerous devotional books (most notably *Samenkörner des Gebets*), as well as postils and sermons for private devotional use. Paul Althaus, *Forschungen zur evangelischen Gebetsliteratur* (Gütersloh: Verlagshaus Gerd Mohn, 1927; repr., Hildesheim: Georg Olms Verlagsbuchhandlung, 1966), 170 (page reference to repr. ed.), rightly says that "the only theologian who brought a special interest [to the study of devotional literature] and worked with the history of collects in a comprehensive way is Wilhelm Löhe."

119 *Three Books*, 178.

120 *Three Books*, 177.

121 Having said that, it should also be said that Löhe did not lightly set aside the sacraments and their importance in the worship life of the church. He wrote early in his career (shortly after his arrival in Neuendettelsau in the summer of 1837) that every preacher should, at least once every year, preach on confession, absolution, and Communion, especially in reference to the present situation and abuses; see "Mitteilung der Windsbacher Predigerkonferenz," *GW* V/1: 51–52.

122 *Three Books*, 167. Löhe was not consistent on this point. Eucharist played an increasingly important role in his understanding of liturgy. As soon as three years later, in 1848, Löhe wrote that the Eucharist was "the highest act of the life of the congregation" ("Vorschlag," *GW* V/1: 251). Even at that, however, he contradicted himself again in 1851: "The return of the Lutheran church is dependent on the correct conception of the preaching office" ("Kirche und Amt: Neue Aphorismen," *GW* V/1: 526). This position is reiterated in the second edition (1858) of the *Prüfungstafel* (*GW* VII/2: 249): "Faith comes out of preaching, out of the Gospel. Faith is strengthened by the sermon, by the Gospel." Russell Briese, in a fine essay, argues for the primacy of the Eucharist in Löhe's theology and ministry; see Briese, "Wilhelm Löhe and the Rediscovery of the Sacrament of the Altar in Nineteenth-Century Lutheranism," *Lutheran Forum* 30 (1996): 31–34, esp. 32; hereafter "Löhe and the Sacrament of the Altar."

123 *Three Books*, 170.

124 *Three Books*, 168. Löhe writes elsewhere that he admired Schleiermacher for his preaching, though he did not think highly of the content of his theology. Schleiermacher was a great man and a great preacher because he controlled himself in the pulpit; see Deinzer, I: 74–76, 80.

125 Wilhelm Löhe, "Prediget das Evangelium," *GW* IV: 119.

126 *Three Books*, 165.

127 *Three Books*, 178.

128 "Dogmatic Constitution on the Church" (*Lumen Gentium*) in *Vatican Council II: The Conciliar and Post Conciliar Documents* (rev. ed.; Vatican Collection Series; ed. Austin Flannery, O.P.; Northport, NY: Costello Publishing Company, 1988), 364;

hereafter "Church," *Vatican II*. Friedrich Wilhelm Kantzenbach, "Persönlichkeit und Zeitgenosse," in *Wilhelm Löhe—Anstöße für die Zeit*, 64, has also noted that Vatican II has rediscovered this metaphor. Theological reflection has generally followed the lead of Vatican II in placing greater emphasis on the church as the people of God. Implicit to this understanding is that location—whether it be theological (doctrinal) or geographic or denominational—is secondary. In the Vatican II document on the church, *Lumen Gentium*, it states that "all men are called to belong to the new People of God. This People . . . is to be spread throughout the whole world and to all ages." Some are baptized into other communions (i.e., some are non-Roman Catholic Christians); others do not yet know God or the Gospel of Christ and his church. These others ought not to be considered as apart from the people of God, but as people in the process of becoming members of the church. In short, such people's knowledge of God, as deficient and inadequate as it may be, should be regarded as "a preparation for the Gospel"; they are the mission field of the church ("Church," *Vatican II*, 367–68). On those with an incomplete knowledge of the Gospel, the document says that "they are exposed to ultimate despair" and that "to procure the glory of God and the salvation of all these, the Church, mindful of the Lord's command, 'preach the Gospel to every creature' [Mk. 16:16] takes zealous care to foster the missions" (368). Elsewhere the document asserts that the Church "receives the mission of proclaiming and establishing among all peoples the kingdom of Christ and of God" (353). A primary characteristic of the church, then, is its orientation to mission and proclamation. The distinction is less one between heaven and hell, or between the saved and the damned, or even those who are Christians and those who are not Christians, than a distinction between those who are Christians and those who are not yet Christian.

[129] Schwarz, *The Christian Church*, 50. See also Hans Küng, *The Church* (Garden City, NY: Image Books, 1976), 157–68, who provides a fine overview of the history of the use of *laos* in the Old and New Testaments. Besides pointing out the broadening of the definition, Küng also notes the eschatological dimensions. He speaks of the "future city of God" toward which Jews and Gentiles journey (167–68).

[130] Schwarz, *The Christian Church*, 50–51.

[131] Peter C. Hodgson, and Robert C. Williams, "The Church" in *Christian Theology: An Introduction to Its Traditions and Tasks* (2d. ed.; rev. and enl.; ed. Peter C. Hodgson and Robert H. King; Philadelphia: Fortress, 1985), 251.

[132] *BC*, 33. To be sure, the identification of the church with the people of God does occur in the confessions, or at least it is implied, but this identification is not stressed. Cf. Apol. 7 and 8 (*BC*, 170); FC, Solid Declaration 5 (*BC*, 562), and also Solid Declaration 1 (*BC*, 516); see also Arthur Carl Piepkorn, "What the Symbols Have to Say about the Church" in *The Church: Selected Writings of Arthur Carl Piepkorn* (ed. and intro. by Michael P. Plekon and William S. Wiecher with an afterword by Richard John Neuhaus; Delhi, NY: ALPB Books, 1993), 48; hereafter Piepkorn.

[133] Heinrich Schmid, *The Doctrinal Theology of the Evangelical Lutheran Church* (trans. Charles A. Hay and Henry E. Jacobs; Philadelphia: Lutheran Publication Society, 1899), 586–87.

[134] *Three Books*, 113. Interestingly, the Augsburg Confession is superseded by the Formula of Concord: "The history of the *Formula of Concord* clearly shows that [the Augsburg Confession], despite its excellence, did not answer all questions.

The *Augsburg Confession* was not final and cannot be final today" (158); see also "Brief an William Sihler" (12 October 1846), *GW* I: 760.

135 This might also be said of Arthur Carl Piepkorn, the influential Missouri Synod dogmatician. In his examination of the confessions, Piepkorn also looked to the biblical witness and arrived at conclusions not unlike those of Löhe. Piepkorn wrote regarding the communion of saints that "it is a sharing, a taking part with other Christians, in the holy things that make them one, rather than a mere abstract being in association with other individuals" (Piepkorn, 24).

136 Among twentieth-century theologians, there have been a few who have shaped the discussion about ecclesiology more than others. One of these is Hans Küng, who, in many respects, is *persona non grata* in the Roman Catholic Church. Nonetheless, his contributions to ecclesiology—both within and without Roman Catholicism—cannot be overlooked. On the contribution of Küng, see Werner G. Jeanrond, "Hans Küng" in *The Modern Theologians: An Introduction to Christian Theology in the Twentieth Century* (2d ed.; ed. David F. Ford; Oxford: Blackwell, 1997), 162–63.

Küng writes that the church is an eschatological community of salvation which "lives and waits and makes its pilgrim journey under the reign of Christ, which is at the same time, in Christ, the beginning of the reign of God . . . the church may be termed the fellowship of aspirants to the kingdom of God. [The church] is an anticipatory sign of the definitive reign of God: a sign of the reality of the reign of God already present in Jesus Christ, a sign of coming completion of the reign of God. The meaning of the church does not reside in itself, in what it is, but in what it is moving towards"; see *The Church*, 134–35. As for the Lord's Supper itself, Küng writes, "Christ's presence in the Lord's Supper is the presence of something that is to come. [It was] a meal which looked forward to the future, full of confidence and hope" (284). The eschatological dimensions of the eucharistic meal become clearer when Küng states that "in the Lord's Supper the reign of the Kyrios is established and recognized and the community constantly reaffirms its dominion" (288). In short, the Lord's Supper "is an anticipation of the eschatological meal" (291).

The similarities between Küng and Löhe are striking. Indeed, it might be said that there is only one major difference between Löhe and Küng. Küng sees a full and perfected eucharistic fellowship as only attainable and possible when the reign of God has come in its fullness. Löhe strove for such a full eucharistic fellowship on earth. That is to say, he attempted to realize the ideal. Küng, on the other hand, is content to note the ideal and to point out that the Lord's Supper is a foretaste of that perfect union.

137 Werner Löser, "Church," in *Handbook of Catholic Theology* (ed. Wolfgang Beinert and Francis Schüssler Fiorenza; New York: Crossroad, 1995), 99.

138 Karl Rahner, *Foundations of Christian Faith: An Introduction to the Idea of Christianity* (trans. William V. Dych; New York: Crossroad, 1989), 322.

139 Admittedly, Rahner and Löhe probably mean two very different things when they talk about the content of the confession, but to this point, at least, there is common ground.

140 On the human being as a social being, see Rahner, *Foundations*, 323; on the people of God as being communally oriented, see 330, 342.

141 Rahner, *Foundations*, 398, 424–25.

[142] Interestingly, Löhe has a companion on this question from a fascinating source. In a contemporary Roman Catholic dogmatics textbook (which is widely used in North America), Michael Fahey writes, "the purpose of these [marks or attributes] has not always been properly understood. What is clear is that none of the attributes was originally intended to be used polemically or apologetically to demonstrate the superiority of one church over another or to imply that one possessed more unity, sanctity, catholicity, or apostolicity." This is exactly the point Löhe made in *Three Books about the Church* a century and a half ago. See Michael A. Fahey, "Church," in *Systematic Theology: Roman Catholic Perspectives*, 2 vols. (ed. Francis Schüssler Fiorenza and John P. Galvin; Minneapolis: Fortress, 1991), 2: 42.

[143] Hefner, "Church," in *CD*, 2: 212.

[144] *BC*, 32, German text. The Latin text is slightly different: "For the true unity of the church it is enough to agree concerning the teaching of the Gospel and the administration of the Sacraments" (32).

[145] Regarding the intent and purpose of the Augsburg Confession, see Wilhelm Maurer, *Historical Commentary on the Augsburg Confession* (trans. H. George Anderson; Philadelphia: Fortress, 1986), 3–57, esp. 10–16, 54. The challenge, Maurer states, was for the reformers to demonstrate that they were in unity with the historic faith. Löhe recognized the catholic character of the Augsburg Confession ("Kirchliche Briefe," *GW* V/2: 852), but he understood *catholic* only from within a narrow Lutheran viewpoint: the catholic character of the Lutheran church was contained within itself.

[146] Leif Grane asserts that the Augsburg Confession is "pre-confessional" in the sense that it does not seek to draw lines between denominations; see Leif Grane, *The Augsburg Confession: A Commentary* (trans. John H. Rasmussen; Minneapolis: Augsburg, 1987), 97. Regarding the unity of the church, Grane writes that Melanchthon "says that the AC speaks of spiritual unity. Therefore he refuses to involve himself with the objections of the Confutation which concern an external, demonstrable unity. All that is needful for this spiritual unity to exist is proclamation and the sacraments. Everything else is understood as human traditions, which may vary without threatening the church" (96).

[147] Robert W. Jenson, "The Means of Grace—Part 2: The Sacraments," in *CD* 2: 349; cf. Eric W. Gritsch, *Fortress Introduction to Lutheranism* (Minneapolis: Fortress, 1994), 117–19; Hans Urs von Balthasar, *Herrlichkeit*, 3 vols. (Einsiedeln: Johannes Verlag, 1961–69), 1: 549–53; Geoffrey Wainwright, *Doxology: The Praise of God in Worship, Doctrine, and Life* (London: Epworth, 1980), 142–43, 234; "The Constitution on the Sacred Liturgy (*Sacrosanctum Concilium*)" in *Vatican II*, 1–2.

3

THE MINISTRIES
OF THE CHURCH

The church is distinct among all organizations in the world by its possession of the Word and the Sacraments. Possessing this unique treasure raises certain questions: How does the church proclaim the Word? How does the church in a given locale—a congregation—effectively go about the task of proclaiming the Word and administering the sacraments? These questions lie at the heart of what Löhe was about in his ministry and theology.

Because the church possesses the Word and the Sacraments, some sort of order or organization is necessary if chaos and disorder are not to reign. The problem from Löhe's perspective was acute. He grew up in an era when the only available theological options were Pietism and Lutheran Orthodoxy. Neither Orthodoxy nor Pietism, he believed, recognized the true strength of the church's most important possessions—Word and Sacrament. Löhe could hardly have turned to Lutheran Orthodox theologians or Pietists for guidance in his thinking.

Both Lutheran Orthodoxy and Pietism were inclined to a somewhat democratic view of the church: Word and Sacrament were available to all. Lutheran Orthodox theologians adhered to Luther's ideal of the "priesthood of all believers" but insisted that "the office of the public ministry is the pastoral office."[1] In essence, a hierarchy was introduced. All Christians were priests, but only some were called to public office; only some were authorized to publicly proclaim the Word and to administer the sacraments. God instituted, established, and ordained the public office of ministry.[2] As Holsten Fagerberg states, "Lutheran Orthodoxy placed *greater stress* on the ordained ministry with the authority (*potestas*) to exercise the Word, Sacraments and the power of the keys. A sign of this change of emphasis is the decreased value on the priesthood of all believers."[3] Yet this greater stress does not mean that laity has no voice. David Hollaz, Löhe's favorite dogmatician, stated, "the right to call belongs to the whole church, and all its ranks and members."[4] God instituted the ordained ministry, but the church called an individual to it. On this point there was un-animity within Lutheran Orthodoxy.

The emphasis on the ordained clergy as the public expression of the priesthood led to a reaction in the seventeenth century. In one sense, Pietism sought to redress the imbalance between the ordained clergy and the priesthood of all believers. The Pietists' program was largely focused on restoring the priesthood of all believers in the life and theology of the church.[5] Philipp Jakob Spener and other Pietists did not want to disman-tle the public office of ministry or reject its unique role. Like Lutheran Orthodox theologians, "the Pietists insisted that the church's pastoral office had been divinely established and instituted and that it was necessary for the church's life and being. This office was essential for the edification of the people of God."[6] Spener asserted that the ordained ministry was necessary for the maintenance of order. He said that to prevent disorder, the ordained ministry

> should sometimes *instruct* their hearers in regard to this spiritual priesthood, and not hinder but direct them *in the exercise of it.* They should *observe* how their hearers do their duty, and occasionally *call them to account.* If they are acting prudently, they should *encourage* them; but if from lack of understanding they make mistakes, they should *correct* them in love and gentleness; and they should especially use precautions to keep them from falling into conceit, contention, and erroneous doctrine as well as from going farther than Christian edification demands. In short, *they should keep the supervision and Christian direction of the work in their hands.*[7]

The Pietists wanted to see a real priesthood of all believers in which the Christian faith was apparent in the lives of both clergy and laity.

Both Pietism and Lutheran Orthodoxy asserted that the essence of the ordained ministry was the preaching of the Word and the administration of the sacraments. They recognized that Word and Sacrament are entrust-ed to a few on behalf of the many, but the Pietists failed to recognize that the true treasures of the church are Word and Sacrament. Löhe tended to take the best of both views.

Löhe looked to four main sources for his reflections on the ministry.[8] He studied the confessions, the writings of Luther, and, of course, the Scriptures. He also read extensively in the Lutheran Orthodox theologians, whose writings from the previous two centuries provided a systematic pre-sentation of the church's faith and practice. Yet a fifth "source" or, better, "influence" can be discerned in certain elements of Löhe's thinking, particularly in his emphasis on the church as a community and his emphasis on the priesthood of all believers: the Pietism of his mother and grandparents.

THE MINISTRY OF THE CHURCH

The Holy Spirit is at work in creation, redeeming creation (Rom 8:22–23). This work of the Spirit is, for Löhe, a preview of the realization of the reign of God's grace.[9] The first and most important feature of the church is that it is the arena where the work of the Spirit is effected, where grace is always being bestowed for the benefit of all creation. At the center of this visible community of the children of God was the pastor. The ministry (*Amt*) played a central role in Löhe's representation of the church. He held firmly to two related themes: the centrality and importance of the local congregation and the centrality of worship in the life of the local congregation. The ordained ministry was the hub from which all other ministry flowed. At the same time the ordained ministry was responsive and responsible to neither the institutional church nor the state, but to the congregation.

This worship, this establishment and preservation of such a *koinonia*, is really a work of priests. But for Löhe *all* Christians are priests.[10] All who are baptized into Christ are baptized into the priesthood of all believers. The priesthood of all believers is the impulse for Christians to live in *koinonia*. Priests are responsible for fostering community, for joining together individuals who have been separated. In their roles as priests, Christians are called to alleviate misery and create community. But because the demands of the priesthood are manifold, the apostles have seen fit to set some apart as deacons. Diaconal service has its origin in mercy and compassion for the poor (Acts 2:44–45).[11] Deacons are set aside by the church for—that is, called to—a service of mercy and compassion. The recipients of this service are the poor. Deacons, one might say, are called to create community where poverty or misery threatens to destroy community.

If humans are united in their misery, united in their need for community, then they are also united in their need for the church. The church is united through the Word of the apostles. The apostolic Word "has always been the uniting force of the church and will continue to be until the end of time."[12] The church, as the apostles envisioned it, is one and indivisible. The apostles consistently spoke against those who would seek to drive a wedge into the church, thus severing one member of the body of Christ from the others. Schisms and parties within the church were not to be tolerated.[13] The church is the union of, the "marriage" between, the divine and the human; as such, it may not be torn apart by humans.

Clearly Löhe sees a unity in the human condition, in the human longing for an escape from sin and its effects. The unity of the church is also a unity of mind and intellectual assent to the church's faith. Löhe does not see the unity of the church as a collection of individuals driven by the same impulses and exhibiting similar patterns of behavior. He points out, "external conduct is deceptive, since pagans, Jews, and Mohammedans often make a good appearance and even the Antichrist does not mind affecting a certain sort of external piety."[14] Yet unity is not merely about intellectual assent; it is, as this statement hints, an assent that moves the soul and the heart to God. Intellectual assent is only the first step in moving the believer to contrite and humble acts of devotion to God. Only a firm faith in the universal grace of Christ will ensure eternal life. This assent is all that is needed, but this assent will necessarily move the believer to acts of love. And this love, this self-giving, agapic Christian love serves the neighbor and reaches out to include him or her in the fellowship of the community called church.

The church clearly arises out of love, but, as Löhe observes, love is precisely the element lacking among Christians. To be sure, Löhe admits, there is a unity in doctrine and confession in the church, but a doctrinal and confessional unity *alone* is not sufficient for an authentic unity. The apostolic command for unity in the church encompasses not only a oneness of faith and confession, but a oneness in order and Word.[15] Löhe was convinced that a new united church must rise again. At present the church lacked the yeast that would cause it to rise anew. That yeast is love.

The love that Löhe envisions is not a soft, passive love that is confessed by "Sunday Christians" who at worship declare that they love all people but immediately forget this declaration of love. Löhe speaks often of an active love that takes seriously the commandment to "Love your neighbor as yourself." Christian love is like the love the Good Samaritan expressed in Jesus' parable, love that moves believers to reach into their pockets and give freely and willingly of their wealth to a stranger in need. It is a love that extends to others in need, a love that gives up all for the community and fosters community. This community has two circles: The first is the narrower circle that cares and provides for those in an immediate geographic proximity; the second, wider, circle extends to all those in need, those often far removed in geography, race, and culture.[16] Löhe challenges believers to be actively involved in ministries that express their love for those both near and far.

MINISTRY IN THE EARLY CHURCH

APOSTOLIC MINISTRY

Ministry in the Christian tradition looks to the Scriptures and the early church for models and exemplars of life given in service. The apostles were those men closest to Jesus and thus most immediately familiar with Jesus' vision for the church and the ministry he entrusted to it. But the apostles are no longer present in the church. Their teaching endures, but they no longer live among God's people. They were a one-time occurrence with no actual successors. For Löhe, the apostles have only a succession of their teaching.[17] Other than the first twelve disciples called by Jesus, there are no other apostles except for Paul and Barnabas.[18] These apostles are the basis of the office of ordained ministry as it has been received by the church.

Among the gifts the first apostles received was the gift of judgment. That is, they received the gift of judging the human heart.[19] The apostles could judge between a pure heart and a hypocritical heart, even without an examination of the person or the situation. They could see directly into the hearts of others.

The apostles also received the gift of laying on of hands. They laid hands on those deacons whose call to service they recognized as legitimate and valid. The apostles also baptized, thus imparting the gift of grace and eternal life. The important point, Löhe says, is not that the apostles' *hands* baptized or were laid on deacons, but that their hands imparted the extraordinary gifts of the Spirit necessary for eternal life.[20] The apostles were merely instruments or means by which the gifts of the Spirit were imparted.

The most important responsibility of the apostles was connected to the call with which they were entrusted. Löhe is convinced that there was—already at the time of the apostles—a universal call of all people.[21] The mission of the apostles was to make this call known, to proclaim that all have been called to priesthood. In short, the most important and immediate responsibility of the apostles was to make disciples.

The Gospel is to be "proclaimed in his name to all nations, beginning from Jerusalem" (Luke 24:47; see also Acts 1:8). This is exactly what happened immediately after Stephen's death. Luke writes that:

[A] severe persecution began against the church in Jerusalem, and all except the apostles were scattered throughout the countryside of Judea and Samaria. . . . Now those who were scattered went from place to place, proclaiming the word. Philip went down to the city of Samaria and proclaimed the Messiah to them. (Acts 8:1b, 4)

The disciples did not just go to God's nation—Israel—or even to favored nations. Rather, the disciples went to all nations—even the nations they did not like. Luke notes:

Now when the apostles at Jerusalem heard that Samaria had accepted the Word of God, they sent Peter and John to them. The two went down and prayed for them that they might receive the Holy Spirit. . . . Peter and John laid their hands on them, and they received the Holy Spirit. (Acts 8:14–15,17)

The apostles even went to Samaria, perhaps the most despised neighbor of Israel, despite an ingrained hatred of the Samaritans. They did this in obedience to the command to "make disciples of all nations" (Matt 28:19).

The apostles went about fulfilling a new task. The old task had been to preach "the kingdom of God" (Luke 9:2), that it "has come near" (Matt 10:7). Furthermore, their old task had been to proclaim this message only to the Jews. Jesus had preached only among the Jews; and the apostles did just as he did.[22] But at Jesus' ascension, the apostles were commissioned with a new task: to preach "in Jerusalem, in all Judea and Samaria, and to the ends of the earth" (Acts 1:8).

The second part of this task was equally as important as the first: to baptize. The command to make disciples continues with the words "baptizing them in the name of the Father and of the Son and of the Holy Spirit" (Matt 28:19b). The Lukan account of the same command implies as much in the context of Baptism: "repentance and forgiveness is to be proclaimed in his [Christ's] name to all nations, beginning from Jerusalem" (Luke 24:47). For Löhe, in the Lutheran catechetical tradition of Baptism as a daily drowning of the old Adam and daily resurrection of the new Adam, Jesus' commission in St. Luke's gospel was clear: In Baptism we daily repent and we daily receive forgiveness of sins.[23] As Paul writes, "we have been buried with him by Baptism into death, so that we too might walk in newness of life" (Rom 6:4). Disciple-making and Baptism belong together.

Löhe notes that the apostolic task does not simply unfold in linear order; the ministerial task is *not* completed with Baptism. The Lutheran understanding of Baptism already witnesses to this fact: Baptism is a daily event, and, as such, it is about daily discipleship. What is daily repentance if not discipleship? What does it mean to daily walk in newness of life if not to walk as a disciple? The "order" of this task, then, is more along the lines of an infinitely repeating cycle. Discipleship leads to Baptism which leads to discipleship which leads to a renewed understanding and appropriation of the meaning and signficance of Baptism. The apostles' responsibility to the baptized then does not end with their Baptism. The apostles are commanded to care for them as well. From the commandment to teach the baptized to obey all that Jesus has commanded the disciples, "it follows that the Apostles are to attend to the people not merely as long as they have not been baptized, but rather that the baptized people were precisely commended to their special care and love."[24] The commandment to care for the baptized carries as much weight as the commandment to baptize. To baptize and disciple is to baptize and care for those who have been baptized.

The main task of the apostles was proclamation.[25] They were to proclaim the universal call of all to priesthood. But this does not entirely answer the question of the content of the proclamation of the disciples. At one time the apostles preached the nearness of the kingdom of God and, at that, only among the Jews. After the death of Christ, though, the content of their message shifted. The nearness of the kingdom of God yielded to the saving work of Jesus as the content of apostolic preaching: "the resurrection of Jesus is the focus of the glorification of Jesus and his work; the preaching of the same is the focus of that preaching which is called evangelical."[26] This preaching is not the same as that of Christ when he walked the shores of Galilee; it is preaching Christ himself.

To preach Christ crucified is to preach repentance and forgiveness of sins. This message is primarily oriented to those who believe and have been baptized. The proclamation is, Löhe notes, often not well received by the stiff-necked. As Paul writes, "we proclaim Christ crucified, a stumbling block to Jews and foolishness to Gentiles" (1 Cor 1:23). Löhe picks up on this Pauline theme, though he does not directly mention the biblical text. He affirms that damnation—the threat of the Law—is to be preached to those who stubbornly and persistently resist God's offer of grace; to those who believe and are baptized, repentance, forgiveness of sins, and life and holiness are preached.[27] In both instances, proclamation is a central task of the apostles. Christ always remains the center of their Gospel preaching.

The apostles founded the first congregations. They gave the church its form and shape. They were the pioneers of the fellowship that became known around the world as the church. For this reason the most loyal, the truest friends of the church, Löhe asserts, follow the example of the apostles. That church does not honor the apostles over God, but rather honors God by honoring the apostles.[28] To reject the authority and example of the apostles is to reject God, as Paul writes to the church at Thessalonica, "whoever rejects this [example of holiness] rejects not human authority but God" (1 Thess 4:8). Peter also called Christians to a life of holiness, as the example of Ananias demonstrates (Acts 5:1–11). The apostles' first tasks, responsibilities, and mission established the tasks, responsibilities, and mission of the church that bears Christ's name through the centuries. To follow the example of the apostles is to carry out the mission of the church.

EVANGELISTS

In Eph 4:11, Paul lists evangelists among the ministers of the church. Löhe speaks briefly to this office using Timothy as the prototype or archetype. This office is closely related to that of apostle; the evangelist's role is to proclaim the Gospel in much the same manner. Evangelists exercise the responsibility of calling, ordaining, and judging presbyters. Löhe asserts that evangelists were called and ordained by the apostles and not by the church, or at least that the apostles played the leading role in their ordination.[29] That evangelists are called and ordained by the apostles points to their subservient position next to the apostles. Evangelists are the apostles' servants: "An evangelist is an assistant apostle, a forerunner, an accompanist, an additional worker of an apostle."[30] Evangelists have the same responsibilities and often exercise the same authority. But this office has not continued to the present age in its original or apostolic form; it existed only in the New Testament church. Today missionaries who are exceptionally industrious are often called "evangelists," but these evangelists are really only the last, fleeting rays of a sun which set long ago.[31] Evangelists in the New Testament or apostolic age are those who can be measured against the standard of Timothy: They were called and ordained by an apostle, exercised similar authority (calling and ordaining presbyters), and accompanied and assisted apostles in their ministry of proclamation.

DEACONS

Another office that existed in the New Testament church was deacon. This work particularly interested Löhe; he dedicated much of his energy to restoring it to a position of honor and importance in the life of the church. What, for Löhe, is the diaconal office? Who are deacons?

Löhe's understanding of the diaconate flows directly out of his understanding of the ministry of the church. All people are called to the priesthood; the church proclaims God's grace and salvation for all. What does it mean to be a priest? It means, among other things, to be about the task of fostering and living in *koinonia*—fellowship or community. Following the example of the Christian community as described in Acts 2, the church devotes itself "to the apostles' teaching and fellowship, to the breaking of bread and the prayers" (Acts 2:42). One way the early church went about this task was to hold "all things in common; they would sell their possessions and goods and distribute the proceeds to all, as any had need" (Acts 2:44–45; cf. also 4:32, 34–35). The key phrase is "as any had need"—the church acknowledges the needs of others. Löhe writes, "The sanctified [*Heiligen*] ought to recognize the needs of others as their own and seek to still these needs through the distribution of temporal goods."[32] The church is not only about the spiritual welfare of its members, but also about their physical welfare.

The diaconate is related closely to the church as community and its concern for the welfare of its members. The members of the church are called to live out their vocations as "a royal priesthood" (1 Pet 2:9). Especially important in this regard, then, is care for the poor. This service to the poor is diaconal service; it belongs to all those who are members of the church. Following in the tradition of the Hebrew prophets in emphasizing justice and concern for the poor, for widows, and for orphans, Löhe says that "diaconal ministry is care for the poor in the sense and the spirit of the church."[33] This ministry is the arena in which the church can most actively and visibly be the church. *Koinonia* defines the church; diaconal service is the expression of this fellowship. To be in fellowship with others is to attend to and care for their needs, especially those whose need is great. Congregations without any poor in their immediate vicinity should look beyond their own membership to the church catholic.[34] Such a congregation properly takes up responsibility for the poor beyond the community to the farthest corners of the earth.

Diaconal service is the service of the church to the poor in its midst. All members of the church share in this vital work.

> All servants of Christ, from the apostles to the [ordained] deacons, are deacons, they are industrious and active in caring for the poor and they carry the Word of life . . . upon their lips bringing in their hands the offerings of the congregation far and wide through which earthly misery will be eased. Diaconal ministry in its broadest understanding is a bond of unity, of interdependence, of remembering others, of love![35]

Diaconal service is an expression of Christian love. It is the expression of Christian love for all others in the community.

Although every believer shares in and supports this mission, some are called and set aside for the express purpose of carrying out diaconal service. These deacons are engaged in the work of caring for the poor on behalf of the church. For this reason the office of the deacon was instituted (Acts 6:1–4).[36] Because of the centrality of their work, deacons are rightly called "the treasure of the church." They are the foot soldiers—so to speak—of the congregation. They engage in other service related to caring for the poor: looking after church buildings, clerical tasks, and other congregational needs. Their work takes place between the clergy and the congregation. They are chosen according to apostolic norms, their election is confirmed by the clergy, and they are consecrated and supervised by the clergy.[37] Although deacons carry out this work of the congregation, they are in many respects independent of the congregation.

The diaconate is part of the presbyterate—the clergy.[38] Deacons are consecrated and supervised by the clergy. They are not peers with the clergy, but like the clergy, they have a distinctive, though subordinate, office. For this reason the diaconate is to be respected as a holy office. Deacons are to be respected even though the congregation selects and calls them (according to apostolic norms). Neither the clergy nor the congregation have grounds to fear the diaconate.[39] The congregation should not fear the diaconate because it has chosen the deacons; the clergy should not fear the diaconate because they have blessed and consecrated them.

By the nineteenth century, the office of deacon had disappeared in Germany. Löhe was much taken by the concept and, in view of the misery that the Industrial Revolution had wreaked upon the people throughout the nation, felt that the times demanded the reinstatement of the diaconate. The diaconate was a powerful means by which the church could involve all its members in the life of the community and world, freeing pastors for the task of preaching the Word and administering the sacraments. Löhe, therefore, reestablished the diaconate to exercise a service of caring on behalf of the congregation.

ORDAINED MINISTRY (*AMT*)

The ordained ministry, Löhe believed, is flexible and responsive to the needs of the people it seeks to instruct in the Word. This flexibility and responsiveness was established early in the New Testament church. The first Christian writings do not provide a *detailed* account of the apostolic ordained ministry. Yet two issues are apparent when one examines the origins and roots of the ordained ministry: Parallels to the ordained ministry may be found in the Old Testament and in Jewish religious life; and the ordained ministry was a necessary response to the demands of communal life.[40] Löhe attempted to establish a biblical and apostolic foundation for the *Amt*, claiming that the office of presbyter "belongs without doubt to the general apostolic practice and is assumed in many apostolic commands and directives."[41] The need for an ordained clergy was also apparent early, in Löhe's view, and that need has remained to this day.

Löhe's missionary activity in North America and his attempt to mediate in the dispute between C. F. W. Walther of the Missouri Synod and J. A. A. Grabau of the Buffalo Synod over the nature and source of the office of ordained ministry (*Amt*) provided the impulse for his writings. In general, the debate contrasted a congregational and an episcopal form of ecclesial polity. Löhe himself had mixed feelings.[42] As to the structure of the church, he favored a more episcopal style of polity; he was deeply suspicious of any kind of congregational polity and in this sense agreed with Grabau.[43] Yet Löhe was conscious that the church had to ensure that all the gifts of the Spirit had an outlet for their expression to the service of God. Practically, Löhe recognized the importance of a democratic element in the church. In North America he attempted to hold this tension in his mediation between Grabau and Walther. Unfortunately, Löhe's efforts availed little. He alienated both Grabau and Walther. In North America Walther carried the day as the Buffalo Synod lost members and pastors to Missouri and other synods. What remained of the Buffalo Synod was small and never did grow large; eventually it was amalgamated into a predecessor body of the American Lutheran Church.[44] This dispute forced Löhe to take a position that mediated between Walther's "congregational" view and Grabau's "episcopal" view of the *Amt*.

Löhe asserted that the office of ordained ministry did not stem from the congregation or from an episcopacy. The ordained ministry has an apostolic foundation but not in the sense that the Roman Catholic Church claimed. At the time of his ascension, Christ appointed pastors and teachers for the equipping of the saints and the building up of the church. Numerous passages in the New Testament establish and attest to the legitimacy of the pastoral office. The pastoral office then proceeds not from the congregation, nor from the episcopacy, but from Christ himself.[45] Christ is the basis of the office of ordained ministry.

Löhe notes that all Christians are called to honor and obey the pastor of the congregation to which they belong. His language hints at his frequent comparison of the church to marriage. Congregations ought to honor pastors in at least two ways: with word and conduct and with the honor of a living income (1 Tim 5:17–18).[46] At the same time pastors are accountable and responsible for their behavior and actions. Those who repeatedly and consciously denigrate, besmirch, or scandalize the office of the ordained ministry should be publicly rebuked. Löhe holds the ordained ministry in high esteem and expects—demands—that others do so as well.

> It is demonstrated how seriously the Lord wills it that we be obedient to the office of ordained ministry. Nobody who views their pastor only as an object of criticism and judgment instead of a superior can be named a Christian (who has to be obedient to the divine command) in truth and deed. Also, nobody can, or [should] attempt to, supplant the ordained ministry that has been established by God without supplanting God's own church order. One turns therefore to obedience to the true servants of Jesus; by that it is not said that one should give honor and obedience to wolves.[47]

To disobey or openly defy one's pastor, to seek to supplant the office of ordained ministry, is to oppose the divinely instituted order for the church. To dishonor the divinely established servants of God is tantamount to idolatry.

For Löhe, ordination to the office comes from Christ and not from the congregation. The pastor continues to be responsible to the congregation as a servant of the congregation. Yet Löhe affirms that the pastor is not a servant in the sense of carrying out the commands of the congregation, but in that the pastor is oriented and sensitive to equipping the members of the congregation.[48] Again Löhe's sense of the importance of mission and ministry among all the priests comes into prominence. The church is a royal priesthood, proclaiming the mighty acts of God in Christ. The office of ordained ministry exists for the purpose of equipping all believers so they might be more effective priests, that is, so God's people might more effectively bear witness to and proclaim the Gospel with which they have been entrusted.

RITE OF ORDINATION

All Christians are called to the priesthood; that is, all are called to live as priests in community. Some of these ministers or priests are set aside by the rite of ordination; deacons, for example, are "ordained" for service to the church and world. But others are set aside into a special ministry that is exercised on behalf of the whole. Ordination is the process or the rite by which these "special" ministers are recognized. These ministers are ordained into a ministry that they exercise on behalf of the whole church.

The rite of ordination acknowledges and celebrates a candidate's fitness for a ministry, then blesses that candidate for that ministry. This recognition and blessing is illustrated by the laying on of hands. Löhe argues that ordination is the same as the laying on of hands spoken of in the Scriptures.[49] Ordination and laying on of hands are the same; "laying on of hands" is the scriptural term for ordination. The New Testament writings record a few instances where people received laying on of hands for the purpose of ordaining them into a ministry. Acts 6 contains the account of seven Hellenist Christians who were ordained. Acts 13 recounts the ordination of Saul and Barnabas.[50] Acts 14:23 records the ordination of presbyters at Antioch. And 1 Tim 4:14 and 5:22 speak to Timothy's ordination by laying on of hands. The scriptural witness seems clear.

The Lutheran church, in Löhe's time, observed only one ordination: into the presbyterate.[51] The church has only one ordained office, the presbyterate, and a person is ordained once; one is never re-ordained.[52] An installation is different from an ordination; it is an installation into a particular setting, for example, a congregation or chaplaincy.

Is ordination a consecration and conferral of the office of holy ministry? Or is ordination the reception of a gift necessary for the office of ministry? In the first view, ordination is a communication of the office; in the second view, ordination is the reception of the gifts necessary for the exercise of the office. Löhe suggests a middle way between these two points of view represented by Lutheran Orthodoxy and Roman Catholicism respectively.[53] Both views, he affirms, are consistent with Scripture. No one should be ordained without a recognition of their call to a specific ministry. Ordained ministry does not exist apart from ministry in a defined setting. And in the case of the second view, Löhe asserts that 1 Tim 4:14 and 2 Tim 1:6 show that the Spirit's gifts for ministry are imparted in the laying on of hands. The presbyters themselves know and understand the gifts necessary for ministry. For this reason the presbyterate bears the responsibility of seeking other able candidates to ordain into the presbyterate.[54] The presbyterate itself seeks and finds candidates, trains and examines them, and finally ordains them. As Löhe writes:

> Ordination, insofar as it is a transmission of the office and a conse-
> cration into the holy office, is the concern of the presbyterate and
> occurs in the name of the Lord and accompanied by prayers to the
> Lord and the participation of the congregation to whom everything
> belongs, even the office which Christ has founded.[55]

The presbyterate then plays the leading role in the ordination of candidates into the ordained ministry.

The congregation, however, also has a significant role to play in the
life of the church with respect to ordination. If the congregation does not
approve of an ordination, it does have "voice" in the ordination process.
Löhe states that the presbyterate ought to listen carefully to the witness of
the congregation, hear the wishes and will of the congregation, and take
their concerns seriously when considering whether or not to ordain a candidate.[56] After all, the ordinand is ordained into a ministry that takes place
in a concrete setting.

Ordination is not conducted by the congregation, and ordination is
not received through the congregation. That is, the ordinand does not
receive the gifts and blessing of ordination through the congregation.
Rather, the ordinand receives the gifts and blessing of ordination through
the presbyterate. The congregation calls, but it does not ordain; the ordination itself is done by and through the presbyterate.

FUNCTION AND RESPONSIBILITY OF THE *AMT*

Amt refers to a public office that exercises rightful authority. The word
has connotations of a wide range of responsibility and authority. For the
church, the *Amt* is properly the ordained ministry. Löhe wrote extensively about this universal office in *Three Books about the Church*. The *Amt* seeks
to be a blessing to those who strive to live in the power of the apostolic
Word; it is the source of nurture and strength to those who seek nourish-
ment. The ordained ministry is the lamp placed upon the lampstand that
all may see and be guided by its light (Matt 5:15). Löhe acknowledges,
"The ministry is a fountain of blessing which is nourished from the apostles who nourished their disciples who nourished their disciples and so
forth throughout time."[57] The ordained ministry exists to serve the
church, to nourish its members, the disciples of the apostolic Word.

The responsibility or task of service to the members of the church necessarily entails a close relationship between pastor and parishioners. The
Amt does not exist to preserve itself; it does not exist to carry out certain
functions or responsibilities for itself. It exists to serve; the *Amt* "exists for

the building up of the church and the preparation of its members."[58] For Löhe, this statement encapsulates the overarching task of the ordained ministry in all its different manifestations.[59] The ordained ministry, though it exists to serve the church, does not exist to give expression to the people's voice.[60] Because the ordained ministry exists to serve Christ and his church—and not the desires of the people—it gives expression to the apostolic Word.

The ordained ministry, then, exists in the often messy and ambiguous space between God and humanity. The *Amt* serves God in proclaiming and giving expression to the apostolic Word. Yet this ministry serves within the arena of human existence. God has given the *Amt* to the church as a gift and a blessing. Yet this ministry is transmitted by a human calling and ordination of a candidate. The *Amt* is hierarchical yet egalitarian. The church is egalitarian: All are called to the priesthood, but in the church some are called to a ministry that sets them in a position of authority and responsibility over others. In the church, Löhe writes, "we see holy aristocracy and holy democracy combined in the work of mercy!"[61] The work of mercy, of embodying Christ's love to others in physical acts, is a concrete embodiment of God's love for all and the Christian's love for others.[62] Ministry, like love, is manifested in many ways.

In 1 Corinthians 12 Paul addresses the issue of spiritual gifts and how they serve to further the ministry of the church of Christ. The apostle writes that there are varieties of gifts, services, and activities given by the Spirit to God's people; to each member "is given the manifestation of the Spirit for the common good" (1 Cor 12:4–7). Later, Paul adds, "For just as the body is one and has many members, and all the members of the body, though many, are one body, so it is with Christ" (1 Cor 12:12). Although there are many gifts and many acts of service in the church, there is but one ministry—the ministry given by Christ to the church, the body of Christ.

After his discussion of the Spirit's gifts to the church, St. Paul pens his hymn on love. 1 Corinthians 13 portrays a community that lives together in concord. "Love lives for the other" might summarize Paul's theme. For Löhe, 1 Corinthians 12–13 represents the heart of his own theology. Love is the bond that binds the church together in its holy calling. The church needs manifold gifts to carry out its one ministry (expressed in various ways) and its calling to do works of mercy and to make known to the world its identity as a royal priesthood. The church becomes like the apostle who wrote, "I have become all things to all people, that I might by all means save some. I do it all for the sake of the gospel, so that I may share in its blessings" (1 Cor 9:22–23).[63] Like Paul, the church is all things to all people for the purpose of sharing the Gospel.

The relationship between the different ministries—between the ordained ministry and the congregation—has elements of hierarchy and equality, of aristocracy and democracy:

> Very simply, what the times demand is, in accordance with Scripture and the truth, the relationship between the ordained ministry and the congregation which we find in the New Testament, in Acts, in the Epistles. There is, at one and the same time, in this relationship something aristocratic and something democratic, something constant and something fluid. An aristocratic element is neither in the state nor in the church to be entirely avoided. There is neither in the world of nature nor in the world of grace a full equality, but rather one finds everywhere great and small, above and below. Where there is no great and no small, loveliness; where there is no above and no below, there is no order. Just as God is certainly a God of order and the Spirit a Spirit of lovely differentiation and union of the great and the small and so forth, so there must certainly be in the state or in the church an aristocratic element. But there must also be something democratic, because without the active participation of the congregation there is no active church and without freedom there is no active participation.[64]

The aristocratic element is the presbyterate or the ordained clergy; the democratic element is diaconal service that belongs to every member of the body of Christ and is entrusted to some—deacons—on behalf of the many. The main task of the presbyterate is preaching. This task was already established by the example of the apostles. The apostles' chief task was to preach the Gospel.[65] The proclamation of God's word of grace is not easy; it has always been laborious and difficult. But the apostles viewed preaching as a labor of love.[66] Preaching, indeed all ministry—service to the other—is done out of a sense of gratitude and thankfulness to God.

Proclamation of the Word belongs to all who belong to the church. This responsibility is fulfilled in many ways. The *Amt* is a ministry of preaching but not only of preaching. Some who are ordained may work more in pastoral care and congregational life or in liturgical and sacramental leadership. Löhe asserts that the presbyterate "is a ministry of 'prayer and the Word,' of liturgy and Sacrament, of preaching, of doctrine, of pastoral care, of discipline, and of order."[67] The *Amt* and its task of preaching takes on many manifestations. In one place and in one person, it emphasizes the liturgy and the sacraments; in another place and in another person, it emphasizes congregational life and pastoral care.

The presbyterate attends to and considers the gifts and abilities of the minister in carrying out ministry in a given location. It also regards the needs of the congregation. Some congregations need more attention in their worship life, others in discipline and order, and yet others in congregational life and parish administration. In this sense, the task given to pastors is that of applying God's mysteries and treasures. An ordained minister is entrusted with the responsibility of properly allotting God's treasures and mysteries—God's Word and the Sacraments.[68] Löhe draws on the Augustana's description of the office of the holy ministry: The church is that assembly where "the Gospel is taught purely and the Sacraments are administered rightly."[69] All who are called and placed in positions of authority and responsibility contribute to the advance and the life of the church.

Clergy are entrusted with the Word and Sacraments. They do not hoard or hide Christ's gifts. Rather, they share the Word and the Sacrament freely, just as Christ freely gave and shared of his precious body and blood. Pastors are servants. They do not govern or rule over congregations as officials of the state govern and rule, Löhe asserts. They direct or manage them.[70] A congregation is not a pastor's fiefdom to do with as the pastor wills. A congregation is a community and the pastor is a member of the community. The pastor stands in need of God's gifts as much as anybody else in that community. The pastor is no better or no worse than anybody else. But a pastor is called by that community to administer the gifts and treasures of God according to the norms established by the apostles. In Löhe's view, the pastor directs and manages the congregation so the people of God in that place might best preserve and honor these gifts so others might come to recognize these gifts too. The pastor is a "supervisor" or "overseer" of the congregation.[71] The pastor serves Christ by overseeing the congregation as a community of love.

The unifying element in the different manifestations of the *Amt* is teaching. In some manner or another, those who are ordained are engaged in teaching or imparting God's Word. Whether it be in explicit teaching and preaching ministries, or in pastoral care and liturgy, or in parish administration and congregational life, the ordained minister seeks to teach the content of God's Word to those to whom he ministers. Löhe summarizes three issues regarding teaching and the ordained ministry:

First, that there could be people outside the presbyterate who have
and exercise the gift of teaching; second, that some presbyters do not
directly possess strength in the work of the Word and of public teaching or are not especially active [in these ministries]; and third, we
must therefore adhere to the example of the apostles that a presbyter
must, to a certain degree, be engaged in instruction.[72]

Proclamation of God's universal call to priesthood and of grace in
Christ has the aim of informing people so they might have a fuller knowledge and understanding of their own call to serve. Both the pastoral ministry and diaconal service contribute to this end.

THE STATUS OF THE *AMT* IN THE CHURCH

The *Amt* occupies a unique position in the church. The members of
the presbyterate—the ordained clergy—are no better or worse, Löhe recognizes, than anyone else; all are simultaneously sinner and saint.[73] Yet the
presbyterate as a whole stands above all other stations and ministries in the
church.[74] Although they stand above all other ministries, the clergy do not
stand apart from them. Indeed, the pastoral office stands in a close relationship with the "ordained" diaconate in the New Testament church.

The apostles knew the congregations and their individual needs and,
therefore, what gifts were most essential for carrying out effective ministry
in the community. Because the needs of the church are not the same in
every place and in every time, the qualifications of the clergy are varied and
broad. While teaching is an important component in the ordained ministry, one need not be an academic theologian to be an effective pastor.[75]
One must instead be recognized by other pastors as being fit and capable
for the ministry to which one is called.[76] It is an ordinand's peers (the
ordained clergy) who recruit the ordinand and acknowledge the ordinand's
call. They then act accordingly in ordaining that candidate for the *Amt*.

CONCLUSION

Few theologians claim that ecclesiology is the center of theology. Yet
ecclesiology often separates denominations. The relationship of local
believers to the whole people of God, of the churches to the Church, is
often determined not by the doctrines of justification or sanctification, but
by the understanding of the church.[77]

In many respects, Löhe's ecclesiology propels his theology. The church
is the "place" where the Holy Spirit is present; it is the arena of the Spirit's
activity. The Holy Spirit is working through Word and Sacrament in the

church.[78] This idea is not, of course, unique to Löhe. At the same time, Löhe addresses the topic differently than the dogmaticians of Lutheran Orthodoxy. In the early eighteenth century, David Hollaz noticed the relationship between the church and the Spirit.[79] The Spirit works through Word and Sacrament, and Word and Sacrament are the possessions of the church.

Löhe is one of the few Lutheran theologians and church leaders to have explicitly developed the connection between the Spirit and the means of grace. He puts forward this strong association because of his elevated view of the church. His contention that the church meets the fundamental human need for community anticipates a sacramental view of the church. Such an elevated or sacramental view necessarily leads to the assertion that the Spirit is at work in the church effecting God's reign of grace.

In his essay on the development of pneumatology in the patristic and medieval eras, William Rusch notes two phases.[80] The first phase, characterized as a period in which the Holy Spirit was benignly neglected as a locus of theological reflection, addresses the question of whether the Spirit can legitimately be named a person of the Trinity. The second phase was preoccupied with the person of the Spirit. In what sense is the Spirit God? In either case, the relationship between the Spirit and the church was not fleshed out.

An obvious place to look for influences on Löhe's thinking on the Spirit and the church is the theology of Luther, the Lutheran Confessions, and the Lutheran Orthodox dogmaticians. Clearly the Holy Spirit plays a much greater role in the theology of Luther than is often acknowledged.[81] Luther recognized the close relationship between the means of grace and the Spirit. Intuitively he perceived that the church is the domain of the Spirit:

> In this Christian church, wherever it exists, is to be found the forgiveness of sins, i.e., a kingdom of grace and of true pardon. For in it are found the gospel, Baptism, and the Sacrament of the Altar, in which the forgiveness of sins is offered, obtained, and received. Moreover, Christ and his Spirit and God are there.[82]

Luther planted the seed for some creative thinking on the relationship between the Spirit and the church. Yet in Luther's lifetime, evangelical writers, including Melanchthon, exhibited a tendency to scholastic thinking on pneumatology and related it more to soteriology.[83] Lutheran Orthodoxy continued the movement away from Luther's "Spirit" theology and reflected the soteriological thrust of the confessions.[84] Luther's conception of the Spirit and the Spirit's active reign in the church did not endure.

In the twentieth century, prominent theologians have articulated the notion of the church as the domain of the Spirit. In the Reformed tradition, Karl Barth states that "a congregation is the coming together of those who belong to Jesus Christ through the Holy Spirit."[85] It is impossible to speak of the Holy Spirit without speaking of the church. More than Barth, however, Dietrich Bonhoeffer highlights the work of the Spirit in the community of faith. His writings proceed along similar lines as Löhe's. Bonhoeffer speaks of the church as the body of Christ, a community that experiences unity with Christ and among its members.[86] His view also leans toward such sacramentalism.[87] Much of theology in the twentieth century thinks along similar lines.

The sacramental view of the church is well known today, but it was not always so. Various factors contributed to this growing awareness: World War I; the Great Depression; World War II; the threat of a nuclear holocaust; and the emergence of younger, indigenously led churches in Africa, Asia, and Latin America. World War I destroyed the optimistic and progressive claims of liberal Protestantism. The Great Depression forced churches and religious communities to overcome any individualistic elements that remained in their midst. World War II revealed the demonic that coexists in the created order. Indigenously led churches, largely untouched by the historical experience of the Enlightenment and the individualism to which Rationalism had given birth, have tended to be community-oriented in their outlook. The end result of these events and trends is an appreciation of the church as a place where community is created and sustained.

In Löhe's ecclesiology, the ministries of the church serve to "build up the body of Christ" (Eph 4:12). All the parts of the body must serve the body (1 Cor 12:7, 12). To frame the answer differently, the ministries of the church work together to build community—*koinonia*.

The church is a community. As such, the church needs different gifts to serve the needs of the community. Löhe seeks to organize the church in such a way so as to serve the community and its chief purpose: evangelism. At the center of this task is the church's possession of the Word and the Sacraments: "The church is the assembly of saints in which the Gospel is taught purely and the Sacraments are administered rightly."[88] For the life of the community itself, it is necessary for the community to be organized such that it fulfills this task. The Gospel cannot be taught purely if there is no one to ensure its purity and the sacraments cannot be rightly administered if there is no one properly set aside for that task.

Löhe's view of the church in this respect corresponds to a more institutional view of the church. Avery Dulles identifies the tasks of teaching and sanctifying as two of the powers and functions of the church. With respect to correct doctrine ("the Gospel taught purely"), Dulles notes that the church "resembles a school in which the masters, as sacred teachers, hand down the doctrine of Christ."[89] In Löhe's conception, pastors have the task of ensuring that right doctrine is taught and proclaimed in the congregation. With respect to the right administration of the sacraments, Dulles notes that the ordained clergy in such a model "are described somewhat as if they were engineers opening and shutting the valves of grace."[90]

Yet Löhe's conception is not nearly as unidimensional as this portrait. The church as the body of Christ and as the people of God are both important images in Löhe's ecclesiology. Löhe also recognizes the church as mystical communion and as the presence of Christ on earth. These images thus act as counterweights to the authoritarianism of the institutional model.[91] Löhe's experience and understanding of the church points clearly to a balanced view of the Spirit, the ministry, and the means of grace. The church is the people of God. As the people of God, the church imparts God's gift of grace to individuals within and outside of the church. In its highest and fullest expression, the church appears in unity, holiness, love, and common confession in Christ. It welcomes the faithful ministry of pastors who serve Christ on behalf of the congregations to which they are called.

The emphasis on holiness, love, and community point to a grand theme in Löhe's understanding of the church: diaconal service. The church is called to such service. Löhe's "innovation" is to restore the diaconate as an office of ministry set apart by the church. His emphasis on the deacon as someone who serves the poor, hungry, and sick on behalf of the church has, by and large, not found widespread acceptance in the Lutheran church or in most other denominations. Yet his interest in reviving the diaconate parallels a common theme in current theological reflection on ministry. Donald Messer highlights the importance of service as a central theme in any theology of ministry.[92] Dulles suggests that the church as servant could be a useful starting point for evaluating any ecclesiological model.[93] The *practice* of ministry, too, must be a key part of all theological reflection on church and ministry.

Bonhoeffer's statement that the church is only the church when it exists for others highlights this diaconal or service theme.[94] Löhe foreshadows an important theme in twentieth-century ecclesiology: The church's ministry is to serve, just as Jesus served in his ministry.

Service permeates Löhe's understanding of the ordering or structure of the church's ministry. A ministry rooted in service enables the church to carry out its commission more effectively. His arguments for such an ordering based on 1 Corinthians 12, Romans 12, and Ephesians 4 are certainly tenable.[95] At the same time, however, his high view of diaconal service seems at odds with his high view of the pastoral office. Löhe's attempt to justify his high view tends to overreach itself. His argument is that the apostles established an office of service which was universal then and ought to be now if the church or a congregation is to make a claim for apostolicity.

The problem with this view is that the New Testament community or even the church which arose out of it was not so homogeneous. Roy Harrisville says that there was never a great golden age in which the first congregations were organized and structured alike.[96] If the primitive church was not uniform and was yet apostolic, then the question must be asked whether the church need be uniform to be apostolic.

Unity is found in adherence to the apostolic Word. Unity suggests uniform adherence to the apostolic Word and a common agreement on the content of the Gospel.[97] Unity, in Löhe's understanding, means uniformity in that each has the same doctrinal interpretation of the apostolic Word. Even in this definition of apostolic unity, uniformity in the ordering of the church's ministry need not follow (though Löhe seems to think that it would be good for the church). "One Lord, one faith, one Baptism" (Eph 4:5) implies that unity is related to faith and its content. It does not necessarily follow that there must be a uniformity in the ordering of the church's ministries in every time and in every place for there to be unity. Nowhere does unity mean uniformity in ecclesiology.

Löhe foreshadowed many developments in theological thinking about the ordering of the church's ministry. His conception of the church's ministry is *charismatic* (i.e., it acknowledges and values all charisms in the church) in that he recognizes that the pastoral office, as it accepts its special responsibility and burden, is responsive to the congregation, though its authority is derived from God. Yet the office recognizes the manifold expressions of its ministry and service to the church and to the world.

NOTES

1 James H. Pragman, "Ministry in Lutheran Orthodoxy and Pietism," in *Called and Ordained: Lutheran Perspectives on the Office of the Ministry* (ed. Todd Nichol and Marc Kolden; Minneapolis: Fortress, 1990), 71.

2 James H. Pragman, *Traditions of Ministry: A History of the Doctrine of the Ministry in Lutheran Theology* (St. Louis: Concordia, 1983), 63.

3 Holsten Fagerberg, "Amt/Ämter/Amtverständnis VII" in *TRE* 2: 578; see also Pragman, *Traditions of Ministry*, 79–82.

4 David Hollaz, *Examen theologicum acroamaticum*, 2 vols. (Stargard, 1707; repr., Darmstadt: Wissenschaftliche Buchgesellschaft, 1971), 4.2.83. Pragman, *Traditions of Ministry*, 69, summarizes the orthodox position: "individuals could not put themselves forward to serve in the church's ministry unless the church had acted through the calling process to place them in that office." See also Fagerberg, "Amt," *TRE* 2: 582.

5 One of Spener's six "proposals to correct conditions in the church" was "the establishment and diligent exercise of the spiritual priesthood" (Philip Jacob Spener, *Pia Desideria* [trans., ed., and with an introduction by Theodore G. Tappert; Philadelphia: Fortress, 1964], 92). See also Fagerberg, "Amt," *TRE* 2: 583; and John Reumann, "Ordained Minister and Layman in Lutheranism," in *Eucharist and Ministry: Lutherans and Catholics in Dialogue IV* (ed. Paul C. Empie and T. Austin Murphy; Minneapolis: Augsburg, 1979), 245. Reumann writes, "Pietism redressed this imbalance and stressed, as might be expected, the *priesthood of all believers*" (author's italics).

6 Pragman, *Traditions of Ministry*, 73.

7 Philipp Jakob Spener, "From the Spiritual Priesthood: Briefly Described According to the Word of God in Seventy Questions and Answers," in *Pietists: Selected Writings* (The Classics of Western Spirituality; ed. with an introduction by Peter C. Erb and a preface by F. Ernest Stoeffler; New York: Paulist Press, 1983), 64. This burden that Spener places on the public ministry can also be seen in his discussion of theological education and ministerial formation in *Pia Desideria*, 103–15 passim.

8 Rudolf Keller, "Reformatorische Wurzeln der Amtslehre von Wilhelm Löhe," in *Unter einem Christus sein und streiten: Festschrift zum 70. Geburtstag von Friedrich Wilhelm Hopf, D.D.* (eds. Jobst Schöne and Volker Stolle; Erlangen: Verlag der Evangelisch-Lutherischen Mission, 1980), 118, persuasively argues that the roots of Löhe's understanding of the ordained ministry can be found in Andreas Osiander; cf. also Rau, *Pastoraltheologie*, 217. This does not, I think, discount the validity of other influences.

9 This idea is latent in much of Löhe's thinking. He speaks often of a type of proleptic experience of heaven, an experience which is effected by the work of the Spirit; see, for example, "Predigt über 2 Chron. 7:3, D.D.F. Pentecostes. 1834 (18. Mai)," *GW* VI/1: 121. See also Sihvonen, "Die schönste Blume Gottes," 140.

10 "Vorschlag," *GW* V/I: 248.

11 "Aphorismen," *GW* V/I: 300.

12 *Three Books*, 62.

13 "Vorschlag," *GW* V/1: 242.

14   *Three Books*, 140–41.

15   "Vorschlag," *GW* V/1: 242.

16   "Vorschlag," *GW* V/1: 246. Löhe writes that we ought to think not only of the poor in our midst but also of those distant from our sight. The Pietists, Francke and Spener, are to be thanked for alerting the Protestant churches to the needs of this wider community; see "Von der Barmherzigkeit," *GW* IV: 517.

17   On the enduring quality of apostolic teaching, see *Three Books*, 74–75.

18   Löhe notes that Barnabas is also called an apostle (Acts 14:14); see "Aphorismen," *GW* V/1: 270.

19   "Aphorismen," *GW* V/1: 271.

20   "Aphorismen," *GW* V/1: 272.

21   "Aphorismen," *GW* V/1: 272; and *Three Books*, 80.

22   "Aphorismen," *GW* V/1: 266.

23   In his explanation of the Sacrament of Baptism in the Small Catechism, Luther says that Baptism "signifies that the old Adam in us, together with all sins and evil lusts, should be drowned by daily sorrow and repentance and be put to death, and that the new man should come forth daily and rise, cleansed and righteous, to live forever in God's presence" (*BC*, 349). Luther writes in the Large Catechism that Baptism encompasses repentance: "if you live in repentance you are walking in Baptism, which not only announces new life but also produces, begins, and promotes it" (*BC*, 445).

24   "Aphorismen," *GW* V/1: 273. Elsewhere, Löhe ("Von der Barmherzigkeit," *GW* IV: 485) states that the apostolic church was ordered around the "merciful love of a shepherd."

25   See page 85.

26   "Aphorismen," *GW* V/1: 267.

27   Löhe cites Mark 16:16 ("The one who does not believe will be condemned") and the Johannine account of the bestowal of the Office of the Keys (John 20:22–23). The thrust of his argument is that believers will be saved and that recalcitrant and intractable nonbelievers are condemned to damnation. See "Aphorismen," *GW* V/1: 266.

28   "Aphorismen," *GW* V/1: 274.

29   "Aphorismen," *GW* V/1: 280. Löhe cites the example of Timothy, who was called by Paul and ordained by the entire presbytery.

30   "Aphorismen," *GW* V/1: 282.

31   "Aphorismen," *GW* V/1: 282.

32   "Aphorismen," *GW* V/1: 299.

33   "Aphorismen," *GW* V/1: 303; also "Von der Barmherzigkeit," *GW* IV: 485. Löhe does not mention the prophetic tradition of concern for the poor and oppressed, but it is difficult to believe that he was unaware of it given his extraordinary knowledge of Scripture. Even a cursory reading of the Hebrew Bible (see, for example, Deut 10:18–19; 24:17–22; 27:19; Ps 146; 82:3–4; Isa 1:17; Jer 7:6; Amos 5:14–15, 24; and Zech 7:8–10) in light of the church described in Acts 2 and 4 would confirm this view. For more on the prophetic emphasis on justice in the Hebrew Bible, see Walter Brueggemann, *The Prophetic Imagination* (Philadelphia:

Fortress, 1978), and *Hopeful Imagination: Prophetic Voices in Exile* (Philadelphia: Fortress, 1986).

34 "Aphorismen," *GW* V/1: 307. The Pauline correspondence is especially rich in expressing a concern and a unity with those parts of the church far removed from a local congregation. Paul mentions to the Romans the generosity of the churches in Macedonia and Achaia in sharing with those in Jerusalem (Rom 15:25–27); he challenges the church in Corinth to take up a regular collection for the church in Jerusalem and, in doing so, again sings the praises of the Macedonians (1 Cor 16:1–3; 2 Corinthians 8–9); and in his letter to the Galatians, he points out that he personally is eager to always remember the poor in his ministry among the Gentiles (Gal 2:10).

35 "Aphorismen," *GW* V/1: 307. Elsewhere, Löhe ("Von der seligen Übung der Barmherzigkeit," *GW* IV: 463) called deacons "servants of mercy."

36 Löhe ("Von der Barmherzigkeit," *GW* IV: 484) remarks that it was an innovation of the New Testament church.

37 Wilhelm Löhe, "Von den Diakonissen," *GW* IV: 450; also "Aphorismen," *GW* V/1: 328.

38 Löhe uses "presbyterate" as a kind of shorthand for the entire ordained clergy. Bishops, deans, superintendents, etc., are included in the presbyterate. All those who are ordained into the ministry of Word and Sacrament belong to the presbyterate.

39 "Aphorismen," *GW* V/1: 303.

40 "Aphorismen," *GW* V/1: 301. William Willimon cautions against reading too much about the origin of ordained ministry into the account of the consecration of the seven Gentiles in Acts 6. He writes concerning ministry and leadership in the church: "Leadership within the church arises from the community's quite mundane but utterly necessary functional needs." See William Willimon, *Acts, Interpretation: A Bible Commentary for Teaching and Preaching* (Atlanta: John Knox, 1988), 59.

41 "Aphorismen," *GW* V/1: 283. In another place, Löhe ("Aphorismen," *GW* V/1: 264) ponders aloud why the church has overlooked the apostolic roots of the *Amt*, and he maintains that the *Amt* is itself a locus of dogmatic reflection but that it has been largely ignored.

42 On this tension in Löhe's ecclesiology, see the section on the church's inner relationships on page 96.

43 Löhe was well aware of the dangers of an episcopal polity. Bishops (or some type of overseer) do not make the church, though they are necessary for good order. Löhe expressed himself clearly in a letter to William Sihler: "I do not want and have never wanted an episcopal system as it haunts us on this side of the ocean in our canon law textbooks" ("Brief an William Sihler" [12 October 1846], *GW* I: 760).

44 For more on the history of the Buffalo Synod, see Nelson, *The Lutherans in North America*, 176–78, 227–28, and 447–48. For a more succinct account, see Todd W. Nichol, *All These Lutherans: Three Paths toward a New Lutheran Church* (Minneapolis: Augsburg, 1986), 67–69.

45 "Vorschlag," *GW* V/1: 243; also "Warum bekenne ich mich?" *GW* IV: 224. Löhe is rather emphatic on this point. He restates this twice more in "Aphorismen," *GW* V/1: 262, maintaining that no support is to be found in the New Testament for the position that the ordained ministry arises out of the congregation. Later, in

his section on presbyters and bishops, he says (*GW* V/1: 294; see also "Brief an William Sihler" [12 October 1846], *GW* I: 760) that there is no support in the New Testament for the position that the ordained ministry is merely the carrier of congregational power and authority. Löhe and his Hessian contemporary August Vilmar were agreed that the *Amt* is derived not from the congregation, but from Christ; see Rudolf Keller, "August Vilmar und Wilhelm Löhe: Historische Distanz und Nähe der Zeitgenossen im Blick auf ihr Amtsverständnis," *Kerygma und Dogma* 39 (1993): 221.

46   "Aphorismen," *GW* V/1: 291–92.

47   "Vorschlag," *GW* V/1: 244; see also *Zuruf*, *GW* IV: 78.

48   "Vorschlag," *GW* V/1: 243.

49   "Aphorismen," *GW* V/1: 313.

50   Gerhard Krodel contends that these two accounts are not unquestionably about ordination and that they are perhaps more likely about a commissioning. See Gerhard Krodel, *Acts* (Augsburg Commentary on the New Testament; Minneapolis: Augsburg, 1986), 133, 228. Hans Schwarz, *The Christian Church: Biblical Origin, Historical Transformation, and Potential for the Future* (Minneapolis: Augsburg, 1982), 258, sees these accounts as ordinations—if not in the same sense as understood today, then at least as precursors of ordination as presently understood.

51   "Aphorismen," *GW* V/1: 314.

52   "Aphorismen," *GW* V/1: 315.

53   "Aphorismen," *GW* V/1: 312–13.

54   "Aphorismen," *GW* V/1: 327.

55   "Aphorismen," *GW* V/1: 311.

56   "Aphorismen," *GW* V/1: 309, 311.

57   "Aphorismen," *GW* V/1: 294.

58   "Aphorismen," *GW* V/1: 264.

59   Löhe argues that the *Amt* includes many different ministries and differences do exist among them that are manifested in the different calls and settings of these ministries. Each of these ministries is recognized and acknowledged with its own unique set of prayers appropriate to the ministry to which the ordinand is being ordained. See "Aphorismen," *GW* V/1: 313–14.

60   Löhe repeated this point often: The *Amt* exists to preserve the catholicity of the church. Pastors serve congregations with a view to the larger, catholic church: "We are not servants of the church, because we do ministry in the individual congregations, but rather because we occupy the office [of ministry] of the entire, undivided church of God, that is, for the sanctification of the congregations ("Brief an Adam Ernst [4 August 1845], *GW* I: 704). See also "Aphorismen," *GW* V/1: 263. Löhe recognized and acknowledged that there might be conflict between the pastor's duty to adhere to the apostolic teaching and the congregation's demands and desires. He reminded pastors that even Paul—an apostle!—had difficulties with the Corinthian congregation; see "Am dritten Sonntage des Advents: 1. Korinther 4, 1–5" in *Kurze Lektionen zu den sonn- und festtäglichen Episteln des Kirchenjahres*, *GW* VI/2: 362–63; and "Am dritten Sonntage des Advents: 1. Korinther 4, 1–5" in "Winter-Postille," *GW* VI/3: 37–49.

61 "Aphorismen," *GW* V/1: 303.

62 This idea of love manifested in works of mercy is an important element in Löhe's theology and ministry. See "Aphorismen," *GW* V/1: 299.

63 See also in this respect Rom 12:4–13 where Paul writes that we, though many, are individually "members of one another." Again the point is made that as Christians we live for one another and not ourselves or some other personally selected ideal.

64 "Aphorismen," *GW* V/1: 325–26.

65 For more on this apostolic task, see pages 85–88.

66 "Aphorismen," *GW* V/1: 262.

67 "Aphorismen," *GW* V/1: 326, also 289. Gerhard Müller, "Der Student Wilhelm Löhe und das Amt: Eine Äußerung aus dem Jahr 1829," *Jahrbuch für fränkische Landesforschung* 34–35 (1975): 595, reports that in an early essay Löhe wrote that the task of a pastor is to lead people such that "they make the right decision for time and eternity."

68 "Aphorismen," *GW* V/1: 289.

69 AC 7; *BC*, 32. For a helpful discussion of the expansion of the pastoral office, see Maurer, *Historical Commentary*, 188.

70 "Aphorismen," *GW* V/1: 288.

71 "Aphorismen," *GW* V/1: 293.

72 "Aphorismen," *GW* V/1: 290.

73 Rudolf Keller, "Reformatorische Wurzeln," 109, rightly notes that Löhe does not want to assign a preferred position either to the *Amt* or to the congregation.

74 Wilhelm Löhe, "Innere Mission im allgemeinen," *GW* IV: 186, as well as "Aphorismen," *GW* V/1: 302. Löhe ("Innere Mission im allgemeinen," *GW* IV: 183) noted that the two are not to be separated; mission is the domain of the presbyterate as well as of the diaconate. They are related to each other as man is to woman.

75 Löhe argues that while there must always be "teachers" (academic theologians and scholars) in the church, it is one-sided to entrust the ordained ministry only to those who are so gifted. See "Aphorismen," *GW* V/1: 326.

76 "Aphorismen," *GW* V/1: 294.

77 Dulles, *Models of the Church*, 9.

78 See page 83.

79 Hollaz, 3.1.318, wrote: "The applying grace of the Holy Spirit is the source of those divine acts by which the Holy Spirit, through the Word of God and the Sacraments, dispenses, offers to us, bestows and seals the spiritual and eternal gifts intended for humanity by the great mercy of God the Father, and acquired by the fraternal redemption of Jesus Christ."

80 William G. Rusch, "The Doctrine of the Holy Spirit in the Patristic and Medieval Church" in *The Holy Spirit in the Life of the Church: From Biblical Times to the Present* (ed. Paul D. Opsahl; Minneapolis: Augsburg, 1978), 66–98.

81 The work of Regin Prenter, *Spiritus Creator* (trans. by John M. Jensen; Philadelphia: Muhlenberg, 1953), is invaluable here. Fred Perry Hall, "The Lutheran Doctrine of the Holy Spirit in the Sixteenth Century: Developments to the 'Formula of Concord' " (Ph.D. diss., Fuller Theological Seminary, 1993), 53, con-

curs, saying that the Small Catechism "demonstrated the centrality of the Holy Spirit in [Luther's] theology."

[82] "Confession Concerning Christ's Supper," LW 37: 368. See also "The Private Mass and the Consecration of Priests," LW 38: 212, where Luther writes, "But where there is a holy, Christian church, there all the sacraments, Christ himself, and the Holy Spirit must be." These two passages clearly demonstrate the close relationship among the Holy Spirit, the church, and the Word and Sacraments in Luther's thought.

[83] Bernard Holm, "The Work of the Spirit: The Reformation to the Present" in *The Holy Spirit in the Life of the Church*, 104.

[84] The dogmaticians of Lutheran Orthodoxy "gradually defined soteriology with an astounding minimal mention of the Spirit." This presentation of soteriology and pneumatology effectively weakens the close link between the church and the Spirit. See Holm, "The Work of the Spirit," 107. Hall has a different view than that of Holm with respect to the theology of the confessions and Lutheran Orthodoxy. He sees essential continuity between Luther and his followers; see Hall, "Lutheran Doctrine of the Holy Spirit," 308–11.

[85] Karl Barth, *Dogmatics in Outline* (New York: Harper & Row, 1959), 141.

[86] This conception especially finds expression in *The Cost of Discipleship*. Bonhoeffer writes: "The Body of Christ is identical with the new humanity which he has taken upon him. It is in fact the church. Jesus Christ is at once himself and his church (I Corinthians 12.12). Since the first Whit Sunday the Life of Christ has been perpetuated on earth in the form of his Body, the church. Here is his body, crucified and risen, here is the humanity he took upon him. To be baptized therefore means to become a member of the church, a member of the Body of Christ (Galatians 3.28; I Corinthians 12.13). To be in Christ therefore means to be in the church. But if we are in the church we are verily and bodily in Christ. Now we perceive the whole wealth of meaning which lies behind the idea of the Body of Christ." For more on the church as the body of Christ, see Dietrich Bonhoeffer, *The Cost of Discipleship* (New York: Macmillan, 1959; Touchstone, 1995), 236–47; quote is on 241. See also Dietrich Bonhoeffer, *Life Together* (trans. and with an introduction by John W. Doberstein; San Francisco: Harper & Row, 1954), 17–37, esp. 8–20; on the unity and catholicity of the church, see 23–26, 37.

[87] See, for example, Bonhoeffer, *Cost of Discipleship*, 239.

[88] *BC*, 32.

[89] Dulles, *Models of the Church*, 34. Dulles has the Roman Catholic Church (especially in the nineteenth century) in mind. His observations on the institutional model of the church are insightful and applicable with respect to Löhe's conception of the church.

[90] Dulles, *Models of the Church*, 35.

[91] Keller, "Reformatorische Wurzeln," 119, correctly notes that Löhe (and Osiander) attempted to argue for the "indelible character" of ordination while at the same time attaching a "functional" view to it; that is, ordination may be indelible, but it is not permanent.

[92] Donald E. Messer, *Contemporary Images of Christian Ministry* (Nashville: Abingdon, 1989), 68. See also Schwarz, *Christian Church*, 322–25; as well as Thomas Franklin O'Meara, O.P., *Theology of Ministry* (New York: Paulist Press, 1983), 32–33; "Pastoral Constitution on the Church in the Modern World" (*Gaudium et Spes*) in

Vatican II, 904–5, 931–32; Bernard Cooke, *Ministry to Word and Sacraments: History and Theology* (Philadelphia: Fortress, 1976), 343.

93 Dulles, *Models of the Church*, 185–86. Dulles writes: "[T]here is nothing to prevent a given theologian from building his own personal theology on one or another of the paradigms in the tradition. If one begins, for example, with the model of the Church as servant, one may then work backward and integrate into this model the values of the other four [models]" (185).

94 Dietrich Bonhoeffer, *Letters and Papers from Prison* (enlarged ed.; ed. Eberhard Bethge; New York: Macmillan, 1972; Collier Books), 382.

95 Others who argue for an ordering on the basis of these texts include Schwarz, *Christian Church*, 250–51; O'Meara, *Theology of Ministry*, 79–81; and T. F. Torrance, *Royal Priesthood* (London: Oliver & Boyd, 1955), 98–101.

96 Roy A. Harrisville, *Ministry in Crisis: Changing Perspectives on Ordination and the Priesthood of All Believers* (Minneapolis: Augsburg, 1987), 23; see also Schwarz, *Christian Church*, 75; O'Meara, *Theology of Ministry*, 76; and Edward Schillebeeckx, *Ministry: Leadership in the Community of Jesus Christ* (New York: Crossroad, 1981), 75.

97 Such a common agreement might be found in Carl Braaten's confessional principle that the Gospel is the proclamation of "justification by faith." See Carl E. Braaten, *Principles of Lutheran Theology* (Philadelphia: Fortress, 1983), 35.

4

LITURGY AND WORSHIP

Doctrine, Löhe affirms, should not be isolated from the authentic Christian life. In a narrow sense, *doctrine* signifies the teachings of the church. In his many writings, Löhe was primarily interested in the *application* of doctrine to the daily life of the church. How is the office of the holy ministry exercised in the congregation? How does the church express its gratitude and thankfulness to its Lord? Löhe returned to these questions time and time again. Of these practical questions on the church's ministries, worship and liturgy commanded Löhe's ongoing interest and attention. He published an *Agende*, prayer books, and numerous tracts on Communion, confession, and other elements of worship and liturgical life.

Löhe was appalled at the state of worship in the Lutheran churches and worked tirelessly to educate those who were liturgically illiterate. His *Agende* was written to be a handbook and textbook for pastors "who are inexperienced in liturgical matters and want more knowledge."[1] The work is a rich mine of Löhe's thinking on liturgy. His interest in community life, the centrality of Word and Sacrament, the importance of the motifs of catholicity and apostolicity are apparent throughout the *Agende*.

The *Agende* represents Löhe's attempt to restore what had been lost in the church. Pastors, by virtue of their theological training, have access to these liturgical elements to greater or lesser degrees. But the liturgy is the great educator of the people. In the liturgy the Christian laity learn about Christ, faith, and the church. The tragedy, Löhe claims, is that these elements have been denied to the laity: "The congregation has been so cheated of its activity in its worship, of its conscience, its prayer, intonation and antiphons, even its hymns at the altar, that scarcely any memory of it remains."[2] The community gathered around Christ had been stripped of its ability to confess and proclaim its faith. Without this treasure, the church loses its identity as a community.

COMMUNITY

One of the central motifs of Löhe's theology, especially of his ecclesiology, is community or fellowship. In *Three Books about the Church*, Löhe writes that "as long as a man is alone he cannot even be blessed."[3] Humans were created for fellowship. There are many fellowships, but only one quenches the thirsty soul—the church of God.[4] Many of Löhe's writings deal at least implicitly with the question of how to create and preserve community among the people of God. Worship is the collective expression of the people of God. It is the church at prayer.

The structure of the liturgy contributes to this sense of community. Each component—the confession of sins, the introit, kyrie, offertory, sermon, eucharistic prayer, and so forth—contributes to the whole. Each component also expresses either the need for community or the realization of community in Christ.[5] The litany is a good example of Löhe's concern for the community. He notes that the litany addresses all the worship and spiritual needs of the community. In the litany, the church

> offers supplications, prayers, intercessions, and thanksgiving to the One who wills that all may be helped . . . the prayers have a magnificent order in which all stations of Christendom are thought of. . . . First one prays for the church and for its concerns, then for the authorities and the peace of the world, and finally for the home and against all evil which threatens the individual members. Institutions of education, of defense and protection, and of physical needs are remembered. Enemies and the harvest are not forgotten. These are the ultimate aims of the prayer, those strong, powerful waves are abated. . . . In this form of prayer, the litany, there can be no sentimentality, no idle talk. This is not acceptable. The succinct character rebels against every sick disease of the one praying. And yet this form of prayer allows, more than any other form, for the expression of specific concerns. It is just as flexible as it is rigid. Any special petition can be included. Here there is a place for every sighing heart. The clear, comprehensible classification of the petitions show to the attentive person where each single petition is to be placed.[6]

Everything that the church needs—everything that the world and universe need—is included in Christian worship.[7] All that is needed and given for the preservation and sustenance of that which God has brought into being is recalled and expressed.

Löhe's understanding of the role of confession is also related to ideas of community. Confession often focused on how community or fellowship was broken. This is particularly true for confession that takes place in the privacy of one's home. Löhe developed a series of questions intended to help his parishioners examine themselves in preparation for Communion. These questions point to the centrality of community life, that is, the worship life of Christian believers.[8] Confession was about confessing the brokenness of relationships; worship was about repairing these broken relationships.

The Lord's Supper is an expression of this community of broken people seeking wholeness in fellowship. The eucharistic meal is catholic in that it gathers many diverse parts into one whole. Löhe quotes Paul: "we all are one bread and one body, because we are part of one bread and drink out of one cup" (1 Cor 10:17).[9] All those who partake of the bread and drink of the cup are members of this catholic community of broken people seeking wholeness.

In worship, people experience community with one another and with God. This community with God is the point and goal of worship. Löhe writes:

> In public worship the Church experiences a special nearness to God; she approaches into the very presence of the Bridegroom, and tastes the blessedness of Heaven even here below. Public worship is the prettiest flower that can bloom on human stems.[10]

The Christian experiences loneliness and alienation during the week. Believers work, play, spend time with family but do not experience that "peace which surpasses all understanding" (Phil 4:7). At worship, they gather together with other Christians to be near Christ. The Bride approaches her Bridegroom.

This emphasis on the communal nature of worship represents a shift away from what Löhe experienced in his youth. The church and its liturgy in the early nineteenth century was profoundly shaped by the ideals of the Enlightenment and Pietism. Moral life for the individual was a central feature of Enlightenment thought, and the personal sense of sin and forgiveness was a major theme in Pietism. Both concepts influenced the liturgical practices of the church. Löhe desired to shift the significance of worship and liturgy away from the individual to the community.[11] Christians are not islands; they live in fellowship. They live in fellowship with God and with one another.

Worship, especially Sunday morning worship, is *the* opportunity for saints to rest in the company of other saints. The Christian, says Löhe, wants to approach God in humble and acceptable worship. He notes that German immigrants in North American often felt lonely and far removed from God and the church and yearned for fellowship:

> When they [the German settlers] were lonely in their new homeland, set in its primeval forests or on the prairies, then every now and again

their home intruded in upon their thoughts, especially if they had to work immediately, and some silent tears ran [down their faces] out of yearning for worship and the blessing of the holy Word of God, which was scorned on German soil. Here one could not hear the bells ringing together for worship, one could not go into a church, hear a sermon, and partake of the sacraments; the infants remain unbaptized, the children untaught and uninstructed and the heart now notices that it was created for God and that it finds no peace outside of God.[12]

Each individual in the community bears his or her own burdens. But gathering together, the community sets aside its individual burdens, sheds the weight of many defeats, and shares the joy of salvation in the Lamb (Rev 7:10).

As important as fellowship with other Christians is, Löhe focuses equally on fellowship with Christ. Particularly important for highlighting this fellowship is the gathering at the Lord's Table. As they stand or kneel at the eucharistic Table, Löhe writes,

The worshipping people . . . know themselves as the Bride of the Lord, their hearts' longings are satisfied in him and through him; but not only through him, also through fellowship with one another; they are the people of God—a unit in their inner life and experience. In the fullness of divine grace they bear in mind the needs of one another, as well as those of the whole world; and humbly wishing each human soul the highest good, they approach the divine Throne in supplication, prayer, and intercession.[13]

In the celebration of the Eucharist, the Christian experiences the fullest expression of fellowship on earth. At the Lord's Table, heaven and earth, the divine and the human, are joined together in a holy marriage.

Word and Sacrament

Word and Sacrament is a dominant theme in all Löhe's writings and theology. The means of grace constitute the inner core of the Christian life, whether understood in its individual expression or in its communal expression.[14] Word and Sacrament are the unshakable center of the church in its worship. In picturesque language, Löhe expressed this truth:

In the inner life and worship of the congregation stand Word and Sacrament like rocks in the sea. Like the sea breaking on the rocks, so do the holy forms of the liturgy crash in upon the center of Word and Sacrament. Like the sea is broken on the rocks, like its rough waters and spray are determined by the rocks, so is liturgical life no arbitrary matter. The waves of the liturgy concentrically orbit the inner circle of the spiritual life which revolves around the poles of Word and Sacrament. Word and Sacrament determine the order of salvation, and these determine the order of worship.[15]

The Word and the Sacraments are closely related to Löhe's understanding of community, confessional unity, catholicity, and apostolicity.

The persistent use of the sacraments is key if the church is to attain its goals. Word and Sacrament alone are sufficient. The task of the church is to unite all its good works under the umbrella of Word and Sacrament. Care of the poor, for example, is a responsibility of the church today, as it was at the time of the apostles. The church also today considers the school its rightful domain; the sick, orphans, widows, and children are all individuals the church is called to serve.[16] For Löhe, all good works are to be united in the ministry of the church. At the center of the church stands the Word and the Sacraments. Together these means strengthen the faith of the saints. Together Word and Sacrament provide the means by which the church will attain its goal: salvation.

WORD

In Löhe's theology, as in any theological system, *the Word* is a complex term, a paradoxical term, meaning at the same time one thing and many things.[17] *Word* refers to Jesus the Christ, the Logos who is before creation (John 1:1). *Word* also refers to the body of knowledge and truth that is received and inherited from the apostles, collected and canonized in the Bible. *Word* also signifies the proclamation of the Gospel, that is, the preaching of Christ crucified and risen. For Löhe, these three nuances converge: The Christ who is the divine Word and who is witnessed to in the Scriptures and proclaimed in worship is the full meaning of *the Word*.

Worship is one of the primary activities of the church. The church cannot sustain itself without a regular, vital worship life. The liturgy, Löhe writes in the foreword to his *Agende*, has two peaks—Word and Sacrament.[18] Everything else is secondary. Both Word and Sacrament point to the centrality of Christ and the grace that is given to us through him.

The Word itself is powerful. It has the power and the ability to give birth and life. The Word can lead the nonbeliever to belief, the faithless to faith, and the dead to life. The Word knows no limitations; through the Spirit, the Word breathes life into those whom God wills. Löhe wrote that "nobody can doubt that the Word gives birth to the congregation and that the Word has power with those who, speaking it, are ordained and with those who, speaking it, are not ordained."[19] The Word works in the hearts and minds of those who hear it regardless of the person who utters the Word that is heard and received.

The Word has a twofold character. On the one hand, it has an accusatory character as "hammer" (Rom 7:7–13).[20] The Word as hammer convicts and kills the spirit. On the other hand, the Word offers life. It offers life as it gives up its own for the sake of the world. To paraphrase the Evangelist, "God so loved the world that he gave his Word" (John 3:16; see also John 1:1–18). This double quality of the Word is necessary for it to complete its work—salvation. The Word speaks to the conscience so the conscience might turn to God: "There is no conscience which perceives every just accusing Word of God, just as there is no heart which recognizes the full power of the blood and the heavenly compassion of Christ. Both make the perfect happiness which is eternal."[21] This Word is powerful on its own. It respects no human in the relentless quest to achieve its goal of salvation.

The Word needs an outlet, Löhe notes, to achieve its ends. It needs people willing and capable of giving it expression, of *speaking* it. To be sure, "the Word is powerful, it does everything in large and small. Who does not know it? Who does not experience it everyday in the ministry? But the Word seeks human channels and even here everything is, at one and the same time, human and divine."[22] The church in its worship provides these channels. The people of God need to hear the Word for their sustenance and preservation. They turn to the church in its worship to hear this Word. And the people give expression to the Word by setting aside one of their own to proclaim this Word in an orderly manner.

The sermon, then, is the fullest expression of the proclamation of the Word. The reading of Scripture is, of course, important, but the sermon provides an opportunity for the congregation to be confronted with the full weight and glory of the Word and the one whom it reveals. In the sermon the congregation meets Christ as well as the community gathered around him. Through the human channel, that is, the preacher, "the face of the Highest is unveiled in the sermon, which in a high sense expresses the communion of the saints, all of whom are glad in the presence of God."[23] For Löhe, the preacher as a channel for the Word is crucial. Preachers do not espouse their own opinions: "The preached Word is God's own Word and not that of the preacher."[24] The preacher's opinion is always secondary, perhaps even incidental. One of the twin peaks in the liturgy, the sermon is paramount, yet it always points to the other peak: the Sacrament of the Altar. The Word opens the way for and prepares the way to the eucharistic meal.

SACRAMENT

Of the two peaks in the liturgy, the Sacrament of Communion is, for Löhe, the higher.[25] Eucharist is the center of the church's inner life as well as its public expression.[26] The Sacrament of the Altar expresses the fullness of the church's message: repentance, forgiveness, Christ's ubiquity, atonement, communion, grace, divine transcendence, divine incarnation. All the essential elements of the church's proclamation are found in the Sacrament of the Altar. Because the central elements of the church's proclamation are present in Holy Communion, it is the higher peak.

The Word communicates through words. The Sacrament of the Altar, on the other hand, communicates at a higher and deeper level. It communicates in words but also in gesture, in physical and symbolic action, and in visual imagery. That the Eucharist so fully expresses the life and proclamation of the church is the reason that Löhe asserts that the Sacrament "is the goal of the Sunday morning worship liturgy to which all of the individual parts of worship point."[27] Each of the individual elements of the liturgy—the order of confession and forgiveness, the kyrie, the general prayer, the prayer of the day, the sermon, the greeting, and the benediction—all serve or express an element that either prepares one's heart for Communion or acknowledges what has taken place. They are steps along the path up the mountainside, the peak of which is Communion. The Christian ascends the mountain with each step, each part of the liturgy:

> In public worship the soul is engaged in an ascent, and the goal is reached at the Table of the Lord. Nothing higher remains in the service—nothing more divine on earth exists than the Sacrament. In the Holy Supper the deepest longings of the soul are satisfied, as the humble worshipper joyfully declares in the Nunc Dimittis.[28]

At the summit, the Christian experiences that most wonderful, mysterious, and fulfilling of events in the Christian life: union with Christ. God's people exult, "Lord, now you let your servant go in peace; your Word has been fulfilled. My own eyes have seen the salvation which you prepared in the sight of every people: A light to reveal you to the nations and the glory of your people Israel." The fulfillment and joy of the Christian life is thus proclaimed.

The liturgy in a certain sense reflects the movement of the Christian life: sin, confession, absolution, proclamation and hearing of the Word, union with Christ, reception of the promise of eternal life, peace, and prayer. At the center of the Christian life is union with Christ, and Communion expresses—realizes!—this unity more fully and deeply than any other element of the liturgy and of the Christian life. The Christian life, Löhe says, is a life centered on Eucharist: "You live, when you are Christians, in a continual movement between preparation for the Sacrament and the partaking of it."[29] Elsewhere Löhe asserts that worship is not worship without the feast. No public worship is complete without the celebration of the Sacrament of the Altar.[30] The Christian life is a life of worship, and worship is incomplete without the celebration of that which nourishes the individual and unites the community.

One of the chief differences between Löhe and his opponents revolved around eucharistic theology. In the wake of Rationalism and Pietism, many churches minimized the real presence of Christ in the Lord's Supper. The Rationalists were inclined to leave the question of the real presence alone and let every communicant decide the meaning of Jesus' words. They wanted to go back to a "common biblical basis, which would effect a unionist and ecumenical liturgy."[31] While the intent may not have been to de-emphasize the real presence of Christ, this was clearly the effect. The Pietists were not inclined to deny the real presence of Christ, but their practice led to a sort of "decision theology."[32] In communing, believers received forgiveness, having made a personal confession of their sins. The import and meaning of Communion was effectively reduced to two aspects: forgiveness of sins and the fruits of Communion.[33] The reception of the forgiveness of sins then prompted an expectation that this forgiveness would bear fruit—"a new life in the sanctification arising out of being born again."[34] This element of "decision theology" was often the more dominant element.

Löhe was certainly partial to the pietistic interpretation of the Eucharist. As a strict confessionalist, he could hardly oppose the orthodox emphasis on the Lord's Supper as a means of grace and the real presence of Christ. He adhered to the confessional Lutheran position that Christ is present "in, with, and under the elements" (FC, Solid Declaration, Art. VII).[35] When he mentioned the redemptive and salvific qualities of the Eucharist, Löhe moved immediately to the real presence of Christ in the Sacrament. Löhe tirelessly taught and wrote that in the bread and wine the true body and blood of Christ are present.[36] This point was so important to Löhe that he could assert that it would be better to die not having received the Sacrament of the Altar than to receive it from somebody who did not adhere to the doctrine of the real presence.[37]

A proper understanding of the real presence of Christ in the bread and wine was important not only because Löhe obediently followed the line of orthodox Lutheran theology. In the Sacrament of the Altar, Löhe states, the Christian really experiences Christ, experiences a real union with Christ. In the eucharistic meal, the Christian partakes of the real body and blood of Christ:

> The altar is—and remains—in every case nothing else than that location at which the sacrificial body and blood of the Lord are united with the elements of Communion and from which these wonderful gifts are extended to us. The altar is the place of the highest revelation of God.[38]

This union or fellowship consists of a double fellowship at the table. The first is fellowship with Christ, effected through the partaking of his body and blood; the second is that with the other communicants.[39] Löhe follows Luther closely. As Leif Grane notes, "The significance of the Sacrament is the fellowship of the saints; the one who receives the Sacrament is united with Christ and all his saints and shares in all their blessings."[40] This second fellowship is not without its consequences. The first consequence of this fellowship with the other communicants is that believers ought not commune with those who do not adhere to right doctrine, especially with respect to the Lord's Supper. The second consequence of this eucharistic fellowship with other communicants is that we are called to care for our brothers and sisters in Christ. We have an obligation to care for those who are in need. Löhe says it best:

> The obligation remains for us to care for our poor brothers, and if we do not hold an agape feast like the ancient Christians, we are not released from mercy. Undoubtedly we go in an unworthy manner to God's table if we do not care for our brothers at the altar, if they do not have, in addition to the heavenly riches of the Sacrament, their allotted share of earthly food also.[41]

The Matthean injunction to disciples to leave their gift at the altar if they remember a brother or sister has something against them is relevant (Matt 5:23–24). For Löhe, the text speaks of coming to the altar repentant and prepared, of coming to the altar in genuine fellowship with your brothers and sisters in Christ. Yet Löhe's linking of heavenly with earthly food also calls to mind the Lord's Prayer. Jesus taught his disciples to pray

"Give us each day our daily bread" (Luke 11:3). In receiving heavenly bread we are invited and moved to share our earthly bread with those who have none. In this sense, Löhe's statement that Christ's blood and compassion are the basis of human happiness has a double meaning.[42] First, Christ's death signifies atonement and salvation. Second, Christ's compassion calls his people to compassion as well. As Christ fed the thousands, we feed those whom we are able (see Mark 6:30–44; 8:1–10).[43]

On the question of whether the Lord's Supper is a physical or spiritual partaking in Christ, Löhe notes that "the Lord did not differentiate between oral eating and spiritual partaking . . . while we receive for the body, in his true body and blood, eternal life, and a food of immortality, our spirits also partake in the fruit of his suffering, life, and blessedness."[44] The eucharistic table should not be a table where some feast while others are distracted from the rich blessings of the redemptive meal because they suffer physical hunger.

With Luther, Löhe notes that believers receive the gifts of the Sacrament at the table, but these gifts demand a response. Luther writes that in feasting at the eucharistic meal

> we may with joy find strength and comfort, and say, "Though I am a sinner and have fallen, though this or that misfortune has befallen me, nevertheless I will go to the Sacrament to receive a sign from God that I have on my side Christ's righteousness, life, and sufferings, with all holy angels and the blessed in heaven all pious men on earth. If I die, I am not alone in death; if I suffer, they suffer with me. [I know that] all my misfortune is shared with Christ and the saints, because I have a sure sign of their love toward me." As love and support are given you, you in turn must render love and support to Christ in his needy ones. You must feel with sorrow all the dishonor done to Christ in his holy Word, all the misery of Christendom, all the unjust suffering of the innocent, with which the world is everywhere filled to overflowing.[45]

The Lord's Supper unites the believer not only to salvation in Christ and the fruits of the Spirit, but also to the suffering, death, and life of Christ. We suffer with Christ as he suffers with those who are hungry and penniless. We die with Christ as he dies for those who hunger and thirst. We live and minister with Christ as he lives and ministers to those in need of spiritual, emotional, or physical support.

Gifts of the Lord's Supper. The blessings of the Lord's Supper are rich. The eucharistic feast is a banquet where Christ gives, as Löhe notes, faith, strength, grace, eternal life, reconciliation, consolation, strength, salvation, forgiveness, and the Spirit. The church in its confession and teaching never exhausts the variety of the gifts and blessings of Communion.

Löhe does not blaze a new trail here. As he followed the confessions on the matter of the real presence of Christ, so he followed the Lutheran writings on the benefits or gifts of the Lord's Supper. The confessions speak of the "forgiveness of sins" (Lord's Supper, SC), of "a comfort for all sorrowing hearts" (FC, Solid Declaration, Art. VII), of "the promise of grace" (Apol. XIII), and of "strength and refreshment" (Lord's Supper, LC).[46] Foremost of the gifts, however, is the forgiveness of sins. Front and center to the Lutheran—and, therefore, to Löhe's—understanding of Holy Communion is that the chief benefit of eating and drinking is the forgiveness of sins. Luther's Large Catechism and the other confessional documents acknowledge and extol this promise often.[47] Löhe also affirms this truth. In an instruction book on Luther's Small Catechism intended for German-speaking Lutherans in the United States, Löhe prepared a series of questions with their answers. One question states: "What is promised and given us for Christ's sake?" The answer: "The forgiveness of sins."[48] This is the classic Lutheran position, and Löhe does not deviate from it.

What does it mean to be forgiven? What are the implications of forgiveness? No established order exists. In various places in the confessions, different benefits are named: eternal life, a soothed conscience, and strengthened faith. Löhe mentions most of these at one time or another. But one benefit emerges most often: union with Christ. To be forgiven is to be reconciled with Christ; to be forgiven is to be united with Christ.[49]

For Löhe, two key words that describe the gifts of the Eucharist are "life" and "strength." He speaks regularly of "eternal life" and of "strengthening the soul." In receiving forgiveness we receive assurance of life. We receive not merely the gift of being, but life in wholeness and health. In one of his prayers, Löhe wrote of coming to the altar "to obtain health and healing."[50] The Christian, who is weakened and burdened by the worries of the week, receives health and healing in the Eucharist. Monday to Saturday the Christian debilitates, but Sunday he/she rehabilitates. The soul and faith are strengthened in the experience of union with Christ. Who among God's people has not felt the burden of everyday worries lifted when one shares them with others in community? The Lord's Supper is, above all, the gathering of the eucharistic people. It is a gathering of people who share their burdens and sorrows with one another and offer them to Christ and receive life and strength in return.

In such a happy exchange, the faith of the Christian is strengthened. On Sunday believers know and feel that they have the strength to face Monday. In Communion their consciences are receiving the salve of life; this, too, is a gift of the Lord's Supper—comfort of the conscience.[51] The Christian is reminded that all those words and actions that hurt God and others are forgiven. They continue their journey in Christ's strength.

Eternal life is a gracious gift of the eucharistic feast. But to receive eternal life and live it *in isolation* is no gift. As Löhe stated at the outset of *Three Books about the Church*, to live alone is as good as to die: "as long as a man is alone he cannot even be blessed . . . [how] could I behold eternal blessedness without looking about for a comrade to share it."[52] Löhe does not expressly say it, but the implication is clear: To live alone in eternity is tantamount to living in damnation. For this reason, when Löhe speaks of eternal life as a gift of the Sacrament of the Altar, he often speaks of it in relation to eternal union with Christ with the communion of saints.[53] As Matti Sihvonen notes, according to Löhe, "in the connection to the hidden life of [the Sacrament] which is in Christ, one receives the source of life. In the Sacrament of Communion believers become members in the new life of the resurrection."[54] The gift of eternal life that is received in the Sacrament of the Altar is closely connected to the human need for community and fellowship. The fulfillment—or, rather, satisfaction—of this need equips and strengthens the Christian.

The Christian faces the week knowing that the Lord's Supper reconciles and comforts. The signs of reconciliation are there: the bread and the wine, the community gathered around the altar, the words—the Word—of absolution and grace. Christians know themselves as a reconciled people, people reconciled to one another and, most important, to Christ.[55] This is the gift that leads one back to Löhe's central theme: community. Among God's people, in the church, reconciliation is practiced and welcomed. Reconciliation, forgiveness, and community belong together.

In speaking and writing about Holy Communion, Löhe often used poetic and vivid language. He was a gifted preacher and his rhetorical and oratorical skills were often demonstrated in speaking and writing about the eucharistic feast. In a certain sense this feast was not altogether unlike a wedding feast. The communicant is received into the family of God by adoption (the imagery is not only familial, but also marital). This sense of adoption, of union with Christ and the church, and of eternal life are beautifully expressed in a petition of a prayer Löhe wrote: "[Christ,] you are my brother and I am your co-heir, since everything you have is also mine. Yes, I am your beloved bride and fully yours, you have acquired me at great cost."[56]

Implications of Löhe's Understanding of the Lord's Supper. What is the significance of Löhe's understanding of the Lord's Supper? What did his views mean practically, pastorally, and theologically?

First, Löhe insisted that Holy Communion be celebrated frequently and regularly. By the nineteenth century, Communion was celebrated rarely in Protestant churches—in many parishes only twice in a year.[57] The opportunity to encounter Christ in the Sacrament ought not be stored up as a treasure in the ground, Löhe notes, but be made available as often as possible. The Eucharist is to be celebrated on a regular—weekly, if possible—basis.[58] The gifts of the Lord's Supper—forgiveness of sins, community, the Spirit, reconciliation—are not to be hidden and grudgingly doled out, Löhe often writes. These gifts are made available and distributed freely and often to God's people.

The efficacy of the Lord's Supper is not a one-time event. Baptism is administered once. One dies to sin and rises to new life. One is claimed by God at a specific moment in time through water and the Word. But the Lord's Supper is different: Just as human beings should eat at least once every day to be sufficiently nourished for the day's labors, so God's people should eat at the Lord's Table frequently. The efficacy and the power of Communion is not restricted to certain times and places in the life of the believer. Christ is always present. The Eucharist is "the greatest divine act of the Lord which is always newly fulfilled."[59] The promise of forgiveness of sins, of grace, of a new life is renewed over and over in this most holy and mysterious of feasts.

For Löhe, St. Paul's words in 1 Cor 11:27–29 were significant: "Whoever, therefore, eats the bread or drinks the cup of the Lord in an unworthy manner will be answerable for the body and blood of the Lord. Examine yourselves, and only then eat of the bread and drink of the cup. For all who eat and drink without discerning the body, eat and drink judgment against themselves." Löhe understood Paul to say that one ought not come to the Table unprepared.[60] To be prepared means to come as one who believes in the words "for you" and "forgiveness of sins." To be prepared to commune with Christ means to come as one who is a Christian. Löhe warned: "One can drink and eat to [one's own] judgment, and does eat to it every time if ones does not come as a Christian. Preaching and Baptism are for the 'becoming' congregation, communion is for the 'has become' congregation."[61] For Löhe, preaching and Baptism are directed primarily to those who are in the process of becoming Christians. Communion is for those who have become Christians. Those who commune and who are not Christians commune to their condemnation.

The practice of confession was important in this respect. The general order of confession and forgiveness was observed at every Sunday morning worship service. The service of the Word preceding the service of the Sacrament had the intent of preparing worshipers for the Holy Meal. Löhe encouraged his parishioners to pray and repent as they sat in the pews and observed others commune at the Lord's Table.[62] The believer repented of his or her own sins and prayed for others as well as for himself or herself. Proper preparation—that is to say, confession—prevented one from communing to his or her condemnation.

Also important in this matter of altar fellowship was the importance of solidarity. Can genuine eucharistic fellowship exist when others doubt the authenticity of some believers? Can believers really experience fellowship with their neighbors if they do not trust their neighbors' sincerity and honesty? These are questions Löhe wrestled with in his writings. His desire was to ensure the authenticity of the communicants' faith as much as possible. Unity in doctrine was paramount, but another kind of unity was critical: The unity of the church needed to be visible.[63] For Löhe, this type of unity was an urgent need.[64] He sought to overcome the chaos and disorder that characterized—in his view—too many Lutheran congregations in Bavaria. He endeavored to overcome "the uncertainty of the congregations in Christian matters."[65] The Eucharist defined the Christian community; boundaries, therefore, needed to be established.

As one who is responsible for the spiritual welfare of all those in the congregation, the pastor must necessarily be vigilant that some do not commune to their judgment. But, Löhe argued, the pastor should not refuse to commune people unless he is convinced of unrepentant sin. As a pastor, Löhe said, he might advise some people against coming to the Communion rail, but he would not refuse such people if they came with believing hearts.[66] Essentially that meant the pastor was a gatekeeper: "Every pastor should be in the position of knowing every communicant and admitting nobody to the Sacrament in whose life or understanding there could be a hindrance to participation in the Sacrament."[67] It was the pastor's responsibility to ensure that, on the one hand, nobody communed to his or her own judgment and, on the other hand, that the eucharistic fellowship remained intact.

If unity was to be maintained on the communicant side of the altar—the believer's life and doctrine—Löhe desired that there be no less a unity on the celebrant side of the altar. Löhe asserted that it would be better to die not having communed than to receive the Lord's Supper from somebody who did not hold to the doctrine of the real presence. Confessional unity, clearly, was necessary among the ordained.[68] But what of those instances where there were no ordained pastors available to consecrate the elements? Could laity administer the Sacrament? Löhe answers affirmatively. Lay persons *may* administer the Sacrament, but for the sake of order it is better if they do not.

Was the Sacrament of the Altar efficacious when administered by laity or, for that matter, erring ministers? Löhe provided a twofold answer. The Sacrament is efficacious whenever Word and element are correctly used. But the Sacrament is not efficacious when administered by someone who errs in the doctrine of Communion.[69] Of course, practically speaking the second follows from the first. Someone who errs in the doctrine of Communion—the real presence—would not use the elements and the Word correctly. The *Amt* was and is the means for ensuring right doctrine and thus the correct use of the elements and the Word.

ORDER

A discussion of order appears often in Löhe's thought and theology. This is no less true in his liturgical theology. The worshiping community and its worship should not be disordered and haphazard. The dedication at the beginning of the *Agende* as it appears in the *Gesammelte Werke* sets Löhe's agenda for liturgy: "All things should be done decently and in good order" (1 Cor 14:40).[70] To this end, Löhe went about the task of writing the liturgies contained in the *Agende*. He was persuaded that the liturgies contained in it would hold up to scrutiny: "A close examination of this Liturgy must convince everyone that it is constructed on that which is fundamentally necessary for the right conduct of public worship."[71] Worship, conducted rightly and in good order, was vital for the church of Jesus Christ.

Löhe wanted to avoid the emotionalism of revivalist worship. He had already encountered "American Lutheranism," a movement that sought to reinterpret Lutheranism so it would be more palatable to an American audience. He had heard about Methodists and their "new measures." Löhe did not like what he heard about either movement.[72] His complaint about American Lutheranism had to do with its lack of confessional depth, while his complaint against Methodists had to do with its excessive emotional-ism at the expense of theological depth.

However, there existed an even more important reason why order was so important to Löhe. An orderly worship life expresses the orderliness of the spiritual life, in fact, the inherent order of creation. The liturgy is a reflection of the orderliness—the balance and symmetry—of the church. "The Order of Liturgy in which this worship is expressed ought to be the image of the inner unity and harmony of the spiritual life—an ecclesiastical aesthetic in concrete form."[73] The Word through which all things come into being is a Word of order, not chaos. This Word is a word that orders and illuminates (cf. John 1:1–5; 2 Cor 4:6). This Word, Jesus Christ, is as appar-ent in the life of the church as in the life of the world.

For the sake of unity and harmony, it would be good to have but one order. The reality, however, is that life is diverse. Good order, of course, cannot save.[74] Good order makes a positive impression and perhaps a good evangelical witness, but it neither saves nor justifies.[75] If there were one liturgy in use in the whole of Christendom, it would serve to witness to the fellowship and unity of the catholic church. But good order or an orderly liturgical life serves yet another purpose. A liturgy that is orderly will include all the components of the apostolic faith. Löhe sought to make his liturgy as Lutheran in character as possible.[76] His liturgy conformed to the forms prescribed by the Lutheran confessions and church orders. The rea-son is that for Löhe the Lutheran church and its doctrine is the purest form of the apostolic faith.[77] Lutheran liturgy is apostolic and catholic.

CATHOLICITY OF WORSHIP

In some ways the most innovative or revolutionary of Löhe's ideas and thinking on liturgy and worship had to do with his sense of the catholici-ty of worship. Thomas Schattauer rightly included catholicity among the distinctive characteristics of Löhe's liturgical thinking: "The communal, historical, and catholic character of the church are among the motifs that highlight [Löhe's] liturgical contribution in particular."[78] Although he rarely used the word "catholicity" in connection with his ideas, Löhe anticipated much of the spirit of the liturgical movement which arose in the 1960s.

Löhe did not often use the word "catholicity" in his writings because he had already been charged with Romanism and "popery." To describe the church and its ministry in this way would have given his opponents that much more ammunition.[79] In the foreword to his *Agende*, Löhe acknowledges that he has been accused of Romanism.[80] Yet he goes on to suggest that the festivals related to Mary should be included in the Lutheran liturgical calendar. The annual feast days (i.e., the Annunciation of Our Lord, the Visitation of Mary, and the Candlemas of Mary) should be celebrated so the entire splendor of the history of Jesus can be placed before the eyes of the people.[81]

Löhe was equal to the accusation of popery. He countered that if one wanted to slander him, then the charge must be laid to all Lutheran liturgies, even to the entire church. Löhe gladly accepted this charge. In essence his argument was that the church—if it really was the church—was necessarily catholic. The Roman Church did not have a stranglehold on catholicity. Indeed, Löhe said, "one could . . . claim—with more right—that the Roman Church catholicizes in those parts of the liturgy in which it agrees with the truly catholic church which on earth is surnamed Lutheran."[82] Elsewhere in the foreword to the *Agende*, he wrote that "the Lutheran Liturgy is an outgrowth from the Roman . . . cleansed from unauthorized additions."[83] In Löhe's view, the Roman Church does not equal the catholic church; the Lutheran Church equals the catholic church.

What does Löhe mean by "catholic"? In a word, he means "inclusive" or "universal."[84] The church is inclusive. It includes all peoples of all times and of all places. The congregation that gathers together to pray and to hear and proclaim God's Word joins itself to the church in every time and in every place. This is catholicity.

Löhe seeks to *catholicize* the church of his day. He will necessarily borrow what is good and helpful from the Roman Church if it serves his ends. Despite his antipathy to the Roman Catholic Church, Löhe freely borrowed elements of the Roman liturgy. He wrote that "one finds individual prayers, which in form and content can scarcely be replaced through a new or different form, from which one can say in the best sense of the word: they catholicize."[85] Löhe was not a romantic idealist when it came to the Roman Catholic liturgies and prayers. He recognized that some, perhaps many, were unsuitable for general use. Some of the collects preserved in the Roman missals were well suited for use in the Lutheran church; some were not.[86] At any rate Löhe researched the missals to find those nuggets which enriched liturgical life. Even the Roman corner of Christendom, despite its many shortcoming and inadequacies, could contribute to Löhe's program.

Löhe's program was most apparent in two elements of worship life. The first was in the collects or prayers of the day. The collects, Löhe said, expressed the desire for fellowship with all the saints.[87] The appointed collects directed the worship community in a given time and place to look beyond itself. The collects pointed the congregation to the church catholic. The collects also pointed to specific events in the life of the church and of Christ which gave a particular Sunday or feast day its own unique character.[88] The collects grounded the worshiping congregation in the particular day or season in the life of the church. At the same time, the collects directed the congregation to look beyond itself to the wider catholic church. To recognize and celebrate the concrete events in the life of the church was to recognize and celebrate with the catholic church.

The second element of Löhe's catholicizing program was the observation and celebration of the liturgical year and its festivals. His liturgical program might be described as an attempt to put catholic "color" into the plain and monotonous liturgy that the Lutheran church had inherited from Rationalism. Löhe endeavored to reintroduce the celebration and observation of the liturgical year and its festivals. He claimed that they contributed to and supported the varied and alternating character of the liturgy. Every worship service ought to have its own distinctive, special character.[89] Worship should not be identical Sunday after Sunday, though it should display a basic unity from one Sunday to the next.

Beyond the variety and the color that a truly catholic liturgy has, a liturgy or liturgical life that observes and celebrates the different seasons and events in the life of Christ and the church *educates*. The observance of Advent illustrates the expectancy and anticipation that accompanies the birth of the Messiah. Epiphany highlights the significance of the manifestation of Jesus as the Savior. Lent recalls one to a renewed life of discipleship in preparation for the resurrection. Easter and the Sundays of Easter proclaim the risen Christ. Pentecost commemorates the establishment of the church, the community of saints, and the gift of the Spirit upon the church. The festivals educate the laity in the life of Christ and the faith of the church. For Löhe, the liturgy was one of the best teaching tools available to the church. Furthermore, the decline in the observance and celebration of the seasons and festivals with their distinctive characters only served to impoverish the community that gathers around the Risen One. He wrote:

> Up until the Reformation, the church year with its celebrations was the great textbook and workbook of the church. One lived through everything in church celebrations which one ought to learn.[90]

A catholic liturgical life educated and drew people into the life of the church. To worship with the catholic church is to live in unity with the catholic church, to live in unity with Christ.

Apostolicity

Apostolicity is closely related to catholicity. If catholicity refers to the universal dimension, apostolicity refers to the historical. The church extends beyond the limitations of a certain time and place. A congregation is not the church in itself. Neither is the worship of a congregation merely the worship of *one* congregation. A congregation at worship today extends to its roots in the New Testament community and beyond to the church that can be found in every place.

The congregation, therefore, does not forge ahead, blazing its own path to God. The forms of the liturgy that have served the church in the past are the basis for the worship life of a congregation. "A true Lutheran," Löhe said, "seems to serve the Lutheran Church most loyally when that person goes forward on the beaten path in one mind and in one spirit with the fathers."[91] The task before Löhe was not to repristinate the liturgy. The liturgy is not a museum piece; it is the expression of a living community of faith that seeks to be true to its God.

The church is a living organic being. It grows. It changes. The church expresses to its God different things at different times in its life. For this reason it cannot merely stand still in its mission or in its worship. The church seeks always to move ahead. But it moves ahead on the trail already broken by its forebears.

Löhe displayed a remarkable sense of the apostolicity and catholicity of the church. Its fellowship extends beyond the limits of time and space: "As a community extended in time, the church is a historical community. . . . [H]istory bears the traces of the fellowship that is the church."[92] To this end, Löhe sought to establish forms that expressed and maintained the historical nature of the community that calls itself the church.

Conclusion

The outstanding features of Löhe's liturgical theology are his sense of the catholicity and apostolicity of the church and its liturgy. These are the organizing and ordering themes in his thinking and writing. In this Löhe anticipates some of the reforms of the liturgical movement which gathered steam after World War II and particularly since the 1960s. The ecumenism of this movement provided the impulse for liturgical scholars to search for those patterns in worship common not only to the early church, but to the church *catholic.*

The most notable—visible—reform undertaken by Löhe was the restoration of the confessional. He did not make private confession mandatory, but he did encourage it.[93] More important, though, was his understanding of the Lord's Supper as not merely a remembrance of a distant event designed to call us to a moral awakening (Rationalism) or as a sign of the assurance of forgiveness. Foremost for Löhe, the Lord's Supper was *communion* with Christ, fellowship in his saving death and resurrection, and union with him. The Lord's Supper was also communion with the other communicants.

This understanding had practical implications. Confessional integrity and solidarity had to be maintained. Real community had to exist not only at the altar on Sundays, but outside the walls of the sanctuary every other day of the week. Gordon Lathrop speaks of an *ordo*—a pattern—that exists both in the church and in the world.[94] Years ago, Löhe spoke of the *ordo* of Christian life, a pattern rooted in love and righteousness. Believers cannot feast at the altar while their neighbors suffer great need.

Löhe was unique and innovative in his theology and ministry. Pietists were more concerned with the notion of the personal forgiveness one received in the Sacrament. Rationalists saw the Sacrament as a reminder to live the moral life exemplified by Christ. Lutheran Orthodoxy emphasized the forgiveness of sins and the sealing of faith.[95] Löhe's emphasis on the Lord's Supper as a uniting event, uniting communicants with one another *and* with Christ, was a hallmark of his theology and ministry.

Community was important to Löhe. The Word creates it. The Word as the Christ who is witnessed to in the Scriptures and proclaimed in worship creates the community called "church." This Word not only creates that community called church, but the Word, Christ, is its organizing or ordering principle, and he preserves the church.

The Word works in close tandem with the sacraments. The preached and written Word points to Christ in whom we find redemption and salvation. The sacraments are the fullest expression of this redemption and salvation.

Within Löhe's theology, the notion of unity plays an important role. In *Three Books about the Church*, he writes that "from the very beginning man was so created that he cannot be happy alone."[96] Humans need fellowship. They need to be in relationship. Only Christ with his bride, the church, can satisfy this need. The sacraments are a real expression of this fellowship; they create and sustain fellowship with Christ and fellowship with those who also participate in the community.

Catholicity and apostolicity compose, then, a two-dimensional picture of the church. Apostolicity corresponds to the historical unity of the church while catholicity corresponds to the breadth of the church. All pictures, of course, consist of three dimensions. What is its third dimension for Löhe? *Christ.* It is Christ who gives the church life and sustains it in its struggle to give witness to the salvation God has offered the world in the Son.

Löhe endeavored in his liturgical reflections and practice to give weight to all the dimensions and elements of the Christian life. He struggled to give expression to the catholicity of the church while being faithful to its apostolicity and vice versa. He struggled to emphasize the real presence with Christ and thus union with Christ when one feasted at the Lord's Table. At the same time, he endeavored to emphasize that union with Christ meant union with all the children of God. Löhe gave weight to the Word but even more important—in view of the times—to the sacraments. He created an atmosphere where the sacraments and the Word could encounter each other to their mutual benefit, as well as to the benefit of the church.

NOTES

1 *Agende, GW* VII/1: 17.

2 William Loehe, "Betstunden," *GW* VII/2: 528. The entire congregation, not only the leaders but also the laity, is to participate in worship, particularly in the Eucharist. See "Predigt am 14. Dezember 1. Korinther 14,40," *GWE* I: 172–73.

3 *Three Books*, 47.

4 *Three Books*, 50.

5 See *Agende, GW* VII/1: 90. Here, Löhe speaks of confession as the "common entrance" of the community into the place (not to be understood merely as a geographic location!) of worship and asks "what could be more natural for the new human than to approach the most holy God with the confession of sins?"

6 *Agende, GW* VII/1: 168–69.

7 See also Löhe's remarks regarding the charge to pray [*Gebetsvermahnung*] which immediately follows the sermon. He writes: "The charge to pray is found in the oldest forms of the common prayer. Every need and necessity of the church, indeed of the world, is named. The congregation is reminded to pray for these needs and to conclude with the Lord's Prayer" (*Agende, GW* VII/1: 202).

8 See especially questions 33–41 in William Loehe, "Prüfungstafel," *GW* VII/2: 240–41.

9 *Agende, GW* VII/1: 338. On eucharistic community, see "Predigt über 1. Korinther 10,16 und 17," *GWE* I: 69–77, esp. 70–71.

10 William Loehe, *Liturgy for Christian Congregations of the Lutheran Faith* (3d ed.; ed. J. Deinzer; trans. F. C. Longaker with an introduction by Edward T. Horn; Newport, KY: n.p., 1902; repr., Fort Wayne, IN: Repristination Press, 1995), xi

(page references are to repr. ed.); hereafter *Liturgy*.

[11] Thomas H. Schattauer, "Announcement, Confession, and Lord's Supper in the Pastoral-Liturgical Work of Wilhelm Löhe: A Study of Worship and Church Life in the Lutheran Parish at Neuendettelsau, Bavaria, 1837–1872" (Ph.D. diss., University of Notre Dame, 1990), 297.

[12] William Loehe, "Ein Versuch, auf die deutschen Auswanderer nach Nordamerika und auf die dortige Kolonisation kirchlich einzuwirken," *GW* IV: 148–49.

[13] *Liturgy*, xiv–xv.

[14] Löhe, "Prediget das Evangelium," *GW* IV: 114, said that Word and Sacrament are the source of the Christian's joy.

[15] *Agende*, *GW* VII/1: 12.

[16] *Three Books*, 166.

[17] See chapter 2 for a fuller discussion of the meaning of "Word" in Löhe's theology. Also see *Three Books*, 61–72 passim. Regarding the slipperiness of the definition of "Word," see Hans Schwarz, *Divine Communication: Word and Sacrament in Biblical, Historical, and Contemporary Perspective* (Philadelphia: Fortress, 1985), 3.

[18] *Liturgy*, xii; see also *Agende*, *GW* VII/1: 13.

[19] "Kirche und Amt: Neue Aphorismen," *GW* V/1: 547.

[20] See Apol. IV. Melanchthon writes, for example, "we teach that a man is justified when, with his conscience terrified by the preaching of penitence, he takes heart and believes that he has a gracious God for Christ's sake" (*BC*, 152). Calvin similarly writes: "The law . . . by accusing moves us to seek grace" (Calvin, *Institutes*, 2.7.3–5, 8–9; quote is section heading of *Institutes*, 2.7.9). The secondary literature is extensive. Good starting exploration points would be Hans Schwarz, *Divine Communication*, 24–28; Schwarz, *True Faith*, 104–06; and "The Means of Grace. Part II: The Word," in *CD* 2: 269–74. Gerhard Forde also has a helpful discussion of the accusatory character of law in the second volume of *Christian Dogmatics*; see Gerhard Forde, "The Christian Life," in *CD* 2: 413–19.

[21] "Prüfungstafel," *GW* VII/2: 246.

[22] "Unsere Lage," *GW* V/1: 490.

[23] *Liturgy*, xiv.

[24] Schwarz, *Divine Communication*, 36.

[25] *Liturgy*, xii; also *Agende*, *GW* VII/1: 13; and William Loehe, "Gutachten in Sachen der Abend-mahlsgemeinschaft: Vor einigen Freunden gelesen," *GW* V/2: 907.

[26] *Liturgy*, xi. For a fuller discussion of this point, see Briese, "Löhe and the Sacrament of the Altar," 31–34; see also Klaus Ganzert, *Vom Heiligtum her* (Neuendettelsau: Freimund-Verlag, 1950), 5–6.

[27] *Agende*, *GW* VII/1: 18.

[28] *Liturgy*, xii. Frieder Schulz has written a helpful essay in which he demonstrates how Löhe altered the order of Holy Communion to highlight the theme of unity in Christ. The position of the Nunc Dimittis was changed. See Frieder Schulz, "Der Beitrag Wilhelm Löhes zur Ausbildung eines evangelischen Eucharistiegebetes," in *Gratias Agamus: Studien zum eucharistischen Hochgebet* (ed. Andreas Heinz and Heinrich Rennings; Freiburg: Herder, 1992), 457–67, esp. 463.

29 "Prüfungstafel," *GW* VII/2: 305; also William Loehe, "Dettelsauer Leben," *GW* IV: 403.

30 *Liturgy*, xii.

31 Albrecht Peters, "Abendsmahl III," in *TRE*, 1: 138–39.

32 Regarding the Pietist tendency, Philip Jacob Spener, for example, clearly affirms the real presence of Christ in the Lord's Supper. Spener, *Pia Desideria* (trans. and ed. Theodore G. Tappert; Philadelphia: Fortress, 1964), 63, writes: "Not less gladly do I acknowledge the glorious power in the sacramental, oral, and not merely spiritual eating and drinking of the body and blood of the Lord in the Holy Supper." Regarding the decision theology dimension of the pietistic understanding of the Lord's Supper, Spener describes the process of preparation: If "each person, especially when he wished to prepare himself for the Lord's Supper, were to describe the condition of his conscience to the whole group and were always to act according to its counsel, I have no doubt that within a short time a glorious advance in piety would result" (114; see also 117).

33 Rudolf Boon, "Child and Church, Communion and culture," in *Omnes Circumadstantes: Contributions Towards a History of the Role of the People in the Liturgy Presented to Herman Wegman* (ed. Charles Caspers and Marc Schneiders; Kampen, Netherlands: J. H. Kok, 1990), 229, summarizes the pietistic teaching on Communion: The piety "around the table of the Lord's Supper and the altar could be characterized as a spirituality of personal religious life. What is important in this spirituality is a personal involvement in the salvation which is preached and an inner assimilation of the doctrine which is taught; it is about being ready to examine oneself and a decision for a conversion to the 'new life', about the resolution to sanctify one's life and about being susceptible of a personal religious experience: the experience of God's work in one's personal life."

34 Peters, "Abendsmahl III," 1: 137. On the actual eucharistic practices of the Pietists, see the instructive essay by Alfred Niebergall, "Abendmahlsfeier III" in *TRE* 1: 287–310; esp. 301–02.

35 The Formula of Concord states that "in addition to the words of Christ and of St. Paul (the bread in the Lord's Supper 'is the true body of Christ' or 'a participation in the body of Christ'), we at times also use the formulas 'under the bread, with the bread, in the bread.' We do this to reject the papistic transubstantiation and to indicate the sacramental union between the untransformed substance of the bread and the body of Christ" (*BC*, 575).

36 For a clear statement of this position, see, for example, *Agende, GW* VII/1: 339.

37 "Prüfungstafel," *GW* VII/2: 308. In *Zuruf, GW* IV: 75, Löhe went so far as to tell German Lutherans in North America that they ought not associate with other denominations even if that meant that they were forced to worship privately as families in their own homes without the benefit of a trained pastor.

38 *Schmuck, GW* VII/2: 561.

39 "Prüfungstafel," *GW* VII/2: 286. For a discussion of the relationship between Löhe and Luther on the meaning and significance of the Lord's Supper, cf. Werner Ost, "Das Bild Luthers und der Reformation bei Wilhelm Löhe (1808–1872)," *Luther* 68 (1997): 128–31, who reaches a similar conclusion regarding the fellowship or union that is effected in the Lord's Supper.

40 Grane, *Augsburg Confession*, 118. In his treatise, "The Blessed Sacrament of the Holy and True Body of Christ, and the Brotherhoods," Luther writes equally plainly:

"Christ and all saints are one spiritual body, just as the inhabitants of a city are one community and body, each citizen being a member of the other and of the entire city. All the saints therefore, are members of Christ and of the church, which is a spiritual and eternal city of God" (LW 35:51). See also Schwarz, *True Faith*, 121.

41 "Prüfungstafel," *GW* VII/2: 287.

42 "Prüfungstafel," *GW* VII/2: 246.

43 Paul Althaus has a good discussion of this same topic. He writes: "As Christ is our food and drink in the Lord's Supper, so we also become food and drink for each other. This means that I give everything which I have to my neighbor who needs it and conversely that I allow him to help and serve me in my poverty." See Althaus, *The Theology of Martin Luther* (trans. Robert C. Schultz; Philadelphia: Fortress, 1966), 321–22; quote is on 321. Hans Schwarz concurs: The Lord's Supper "will prod us socially to indicate that the solidarity around the table needs to extend beyond the Lord's Table to include every home and nation" (*Divine Communication*, 135).

44 "Prüfungstafel," *GW* VII/2: 285; see also *Agende, GW* VII/1: 338. Löhe suggests that we who are imaged or embodied in Christ by faith and by love should give ourselves to our neighbors in like manner.

45 LW 35:54.

46 *BC*, 352, 577, 211, 449.

47 *BC*, 449. See also Althaus, *Theology of Luther*, 347, who writes that "the forgiveness of sins [is] the real gift of the Lord's Supper."

48 Loehe, *Questions and Answers to the Six Parts of the "Small Catechism" of Dr. Martin Luther* (2d. ed.; trans. Edward T. Horn; Columbia, SC: W. J. Duffie, 1893; repr., Fort Wayne, IN: Repristination Press, 1993), 175 (page references are to repr. ed.); hereafter *Questions & Answers*.

49 "Prüfungstafel," *GW* VII/2: 300.

50 Wilhelm Löhe, "Hausbedarf christlicher Gebete für Augsburgische Konfessions-verwandte," *GW* VII/2: 156; hereafter "Hausbedarf." See also "Hausbedarf," 157, for a trinitarian expression of the gifts of forgiveness, life, and healing.

51 *Agende, GW* VII/1: 337.

52 See *Three Books*, 47–49; quote is on 48. Löhe writes that "from the very beginning man was so created that he cannot be happy alone" (47). Even with Christ, you cannot be blessed if you are alone with Christ: "He and his eternal blessedness are much too great a burden for a soul which has no kindred soul near it. . . . Even if one should in all seriousness wish to be alone with God for eternity, that wish could never be fulfilled. For just as the Lord did not create an earth for only one man, so he also did not create a heaven for just one man" (49).

53 *Agende, GW* VII/1: 338.

54 Sihvonen, "Wer sein will," 454.

55 "Prüfungstafel," *GW* VII/2: 290; see also "Prüfungstafel," *GW* VII/2: 303–04.

56 Wilhelm Löhe, "Rauchopfer," *GW* VII/2: 464.

57 Neuendettelsau apparently was one of these when Löhe arrived. See Schattauer, "Announcement, Confession, and Lord's Supper," 291–92.

58 "Prüfungstafel," *GW* VII/2: 290. Löhe, *Zuruf, GW* IV: 75, even encouraged those in North America who lived far removed from a Lutheran church to make the

effort to partake in the eucharistic meal at least once (or more) in a year. The effort would be rewarded with the reassurance that one does indeed belong to a heavenly community. Luther, in the Large Catechism, also argued for a frequent, regular participation in the Lord's Supper; see *BC*, 450–57.

59 "Unsere Lage," *GW* V/1: 390.

60 Löhe, "Predigt am 7. Dezember 1. Korinther 11,28ff," *GWE* I: 164–70. Löhe was not alone in this. He drew support from the confessions. See, for example, the Solid Declaration, Art. VII (*BC*, 580).

61 Wilhelm Löhe, "Mitteilung der Windsbacher Predigerkonferenz (am 7. November 1837): Vom Abendmahlsgenuß," *GW* V/1: 47; hereafter "Vom Abendmahlsgenuß."

62 "Prüfungstafel," *GW* VII/2: 291.

63 Schattauer, "Announcement, Confession, and Lord's Supper," 303. This is clear in *Zuruf*. Here, Löhe says that "neither fraternal love, nor friendship, nor blissful common living will fall away where one is united in doctrine. . . . While we praise the bond of the invisible church above everything, we are also bonded to the visible church" (*Zuruf*, *GW* IV: 82; see also "Eine Verteidigung," *GW* IV: 231).

64 Löhe, "Predigt über 1. Korinther 10,15 bis 17," *GWE* I: 63.

65 "Vom Abendmahlsgenuß," *GW* V/1: 49.

66 Löhe, "Brief an das Dekanat (24. Februar 1840)," *GW* V/1: 70.

67 "Prüfungstafel," *GW* VII/2: 264.

68 "Unsere Lage," *GW* V/1: 389; see also Löhe's exhortation to clergy and church leaders in *Zuruf*, *GW* IV: 80–84.

69 "Unsere Lage," *GW* V/1: 486. Cf. also the Large Catechism (*BC*, 448).

70 *Agende*, *GW* VII/1: 6.

71 *Liturgy*, xi.

72 Regarding Methodists and their new measures, Löhe wrote the sincere preacher "despises any sort of Methodism" (*Three Books*, 168). Regarding American Lutheranism, Löhe wrote to his friend Karl von Raumer in a letter dated 3 July 1843 that he had received a copy of Schmucker's *Portraiture of Lutheranism* and expressed some alarm about the ideas Schmucker presents (*GW* I: 637).

73 *Liturgy*, xi.

74 In this respect, Löhe could even assert that a uniform order of worship in universal use could get in the way of authentic unity on the basis of the apostolic Word; see Löhe, *Die bayerische Generalsynode vom Frühjahr 1849 und das lutherische Bekenntnis: Eine Beleuchtung der Synodalbeschlüsse in Betreff der Petition* "Wahrung des Bekenntnisses und Einführung desselben in seine Rechte," *GW* V/1: 338.

75 "Unsere Lage," *GW* V/1: 461.

76 *Agende*, *GW* VII/1: 17.

77 *Three Books*, 111–15. Löhe says that the Lutheran church has the mark of the pure denomination; it is the apostolic church *par excellence* (111).

78 Thomas H. Schattauer, "Sunday Worship at Neuendettelsau under Wilhelm Löhe," *Worship* 59 (1985): 383.

79 Having said that, Löhe did consider himself a "catholic Christian." He wrote, "I will not be ashamed of [Luther's] name so long as I can call myself—without being

misunderstood—what I truly am: a catholic Christian in the true and correct understanding of the word" ("Warum bekenne ich mich?" *GW* IV: 221).

80 *Agende, GW* VII/1: 21–22. The anointing of the sick episode in 1857–58 is also indicative of Löhe's supposed "Romanizing" tendencies. See "Nach Bekanntwerden der Krankenölung (Ende 1857–Frühjahr 1859)," *GW* V/2: 719–43; and "Kirchliche Briefe," *GW* V/2: 845–47, for Löhe's response to the charges against him. Regarding the charges against Löhe and the potential consequences, see Ganzert's editorial comments in *GW* V/2: 1053. Regarding Löhe's relationship to Roman Catholicism, see Wilhelm Mauer's helpful essay, "Wilhelm Löhe und der römische Katholizismus," in *Wilhelm Löhe—Anstöße für die Zeit*, 69–88.

81 *Agende, GW* VII/1: 27.

82 *Agende, GW* VII/1: 11.

83 *Liturgy*, ix. Elsewhere, Löhe rhetorically asked, "What is more catholic than the Augsburg Confession and its Apology?" See "Warum bekenne ich mich?" *GW* IV: 223.

84 *Three Books*, 57–59; see also "Aphorismen," *GW* V/1: 273.

85 *Agende, GW* VII/1: 12; see also *Liturgy*, xi.

86 *Agende, GW* VII/1: 127.

87 *Agende, GW* VII/1: 101.

88 *Agende, GW* VII/1: 126.

89 *Agende, GW* VII/1: 13.

90 *Agende, GW* VII/1: 126. The great advantage or gift of the Reformation was the emphasis on Scripture, on making Scripture available to all. Unfortunately, this was to the detriment of interest in and emphasis on liturgical life. Löhe wrote that in the Reformation there was a decline of interest in the church year and its celebrations while the written Word gained more emphasis.

91 *Agende, GW* VII/1: 18.

92 Schattauer, "Sunday Worship," 383.

93 Private confession was at the center of Löhe's theology of pastoral care; it was indispensable. See *Zuruf, GW* IV: 83.

94 Gordon W. Lathrop, *Holy Things: A Liturgical Theology* (Minneapolis: Fortress, 1993), 207. Lathrop writes: "The liturgy is a social event and its order proposes a vision of ordered society within a larger ordered world. . . . [The local] assembly is itself the full presence, in this place, of all that Christians have to say about the ordering of place, time, and society."

95 Schmid, *Doctrinal Theology*, 557. Regarding the forgiveness of sins and sealing of faith, see 579–80. Noticeably, the one Lutheran Orthodox theologian who places emphasis on the Lord's Supper as a union both with Christ and our neighbor is David Hollaz. And Hollaz was influential for Löhe. Schmid quotes Hollaz: "Being united through the Holy Supper with Christ, the Head, they are also united with one another as members of the mystical body, and thus the Eucharist is the basis of love between us and our neighbor" (581).

96 *Three Books*, 47. Martin George, "In der Kirche leben," 222, notes that Löhe oriented his theology to the New Testament model of *koinonia*, of a community of love and service, which was centered in the Sacrament of the Altar.

5

MISSION AND PROCLAMATION

Mission was, next to ecclesiology and liturgics, central to Löhe's ministry and theology. The nineteenth century witnessed something of an explosion in missions *practice*, as well as in theological discourse on missions. In the first centuries following the death and resurrection of Christ, the growth of the church was propelled by personal conversion. People were attracted to the Christian church because of its example and witness. Christianity offered a confidence, a burning conviction for the message the church proclaimed.[1] Mission strategy in the first five hundred years of the church's existence was characterized by personal witness and evangelism.[2] The conversion and baptism of Clovis, king of the Franks, marks a new trend in mission strategy.

When Clovis was baptized on Christmas Day, 496 A.D., so were his soldiers. This marked the beginning of what one might term "conversion by conquest." This strategy was perfected by Charlemagne. Stephen Neill describes a typical situation: "Once a German tribe had been conquered, its conversion was included in the terms of peace, as the price to be paid for enjoying the protection of the emperor and the good government that his arms ensured."[3] Such a strategy reflected the colonial and "imperialistic" character of much mission activity in the life of the church.

Mission in this early period also owes much to the monastic orders. The ministry of the monks in non-Christianized areas was twofold.[4] They lived as the people did. They worked the land and provided for themselves just as the indigenous populations. They were also committed to the local language and culture that was worthy of preservation in its own right. The monastic model and the conquest model of mission struggled for ascendancy. As the church became more powerful and centralized, the conquest model became, in many ways, more predominant.

By the nineteenth century, mission theology was beset by a number of difficulties. Missions were often characterized by colonialism.[5] On a purely theological level, "the majority of Protestant missionaries had no strong sense of the church-at-large. In most cases missions had been undertaken as the personal effort of devoted Christians, and not as the responsibility of the churches as a whole. This was true even of the Roman Catholic Church."[6] It also seems to be particularly true of later Pietists.[7] But this charge cannot be leveled at Löhe. His theology of mission is characterized by a strong ecclesiology at its center.

Löhe was moved by his reading of Paul and the Acts of the Apostles to orient his ministry around mission. The apostle, he wrote, "spoke with ardent love of that which we call mission."[8] The same convictions moved Löhe. Prior to Löhe's mission activity there were no mission organizations in Bavaria supported by the Lutheran church. Even Löhe's efforts received no official support from the leadership of the Bavarian church.[9] His interest in mission began while he was still a young theological student at Erlangen. On November 10, 1827, he presided at the first meeting of a mission circle. In its official diary, he wrote, "Today I held my first mission circle in the name of God. It is a small beginning, but if one cannot do more, even a little is enough."[10]

Already in these early years, Löhe seems to have anticipated his later interest in missions. Within fifteen years of the first meeting of that small mission circle, consisting of only a handful of people, Löhe became the editor of a periodical dedicated to mission activity in North America (*Kirchliche Mittheilungen aus und über Nordamerika*) and was training men and sending them to North America. In that first mission circle, he suggested to the other members that the circle subscribe to periodicals dedicated to mission. The reason was so the members might hear about God's blessing to the church in faraway lands. Yet Löhe also insisted that the more they hear about missions, about God's blessings, about the heathen and their desire to hear the Gospel, the more they will have their desire stirred up.[11] Löhe's own experience, particularly in the 1840s as the North American missions were flourishing, confirmed his insights.

In his little book, *Die Mission unter den Heiden* [*Mission Among the Heathen*], Löhe suggested that Lutherans read aloud to each other the *Dresdener Missionsnachrichten* [*Dresden Mission News*]. The *Dresdener Missionsnachrichten* was not as easy to understand as other mission periodicals, but it was confessional and evangelical. In this way Lutherans could know what the only Lutheran mission organization in Germany was doing. Moreover, Löhe wrote, "you can distribute it with a clear conscience."[12] Confessional integrity and right doctrine were important in missions too.

Confessional integrity and right doctrine were important in the *mission field* as well. Löhe was not inclined to join forces with mission organizations he felt were not sufficiently Lutheran and confessional. Initially he supported the Basel Mission but withdrew his support after he decided that it was insufficiently confessional.[13] Why should right doctrine be so important? After all, did not most questions of doctrine address the finer points of theology which were the concerns of those nourished by "solid food" and not "milk" (Heb 5:12–14)? Löhe points out that most Christians are eventually weaned from milk to solid food, from the basic questions to the more complex questions. As long as the heathen remain at the beginner's level of Christianity or intentionally want to maintain it, they will finally come to every question the church has already encountered. Mission churches will have to struggle with these questions, too, because human nature is the same in all times and in all places. The same errors, mistakes, and sins emerge over and over again where one does not make the whole truth known to people. Löhe wanted to ensure a satisfactory answer for every question that arises so a lasting calm might prevail for every need.[14] New Christians should be introduced to right doctrine at the beginning so they do not have to struggle with the same issues and heresies of the past.

Löhe was always looking for ways to become more actively involved in missions. In the mid-1830s, he considered traveling to the Middle East to survey mission opportunities there, but the plan fell through for financial reasons.[15] Löhe was also prepared to support a missionary in the East Indies, but this plan was never realized because the instigator, Johann Merkel, died.[16] During the 1830s, Löhe satisfied his desire to evangelize by being involved in at least a couple of tract societies.[17] His interest in tracts waned, however, by the end of the 1840s. In the late 1850s, Löhe once again turned his attention to tracts.[18] But his interest was motivated by purposes other than mission and evangelism.[19] Initially tracts were a means of evangelism, but by the 1840s he saw evangelism in other, more personal, terms. Löhe's zeal for mission did not diminish at this period; instead, it took other forms. He sought to support foreign missions through many avenues.

In December 1840, while visiting in the home of his friend and former professor, Karl von Raumer, Löhe saw an article written by Friedrich Wyneken in the *Zeitschrift für Protestantismus und Kirche*. He immediately perceived an opportunity to be more directly involved in missions. After writing an article for the *Sonntagsblatt*, Löhe began to receive money, and two volunteers for mission appeared on his doorstep in Neuendettelsau. This was the beginning of his mission activity in North America. Mission work became his passion. He sought to share this passion with others and to inspire them toward efforts to evangelize the heathen. The closing words of a lecture Löhe delivered to the general assembly of the *Protestantische Zentralmissionsverein* [Central Protestant Mission Association] titled *Die Heidenmission in Nordamerika* [Heathen Mission in North America] reveal something of his fervor:

> I wish that every congregation of the Lutheran confessions may rec-
> ognize their calling to be mission congregations to the Indians. I
> wish that our partners in faith [in North America] may soon be
> strengthened—both within and without—such that they support
> mission like the Romans and go further than them in every corner
> where heathens are found, that it become known that the true God
> is in Zion. May every land—even North America from New York to
> the waves of the peaceful ocean—be engulfed with the recognition
> of the unspoiled truth and may the honor of the Lord of the Sabaoth
> become complete.[20]

Löhe's passion for mission cannot be better expressed than in his own wish for the Lutheran church.

Mission—both inner and outer mission—were at the heart of Löhe's theology and ministry. Indeed, in his view, a church not in mission was not a church at all. To be church was to be in mission. Löhe maintained that "there is no such thing as zeal for religion without zeal for mission in Christianity."[21] To paraphrase the Epistle of James, one could say, "just as the body without the Spirit is dead, so faith without mission is dead" (Jas 2:26). Faith and mission are inseparable.

MISSION: THE WHY AND THE WHAT

Löhe defined mission as "sending out." He further wrote that "by mis-sion one means sending Christian preachers out among non-Christian peoples, namely among the heathen."[22] His definition seems traditional. As one commentator notes, "mission has often been identified with over-seas mission and been thought of in isolation from the mission of the church in its 'home' environment."[23] Although Löhe characterizes mission as "Christian preachers out among the heathen," his understanding of mis-sion is actually broader. Missionaries carry out the work of the church in a foreign setting. But missionaries do the same thing in a foreign setting that a farmer in Neuendettelsau does in his community. In its broadest sense, a missionary is nothing more than a Christian living his or her faith among non-Christians.

Missionaries were regular Christians who lived on foreign soil. They did not necessarily do anything so different from what any other Christian might do in the same situation. Missionaries were Christians who exercised the office of the priesthood in an alien land. This becomes clear when Löhe asserts that those best placed to carry out mission work are those in the immediate vicinity.[24] Those congregations located nearest to heathens should take the lead in mission activity among those heathens.

Why did Löhe feel so compelled to contribute to missionary efforts? Why should anybody contribute? Löhe responded to these questions not by pointing to the Great Commission (Matt 28:19), but by pointing to Acts 2. In particular he was motivated by the description of the early church:

> They devoted themselves to the apostles' teaching and fellowship, to the breaking of bread and the prayers. Awe came upon everyone, because many wonders and signs were being done by the apostles. All who believed were together and had all things in common; they would sell their possessions and goods and distribute the proceeds to all, as any had need. Day by day, as they spent much time together in the temple, they broke bread at home and ate their food with glad and generous hearts, praising God and having the goodwill of all the people. And day by day the Lord added to their number those who were being saved. (Acts 2:42–47)

One of the key elements in this description of the activity of the early church is that of fellowship or community. Luke describes the fellowship that existed in the church and concludes that "the Lord added to their number." Mission, in this sense, means to love others, to reach out to them in love.[25] Löhe tied mission and fellowship together.

Löhe answered the why of mission with a variety of answers. The first and most obvious answer is that the Gospel of salvation is to be shared with those who might otherwise be condemned to damnation. Both temporal and eternal misery is the lot of the heathen. How could Christians not be aroused to compassion by the temporal and eternal misery of the heathen? "Indeed," Löhe wrote, "who can read or hear what you, my dear ones, have often read and heard—the innumerable and dreadful violations of the innate human laws by the heathen, the disorder, the destruction of all happiness and peace, the dissolution and destruction of every natural bond as they result from these violations and indeed must result?"[26] The Christian Gospel brings order into societies ruled by disorder, lawlessness, and chaos.

For Löhe, temporal misery is bad enough, but it only affects the mortal body. Eternal misery is another matter; it affects the immortal soul. The threat or the danger of eternal misery is real: "every day hundreds of thousands of unfortunate souls with conscious grief go out the gates of time and enter into the gates of eternity."[27] The thought of souls destined to eternal suffering should alone be reason enough to arouse Christians to mission. Those who are baptized and saved have a responsibility to do what they can to save those whose fate is uncertain.

Löhe also answered the why of mission by pointing to the innate human need for community. He stated at the outset of *Three Books about the Church* that "as long as a man is alone he cannot even be blessed."[28] This notion that humans ought not be alone was the impulse for mission. The goal of mission was to bring others into fellowship. Why should adherents of other religions be excluded from Christian fellowship because of an accident of birth? Löhe was unequivocal in his view that one could not find salvation outside the church. Christians are to go "to the ends of the earth" (Acts 1:8; see also Matt 28:19; Luke 24:47; and Acts 10–11).

> The Hindu, just because he was born humble and poor, should not be excluded from the blessings of religion, he should not be accursed, an outcast, and lead a wretched existence! The peace of God, which the Gospel brings, should seize every heart and bring bliss. Love should be passed from person to person and the thought of brotherliness— of humanity—as one family of God should be captured in the desolate hearts of heathens.[29]

Mission is about sharing the peace of God with others and inviting them into that fellowship where God's peace and love are found. It is about inviting others into the church.

The church is that place where one can experience the deepest and most sublime of all forms of community. In the church one experiences— in the celebration of the Eucharist—the living presence of the risen Christ. It is on account of this encounter that Christians are so happy. Löhe was characteristically pointed on this issue; he states that "Word and sacrament are the fountains of our happiness."[30] Should Christians not share their happiness with others? The joy of the Christian message is meant to be shared. By virtue of their membership in the priesthood of all believers, all Christians ought to be moved to expand the membership of the priesthood. The impulse to mission, Löhe says, is borne out of our vocations as priests; it is not limited to those who are ordained.[31] Our vocation as priests of the church calls us to be engaged in the activity of the church—

reaching out to all those who are not presently part of the community of the baptized, reaching out to all those who do not experience the joy and peace of the eucharistic feast.

The most important reason that the church should be engaged in mission, however, is not because of love and compassion for those condemned to misery. Nor should the church be engaged in mission because it wants to invite others into its fellowship. These are good reasons, to be sure, but the main reason, Löhe affirmed, is found in the words of Acts 10:42: God "has commanded us to preach to the people." In a sermon, Löhe commented on this command:

> Who has commanded? God has commanded. What has he commanded? To preach. To whom shall one preach? To the people. To which people shall one preach? Perhaps only to the Jewish people? Cornelius and his house-church are indeed heathens, and we and our fathers are also heathens! Thus, as the Scriptures elsewhere say, to all people and all peoples. As the Scriptures also say, "to all creatures."[32]

It is good to have compassion for heathens, and it is good to reach out and share the fellowship and community we experience with others. But these reasons are penultimate. The most important reason for Christians to be active in mission is because *God* commands it.[33] God commands that we love our neighbors as ourselves. God commands that we reach out and draw into the household of God those who do not yet know about genuine community. The church need not be overwhelmed by the task. To be sure, there are many who have not yet heard the Gospel and many who have not received it. Nonetheless, Christians are encouraged precisely because the command to proclaim the Gospel is a command from God:

> We know that all of God's commands are accompanied by a promise of success. And we know that the last commandment of the Lord is accompanied by the promise "remember, I am with you always, to the end of the age." Therefore we can lift ourselves up with courage and strength, we can open up our sails with joy and allow our ship to be driven by the power of the command of Christ in quiet confidence to the destination which we desire.[34]

The command, far from being a source of anxiety, is a source of confidence as the church goes forth in mission, seeking ever more souls in its quest to extend its community.

The need was—and is—great. God has commanded the church to be in mission. All God's people are called to make mission a central part of their life. Mission is discipleship; it is a witness to God's Word of grace. But who should go in mission to heathen lands? Löhe affirmed that true successors to Peter were needed, gifted, strong, and heroic souls who have been purified by God's Spirit.[35] A commitment to pure doctrine was, of course, a product of cleansing by the Spirit. Anything less than pure doctrine posed a danger of leading those less mature in the faith astray. Many missionaries were needed, but they had to be genuine successors to Peter and the apostles.

Löhe did not mean to accept indiscriminately anyone who wanted to join the church. No one, of course, should be prevented from joining the church. At the same time, right doctrine and right belief is important. Right doctrine ensured right belief. For Löhe, right understanding of doctrine ensured that one received the Gospel in its purity and fullness: "one finds one's way better at high noon than by the light of evening stars. The more complete the knowledge, the more complete life can be and will be."[36] To water down the Gospel or to present a false picture of it was tantamount to leading others astray. Löhe wanted to invite all people into community, but false doctrine serves only to lead one to a false sense of community. The church invites others into the community but not at the expense of authentic fellowship with Christ and his body.

The church is a new world. Humans experience the brokenness of the physical world in which they live as well as the brokenness of the social and cultural worlds. The church represents a different world. It is the manifestation of God's kingdom, of God's world. To become a Christian was to encounter—even if incompletely—the fullness and perfection of God's world:

> The awakening into Christendom opens to a person a world which was previously unknown to that person. An entirely new view of life will usually arise. One no longer seeks the goal of life here, but rather beyond. The world is transformed into an institution for the bliss and salvation of humanity.[37]

Mission was not only about inviting people into a community. It was also about inviting and introducing people into a new world, a world where one finds bliss and salvation.

MISSIONARY TRAINING AND EDUCATION

Mission is a multifaceted task. Löhe expected missionaries to have a well-rounded, though not necessarily extensive, education.[38] A brief look at the curriculum at the mission seminary in Neuendettelsau illustrates his goals. In winter semester of 1858–59, the following subjects were taught: music (voice, piano, and violin), German, Latin, Greek, Hebrew, basic medicine, rhetoric, biblical history, Bible interpretation, dogmatics, homiletics, and orthography. In the following summer semester, the courses were similar: music (voice, piano, and violin), German, English, French, Latin, Greek, rhetoric, biblical interpretation, dogmatics, biblical history, and church history of North America.[39] Missionaries proclaimed the Gospel not only in words, but in actions. Missionaries were expected to embody the Word as well as proclaim it.

Another reason why the education of missionaries was so broad at Neuendettelsau is that Löhe did not see missionaries as pastors among the heathen. A more apt comparison is that of a schoolteacher. In *Die Heidenmission in Nordamerika*, Löhe wrote that

> Missionaries, whom we have trained up until now, are very different in their training from those servants of God who minister within the church. A missionary and a German preacher will relate to one another . . . much like schoolteachers and pastors relate to one another. Mission seminarians and schoolteacher seminarians have much in common.[40]

Just as the education of a teacher is different from a pastor and complements the work of a pastor, so is the education of a missionary different from a preacher. A missionary's work, then, complements the work of a preacher.

Löhe had high expectations of those men he sent out as missionaries. He sought individuals who could say with the prophet Jeremiah, "I have not sought human days, you know that. What I have preached is right in front of you" (Jer 17:16).[41] Löhe commented that "there are sufficient people who offer themselves to the ministry among the heathen, but send twelve such as those we need, then the heathen shall rejoice and hell shall be filled with the sound of grinding teeth and the world shall become aware that there is another kingdom besides that of the visible."[42] Many Christians feel called to be missionaries; sometimes their skills and gifts vary greatly. At first, Löhe considered Georg Burger, the second man to volunteer for ministry in North America, to be unsuitable. It was only because of Burger's enthusiasm and persistence that Löhe finally decided to accept him.[43] The right person, he recognized, could achieve more than ten who are not meant for the task. To paraphrase Matthew's gospel, one might say that many are called to mission, but few are chosen (see Matt 22:14).

It is here that one encounters a paradox or ambiguity in Löhe's theology. On the one hand, he suggests that all Christians are missionaries, just as all Christians are priests according to the doctrine of the priesthood of all believers. On the other hand, Löhe rejected an *ordained* mission ministry, since all Christians are called to be missionaries.[44] As Löhe distinguished between the ordained ministry (*Amt*) and the priesthood to which all Christians are called through their Baptism, he also held to a similar distinction with respect to missionaries. All Christians are called to mission and personal evangelism. At the same time, some are chosen to exercise this work in an intentional way. It is these missionaries who receive training in preparation for the special work which they will carry out.

Löhe does not state whether missionaries chosen for this service need to be ordained. He asserted that missionaries are more like teachers than pastors.[45] This would suggest that missionaries need not be ordained. He also insisted that there is no "missionary *Amt*." Löhe argued that the *Amt* exists today chiefly in the forms of shepherds and teachers.[46] However, nearly all the men who passed through Neuendettelsau were eventually ordained, including those who went to the Michigan colonies. In any case, it is clear that those who are set aside as missionaries need a different education. Löhe even recognized the shortcomings of the training at Neuendettelsau in light of the standard theological education in Germany.

Löhe did not entirely break new ground with his approach to missionary training. Indeed, he compared his first missionaries—Ernst and Burger—to the first Moravian missionaries. They were not educated theologians like pastors in Germany. Löhe wrote to L. A. Petri that Ernst and Burger "are going out . . . with a purified confession, like the first Moravian missionaries, dependent on the blessing of the Almighty, waiting and believing, he will show them the path to their goals."[47] They were going out with more enthusiasm than expertise. That is not to say that they were ignorant and uneducated.[48] The phrase "purified confession" points to their training; they were simple people, armed with the truth of God's Word, and equipped for the reality of the North American situation.

The mission seminary at Neuendettelsau had developed a curriculum intended to address the reality of mission work. Löhe nevertheless saw this education as only the beginning; he fully expected that candidates would receive more theological training once they arrived in North America. This reality gave rise to the idea of establishing a seminary nearer to the mission field. Löhe realized that a seminary offered missionaries access to teachers who were themselves experienced in the mission field.[49] Missionaries should be further trained in the context in which they will serve.

The establishment of the seminary in Fort Wayne in 1845 was a logical consequence of his experience with the Ohio Synod. At the beginning, Ohio requested and Löhe sent men and books. The church severely needed willing men to serve as missionaries there, and the seminary desperately needed books for its library.[50] After the relationship between Ohio and Neuendettelsau was severed, Löhe looked for new ways to continue his missionary work in North America. The Fort Wayne seminary was an easy decision. Missionary candidates from Neuendettelsau and elsewhere were sent to Fort Wayne to receive theological training on location. Löhe established the seminary at Fort Wayne as a means by which he could ensure confessional (and linguistic) integrity. Through the seminary, its professors, and its stream of students, Löhe desired to influence the church in North America.[51]

MISSION COLONIES

Mission is at the center of a life of discipleship. For Löhe, mission was not something that certain people did in distant lands or in the tough urban neighborhoods. His mission seminary trained men for a variety of contexts. The "Annual Report of Mission Institute in Neuendettelsau for the Academic Year November 1, 1859 to October 15, 1860" [*Jahresbericht der Missionsanstalt in Neuendettelsau für das Schuljahr vom 1. Nov. 1859 bis zum 15 Oktober 1860*] points out that the Neuendettelsau mission seminary is the only organization of its type. It coordinates and supports mission among American Indians as well as German Lutherans who have emigrated to the United States.[52] Genuine mission activity supports and encourages both the newcomers as well as indigenous peoples.

Löhe was eager to move beyond evangelizing the converted in North America. He was not satisfied merely to send out pastors to the German Lutherans who had settled in the New World. He wanted to be more actively involved in evangelizing those who had never heard the Gospel. By 1846 Löhe was actively campaigning for support for mission activity among the Indians in North America. He began his lecture to the General Assembly of the Protestant Central Mission Association by asking where the church should next direct its attention. Where should it next direct its energies? Löhe answered, "I vote for the red Indians in North America."[53]

His motives are interesting. In addition to the reasons outlined above, Löhe included another motivation for German Lutherans to support mis-

sion activity among the Indians in North America.[54] He noted that the
Indians in North America had been driven out from their traditional
homelands and that in some places terrible atrocities had been perpetrated against them. One could say, Löhe wrote, that

> what Protestants have been responsible for, Protestants should cor-
> rect and pay for. One could justify this sentence by saying: "Indeed
> German Protestants have not taken that responsibility upon them-
> selves, but all the churches which emerged out of the Reformation
> nonetheless have something in common." One could acknowledge
> the responsibility of another as one's own.[55]

German Protestant churches had sufficient motivation to be involved in
the evangelization of Indians in North America.

One of the most important of Löhe's "experiments" was the establishment of the "mission colonies" in Michigan. In a letter to L. A. Petri in
Hannover, Löhe noted that in a neighboring parish neglected by its pastors he had "many, very solid followers."[56] Of these, 105 had committed
themselves to emigrating to Michigan to establish such a mission colony.[57]
Their pastor would be August Crämer, at that time still a student at the
mission seminary. But Crämer would complete his studies by the time the
group departed for the United States and ably serve the people in their
new home.

At the outset these colonies were settled by those who were moved by
the opportunity to break "new ground" and to evangelize Indians in the
American West. These were able men and women who freely chose to go
to the New World. In the *Kirchliche Mittheilungen*, Löhe wrote that they
were strong youth, well-known to the editor and worthy of the challenge.
They were not simply fleeing the fatherland; they were motivated by the
desire to found a starting point for heathen missions in the wasteland of
the New World.[58]

Later colonies were established for those who had no prospects in
Germany. Löhe was sensitive to the plight of those who did not have the
means to buy land to farm or who could not get established into a vocation.[59] It took some years to realize an idea that had first arisen in 1845. In
a letter to L. A. Petri, Löhe mentioned that an old pastor in the area had
an idea for financing the colonies.[60] A floating capital fund of 30,000–
50,000 florin would be established. With these funds, land could be bought
and sold to emigrants who were prepared to support a Lutheran pastor.
The proceeds from the sale of land would then be used again in the same

manner. It was this idea that was the basis for the third of the Michigan mission colonies, Frankenlust.

The basic idea remained the same in establishing the Michigan mission colonies. Mission colonies of German Lutherans would be established near American Indian settlements. These colonies would form a foothold from which Indians could be evangelized. Löhe's perspective was that the personal interaction with the American Indians nearby would witness to the Christian message of salvation. He was convinced that these Indian settlements were rich mission fields waiting to be harvested.[61] Those who lived in the mission colonies need not do anything more than be Christians.

Always at the center of these mission schemes was the notion that mission began in the congregation. This was how the early church began. The apostles would go to a new area and establish a base from which they would evangelize. In similar manner, Germany was evangelized by monks and nuns from the British Isles. The piety and charity of these missionaries were enough to persuade the German heathen to convert.[62] The Michigan mission colonies were to function as springboards to mission among American Indians. The German settlers would support their pastors and missionaries and be actively engaged in evangelistic activity. The congregations would serve as models of Christian life and discipleship.[63] In this way, Löhe hoped, "colonization, inner and outer mission could go together."[64] Congregational life and mission were always closely linked in Löhe's theology.

This linking of congregational life and mission is important. Löhe's comment to L. A. Petri on the neighboring parish neglected by its pastors revealed one of the recurring arguments against foreign mission at that time: Why should the church expend its resources overseas when there is more than enough to do at home? Why should the church not focus on the needs at its doorstep? Löhe anticipated this challenge. He responded that there was always work enough for all the preachers and candidates for ministry even if their gifts were used to their fullest extent. But, he added, ten or twenty times as many preachers and candidates could go among the heathen. Even if the German church sent as many missionaries as Löhe wanted, they would not be able to withdraw the claim that "the heathen only eat the crumbs which fall from the Christians' table."[65] Foreign missions, in Löhe's opinion, were not a threat to the viability and vitality of ministry at home.

Löhe went further. Overseas mission work was not a threat to local congregations because most of those who were sent were not sufficiently educated and qualified to serve in Germany. It was "mostly people from the uneducated classes who decided to go among the heathen."[66] In fact, a high level of education was often unnecessary for those who chose to serve overseas. Some heathen were more educated and, therefore, needed educated preachers. But those who were not so well educated did not need preachers with strong educational backgrounds.[67] In a certain sense, overseas mission work provided ministry opportunities for those who wanted to serve but were not qualified to serve at home. Mission work allowed the church to deploy people more efficiently by providing places for these people to serve according to their gifts and level of education. It allowed the church to more effectively use the gifts of all the limbs of its body.

At the same time, mission was not simply to be equated with ministry to those who have already been baptized. Löhe quoted the Sermon on the Mount: "Do not give what is holy to dogs; and do not throw your pearls before swine, or they will trample them under foot and turn and maul you" (Matt 7:6). Certainly there was a need for pastors in Germany, but the need was greater among those who were not yet baptized. One had to be cautious in throwing pearls to the baptized in Germany at the expense of the unbaptized elsewhere:

> The truth appears indeed as it is found at the trough. For those who, like pigs, merely want to be fed, the basic claim is valid. Among them the better wisdom of Christian love is like pearls beneath the feet of sows and like holiness among sins. . . . I remind you that there is a big difference between someone who changes religion and someone from the Ziller Valley. What the person from the Ziller Valley gives up is not a trough, but does the heathen give up religion? They should apologize for such an unworthy comparison.[68]

Too many Christians are indolent in their discipleship. The efforts of the church may often be better rewarded in reaching out to the unbaptized.

In this respect Löhe noted the eagerness of the American Indians in Oregon to receive the Gospel. The Roman Catholics had been successful there without really having to work at it—at least not to the extent that the church had to work elsewhere. The Indians in Oregon had actually sent emissaries to the Jesuits in St. Louis to hear and receive the Gospel.[69] Simply by establishing a chapel among the Indians, the Jesuits were able to establish a foothold for ministry in Oregon.[70] In Löhe's mind, there was no reason why Lutherans could not do the same.

Löhe's theology was important in his advocacy for mission work as well. He wanted to provide an opportunity for the heathen to participate in the community of the body of Christ. His reasons for mission work were entirely based on practical assessments of what work among the heathen would yield. In *Three Books about the Church*, he asserted that the Lutheran church preaches a doctrine of universal grace.[71] In the sacrificial work of Christ, God offers his grace and salvation to all people. Those who are baptized and refuse to participate in the life of the church do so at their own peril. On the other hand, those who are not yet baptized are an entirely different matter: "There is certainly a big difference between heathens who are lost and between Christians who are lost. The latter, despite being in the rich possession of all the means of grace, are lost; the former meanwhile go lost without a saving hand having been extended to them."[72] Christians who refuse to drink of the community for which humans thirst can hardly be forced to drink of that cup. Heathens who have never even had the cup offered to them are a completely different matter.

Löhe's reasons for advocating a stronger mission presence among the heathen were, in the end, primarily theological in nature. The church's effort might be better "rewarded," that is, bear more fruit, in reaching out to the heathen. Missions also allowed the church to more efficiently use the gifts of the entire body. Most important, though, Löhe affirmed that God is the God of the heathen as well as of Christians.[73] His passion was evident: "one could just curl up one's fist against Christians who are able to forget whose Spirit they should be children of and one is aroused by mercy for the millions of Blacks."[74] God reaches out to everyone and desires that all people experience the sense of belonging and community found only in the church. The Spirit is constantly blowing where he wills, seeking souls for the church. Some heathen, at some subconscious level, are ready to hear the Gospel. The Ethiopian eunuch (Acts 8:26–40) and the Roman centurion Cornelius (Acts 10:1–33) are two examples of people who were receptive to the message. In every place and every time, people who live among the heathen have earnestly sought after Christ:

> There are, among the heathen, souls which perceive and yearn, there are some Corneliuses in the wide world of the heathen who, unsatisfied with the worship of idols which has been bequeathed to them, sigh for the satisfying of their souls and pray. There are some heathens who, if they could, would appear to us in our dreams at night and with piercing screams call out, "Come over here and help us!"[75]

The Spirit seeks to work in all people. Mission is, moreover, an integral part of the history of the church. Löhe pointed to the gospels and especially to Acts as mission accounts. Acts is an account of the expansion of the church. It is a history of the earliest mission activity of the church among the Gentiles, who are, from the Jewish perspective, the heathen. Pentecost, Löhe writes, was recognized by the early church as the beginning of the expansion of the church: "the history of the church and of the world since then shows us . . . only a continuation of that majestic and divine beginning on Pentecost."[76] Since then the church has not rested; it has always sought to reach beyond itself. Church and mission are inseparable; the church is not the church if it is not engaged in mission.

If mission is commanded by God, then the church is commanded to be the church. It is commanded to be a community of love, grace, and mercy.[77] Will the church be obedient to the command to proclaim the Gospel, to the command to be engaged in mission? These are the questions Löhe posed to his readers. Mission, he says, "is the obligation of the Christian."[78]

A church engaged only with itself is a church *loving* only itself. For Löhe, the church is a community that reaches out in love *to others:* "Pentecost and mission are nothing other than the church's powerful life of love directed outwards. . . . In a certain sense therefore, Pentecost and mission mean the same thing."[79] Mission is essentially the expression of the love necessary for the inner life of the church now to those who are not part of that community. Mission is the external expression of the life of the community.

Löhe's call for expanded mission efforts on the part of Christians is urgent. The Word is sent to the church and gathers people into one holy body. For this gathering to take place, the Word must be unleashed and proclaimed so that all people might be gathered into one. This is the essence of the universal call. For this reason Löhe rejected the doctrine of predestination. This doctrine "can cripple all desire to reach the nations with God's gospel."[80] The Lutheran church, he said, believes in universal *grace*—a completely different matter than universal *salvation*. In Löhe's writings, the one "who wantonly and maliciously opposes the Word" is condemned.[81] All are called by the Word and invited to participate in the community of the Word.

The church, as the community of the Word, seeks to gather all people into its community. The point of the account of Peter and Cornelius in Acts 10 is that God "wanted to prove that heathens of Cornelius' noble type should be gathered to Christ, that heathens could and should become Christians."[82] This is the meaning of Peter's confession that "I truly understand that God shows no partiality, but in every nation anyone who fears him and does what is right is acceptable to him" (Acts 10:34–35). This text then—as now—was commonly used as the basis for the argument for universal salvation. Löhe argues that the text does not say that anyone who fears and does what is right is accepted by God; the text merely states that such a person is acceptable. The church is not restricted by race or ethnicity; it is open to all. God calls all people to join the community of the baptized.

GERMAN LANGUAGE AND CULTURE

The mission colonies had another important purpose. They could serve as outposts, bastions, of the German language and culture in a "hostile" environment. Löhe recognized that it was difficult to maintain the German language in the midst of foreign elements.[83] The church would do well to establish colonies of German settlers where their faith and language could be preserved.

Language was important, especially in the early years of Löhe's activity in North America. "For Löhe, faith and the language in which that faith is expressed could not be divided."[84] The confessions were written in German. The Lutheran church was German through and through. For these reasons, Löhe insisted that German be the language of the North American church.

Language was a determining factor in the split with the Ohio Synod. The synod chose to make English the language of instruction. Löhe instructed his men to withdraw from the Ohio Synod and seek fellowship elsewhere. Löhe wrote, "The German language of your German church lives and reigns in your houses, in your villages, in your cities, in your schools, in your churches, in your synods."[85] German immigrants, especially those in the mission colonies, were expected to retain the German language. It was even to be the preferred language for worship. In his instructions to missionary Georg Wilhelm Hattstädt, Löhe wrote that a suitable candidate

> recognizes the importance of the German language for the German faith . . . if one can—without being misunderstood—call the faith of the evangelical Lutheran church a German faith. Therefore you will not form any relationship with a congregation which allows room for those who speak English in the pulpit or in the classroom. The German language and morals are the vanguard of the evangelical Lutheran faith.[86]

Löhe's writings in this early period in the mid-1840s are full of references to the necessity of the German language for the Lutheran church in North America. To nearly every missionary, he repeats this charge to align with a German-speaking congregation.[87] A Lutheran church—a church with right doctrine—was properly a German-speaking church.

Of course, Löhe did not limit himself to telling his missionaries to align themselves with a German Lutheran congregation. He was regularly suspicious of wolves in sheep's clothing, of false doctrine perpetrated by other churches on innocent believers; he, therefore, told German Lutherans in North America to avoid other denominations.[88] It would be better to forsake the blessing of community and to worship privately with one's family at home than risk association with a heterodox congregation or denomination.

Yet Löhe did not believe that German Christians alone were Christians. To be sure, the church could praise God in any language.[89] His point was that German Christians were Lutheran; the language of Lutheranism was German. In Löhe's day, Lutheran theological literature in English was extremely rare. His position was not rooted in arrogance or conceit. German was necessary, he sincerely held, if German-Americans were to sustain their Lutheran faith. German preachers and pastors were not necessarily better than their English or American counterparts, but they had access to the piety of their parishioners. Löhe felt that, since there was limited Lutheran literature in English, German-speaking preachers had an advantage. Those who could not read German were reduced to reading the literature of the Episcopal church and other denominations. It was not that the Lutheran church was in danger of falling away, but that the German language would strengthen its confessional identity.[90] An English Lutheran church could only build on a German Lutheran church.

That English Lutherans risked losing access to Lutheran theology and piety was the heart of Löhe's insistence on German. Yet Löhe did not propose that people should learn German before they could hear the Gospel. He was not a cultural imperialist in the sense that the heathen had to learn German and become Europeanized to be genuinely and authentically Christian. He wrote that "we have no right to demand that heathens and wild peoples shall live in a European Christian manner as soon as they have heard the Gospel and have given themselves to its influence."[91] Löhe likely thought European—especially German—culture was higher and better than that of the heathen, but he neither demanded nor expected that heathens should leave behind their old ways.

The German connection was important not only in North America. In an address to Bavarian Lutherans in 1841, Löhe asked his readers quite pointedly if they did not care about their German brothers, sisters, sons, and daughters in North America:

> Thousands, even hundreds of thousands, have left Germany and sailed over the sea to seek a new home. The children of German fathers and German mothers, the siblings of German brothers, the family and friends of Germans, the friends of German youth walk under a different sky on another earth in great remnants. Has love left with their bodies? Have thoughts of a faraway love died? Fathers, do you not ask about your children? Mothers, do you not care any longer who cares for your brood? Is it so cold in Germany that the love which is in every breast—the love of parents and children, the love of blood relatives—no longer thrives? Have the German people forgotten? Has the Fatherland of familial love changed?[92]

Löhe used the German connection to arouse interest and support for missions in North America. He often described the situation in North America: few congregations, even fewer pastors, German Lutherans were in danger of either being lost to the Roman Catholic Church or to sects.[93] Löhe reminded his readers that "we believe in one holy, Christian church which encompasses heaven and earth! We love over the sea, into the forests of America, in the mountains which divide, over the wide streams—everywhere where humans live who confess the pure Word, who confess the unmistakable power of the sacraments!"[94] The bonds of Christian love were even stronger than those of blood.

The German connection was not only used to persuade Germans to support their brothers and sisters and daughters and sons in North America. In his effort to drum up support for mission among the heathen, Löhe reminded Germans of how Germany became christianized:

> We ourselves, we Germans of all tribes were led to Christ by missionaries [sent out] by peoples who were already converted. Boniface, Willibald, and many others like them—the teachers and pastors of the German tribes—encountered our land as we encounter the lands of heathens. Our land became a dwelling of Jesus and his kingdom as a result of missionaries whose work was blessed by God, the lands of heathens can become like ours as a result of our ambassadors [sent out] to the heathens, ambassadors whose work is blessed by God.[95]

Löhe used the bonds of nation, language, and culture to remind other Germans that they should be emissaries of God's Word, since they had benefited from the work of emissaries sent out from other lands.

Having established that Germans ought to support mission effort in other lands far removed from Europe, Löhe stated that there was much that they could do to support mission overseas. Financial support was always pressing. Prayer was also important: "Pray," Löhe wrote, "to the Father of all good gifts, who has promised to hear all of our prayers in Christ Jesus, for truly miraculous people to go to the heathen."[96] Christians can pray that the Gospel be proclaimed in foreign lands and that willing and able people be found to proclaim the Gospel in these lands.

Löhe was eager to emphasize this point. Given the shortage of capable men willing to serve as missionaries, he encouraged anyone who would listen to him to pray. Capable volunteers for mission were hidden. How were they to be found? God knows who is capable, who is suited to be a missionary. Jesus said, Löhe noted, "The harvest is plentiful, but the laborers are few; therefore ask the Lord of the harvest to send out laborers into his harvest" (Luke 10:2, also Matt 9:37). Already the command to pray for missionaries is to be found in the ministry of Jesus.

> Look, here we have pointed out [to us], in the words of Jesus, our most intimate, true participation in mission. It consists in prayer—in prayer to God for equipped and blessed workers who have been sent out into God's great harvest. Mission organizations should be prayer organizations. If they are not, then they work in the kingdom [*Heiligtum*] with unclean hands. Whoever cannot pray has lost the most beautiful and, I think, the greatest effectiveness for mission.[97]

Prayer is the true—and the most important—work of those who support the church in its ministries, most of all in its work of mission.

Readiness for outer mission was integral to inner mission. One of the areas of responsibility for the *Gesellschaft für innere Mission* was to support the mission seminary in Neuendettelsau. The students at this seminary were largely prepared for the preaching and teaching ministries among congregations in North America. The idea was that in Neuendettelsau young men were trained in the basics (history, geography, literature, Bible, dogmatics, etc.), then sent to North America. These men would present themselves to a synod there and ask to be suitably trained for ordination in that synod. In some cases the men were ordained without further education, but in most cases they would spend a year or so at the seminary of that synod. Löhe established relationships first with the Ohio Synod, later with the Missouri Synod, then finally with the Iowa Synod. "The Iowa Synod, along with the seminary in Wartburg, can rightly be viewed as a daughter of this mission seminary," proclaimed the annual report of the *Gesellschaft für innere Mission* in 1864.[98] Inner mission explicitly assumed outer mission. Indeed, an important task of inner mission was to support the efforts of missionaries overseas.

Although a distinction is often made between inner and outer mission and Löhe often used this distinction, he was quick to emphasize that they were two parts of a whole. Inner mission and outer mission are a unity.[99] This was in effect another way of expressing Löhe's assertion that all Christians are missionaries. It illustrates the unity for which he strives in his theology. Mission is an expression of discipleship; and inner mission is one with outer mission.

Central to mission in Löhe's view was worship. In worship the individual is nourished by Word and Sacrament. The Christian is lifted up and encouraged by the community as well as lifting up and encouraging the community and its ministry. Mission is not merely about the intellectual appropriation of a set of values and doctrines. Mission is about bringing someone into a community, a specific community. This community is the people of God or the body of Christ. This community is defined by its worship, that is, its proclamation of the Word and its celebration of the sacraments. For this reason, worship played an integral role in the formation of students at the mission seminary. There was a short devotional service every morning, and every evening there was a full liturgical service.[100] These services were intended to teach the students liturgics, the art of leading the body of Christ in worship.

Worship was central to the being of the church. A mission church had to have a vibrant worship life if it was to survive. Strong preaching and powerful acts of witness were inadequate to sustaining the faith of Christians. Orderly worship and regular celebration of the Sacrament of the Altar were necessary. For this reason, Löhe considered it essential that an order for worship be developed for use in the North American congregations. He wrote the *Agende für christliche Gemeinden des lutherischen Bekenntnisses* at the request of Friedrich Wyneken.[101] Christians are only individuals until they worship together. To worship together is to form a community of faith. To be *church* is to worship together as a community of faith.

This task of forming a community occupied Löhe's thoughts. He was convinced that true community could only exist when there was doctrinal unity. He was not inclined, therefore, to relax his emphasis on the confessions or on the *Amt* as the protector of the apostolic Word. In the *Rechenschaftsbericht*, Löhe reported that many pastors took calls into congregations that appeared to have authentic Lutheran constitutions, but parish life turned out to be something different. He called for strict confessional conformity from the beginning when a pastor began work in a congregation. The relaxation of strict adherence to the confessions led congregations down a slippery slope away from a genuine Lutheran church. He wrote:

> No single congregation, among all those which have been founded by our friends, remained without divisions no matter whether a stricter or softer type of pastor sought to lead them on the right path. The more a pastor retreats from confessional decisiveness at the founding of a congregation, the more yielding he proves himself to be to congregational members in the hope of a better [confessional] understanding in the future, the more he has had to repent for afterwards. We could tell many more individual cases for proof. But the more these experiences show themselves to be accurate, the more both we as well as our brothers in ministry over there recognize that it is difficult to found genuine Lutheran congregations in those areas in which, because of living next to sects of all types and because of the efforts of the Methodists (these vermin of the New World), because of unionistic fanaticism, because of living next to the English, the English language has gained the upper hand.[102]

The English language and the culture attached to it presented a real threat to the type of community Löhe envisioned for Lutheran congregations in North America.

Worship, inner mission, outer mission, colonization, discipleship, and the Christian life pointed to an important theme in Löhe's understanding of mission. To be about evangelism was to be about making the invisible church visible. He wrote to his first missionary, Adam Ernst, that the evangelistic task was to realize the idea of the holy church.[103] Missionaries were to do everything humanly possible to further the holy church. Mission at its heart was about being the church. It was not merely about converting people. It was about simply being the church in ministry. These other things—converting the heathen, regaining the lost, holding on to the saved—were products of this aim. Being the church was all of these things.

Löhe's perspective is profound. Most pastors, it seems, could not possibly bear the weight of the burden of "being the church" and "making the invisible church visible." The church preaches the Word, administers the sacraments, feeds the poor, and cares for the sick, the widowed, and the orphaned. The ministry imposes a heavy burden on its servants. The most important burden, however, has been borne. The most important task is finished: "The Lord did that which is necessary and best for the salvation of the heathen long ago. The word, 'It is finished,' which the Son of God cried on the cross is valid for the heathens also. Even for them is eternal salvation complete."[104] The church has a heavy burden to carry, but God has already done the necessary thing.

Christians do not have to consciously go about trying to convert others. One need only go about the task of being a Christian in a given location. A congregation need only go about the task of being the church in its location. God, through the Holy Spirit, converts people. This does not mean that Christians relax, that they are exempt from the responsibility of witnessing to the Gospel. Löhe wrote, "Remember that the almighty God wants and commands the active participation of the church in the work of converting heathens. Remember that God converts people through people and wants to make humans co-workers in the working of God's grace."[105] Again Löhe wants to avoid the notion that humans can evade responsibility in the establishment of God's reign on earth. Insofar as mission is part of this work, God will not allow it to be undermined by a doctrine of predestination or of universal salvation which releases humans from the responsibility of the promise into which they are baptized.

Conversion is the work of the Spirit. Christians need only go about the task of being Christians, of being the church in a given place. For Löhe, this necessarily points to diaconal service. All Christians are called to diaconal service.[106] To be a deacon is to be engaged in service to the poor; it is to be engaged in a service that seeks to alleviate misery. Christians are to follow the example established by the first Christians. They are to dedicate themselves "to the apostles' teaching and fellowship, to the breaking of bread and the prayers" (Acts 2:42). Löhe said that Christians "ought to recognize the needs of others as their own and seek to still these needs."[107] This sense of diaconal service extended to mission.

Christians who live in mission settings are called to do no more and no less than be Christians in that setting. They are to seek to still the needs of others—whether they are Christians or not—in that location. They may succeed in winning human hearts and souls to Christ, but they might not.

Conversion is the work of the Spirit, but, as Löhe said, "If mission had accomplished nothing else, by [its diaconal service] it would have earned the compassion of every human heart which has not been hardened. But it has done—and does—more."[108] Mission in the form of diaconal service makes us human, it awakens compassion and sympathy in our hearts in the face of misery and suffering.

People may forget their call to diaconal service. They may lose their compassion and sympathy, in short, their humanity. They may neglect their part of the baptismal identity. God, however, will not forget his promise. God promises to be with the church "to the end of the age" (Matt 28:20).[109] Mission—the work of the church—is a partnership between God and humanity. God is forever seeking the sheep that is lost (Matt 18:12), forever seeking the lost coin (Luke 15:8). The church is called to join God in this task of seeking souls and gathering them into the community of the baptized.

Excursus: *Zuruf aus der Heimat an die deutsch-luth. Kirche Nordamerikas*

One of the fullest expressions of Löhe's theology of mission is contained in *Zuruf aus der Heimat an die deutsch-luth. Kirche Nordamerikas* (1845). Klaus Ganzert, the editor of the *Gesammelte Werke*, writes that "one can, with some right, say that the *Zuruf* is the [*magna*] *charta* of German Lutheran mission in North America."[110] It contains instructions to those who live in isolated areas, to those who live in larger settlements and cities, to pastors and church workers, and finally to all fellow German believers in North America. It is helpful to briefly examine its contents.

The main themes of the *Zuruf* have to do with confessional integrity and the importance of education. Confessional integrity in the North American setting is often equated, in Löhe's mind, with the German language and culture.

In the first section of the *Zuruf*, directed to those living in isolated areas, Löhe exhorts these settlers to keep the faith. He knows that these people often live some distance from a Lutheran church. Nonetheless, Löhe writes, "do not forsake any longer the hymns of praise of the congregation, the prayer of the holy church, the blessed sermon, the blessings of the Trinity, the mysterious and wonderful words of God in the sacraments."[111] Regular worship, prayer, and Scripture reading are essential for the Christian; they maintain the ties that bind believers to the apostolic faith.

Löhe was well aware of the dangers that faced these settlers. Many of them lived far removed from Lutheran preachers. It would be easy to have one's thirst for the Word quenched in a Methodist or Roman Catholic church. But for Löhe this was no solution because it would only lead one to waver in the apostolic faith.[112] The Lutheran church alone possesses the apostolic faith in its purity. Why turn to a diluted—or poisoned—version of the apostolic faith?

Löhe's solution is, in a sense, ingenious. He recommended that those who lived in isolated areas far away from a congregation should have worship services in their homes. "Praise God!" he writes, "that we can name, advise, and recommend something rich in blessings to you. It is the house worship service and conscientious loyalty in God."[113] This was a daring proposal. Löhe was shaped theologically by Lutheran orthodoxy, a movement not inclined to support private churches. His recommendation hints at pietistic influences. Pietism was renowned for its small meetings in the homes of believers; these house gatherings were eventually declared illegal in many areas in Germany. Given the circumstances—the need for confessional integrity on the one hand and the need to worship on the other—this solution was rather ingenious.

Löhe justified his recommendation by appealing to Luther's doctrine of the priesthood of all believers. It is not just the right of a Christian to exercise the priesthood in this manner, it is the Christian's *obligation*.[114] All who are baptized into the church are baptized into the priesthood. Those who are baptized can lead worship in their homes just as Abraham, who lived in a strange land, led worship at a house altar dedicated to the Lord.

What does one need for house worship services? One needs only a Bible (Luther's translation was preferred), the *Book of Concord*, some hymnals of the Lutheran church, and devotional and doctrinal books of the Lutheran church.[115] In short, one needed only those things that everyone should have readily available. Löhe asked only that Lutherans have materials appropriate to Lutherans and that they exercise the priesthood given to them in their Baptism. Worship should not be the *exclusive* domain of those who are ordained nor need it be restricted to churches.

Worship is central to the Christian life. For this reason, Löhe encouraged Lutherans to worship at home with prayer, readings, and singing. All these elements were equally important. For those who felt uncomfortable praying in their own words, he recommended prayer books. Doctrinal books were necessary for the correct exposition of the Christian faith. God should be praised in song, so Löhe encouraged those who could not sing to learn to sing.[116] Hymns were important not only for their value in praising God, but also as means by which the faith was transmitted. Hymns and music are indispensable to an authentic worship life.

In this connection, membership in a congregation was also important. To be a Christian was to live in a community. It was to belong to the community of Christ. One cannot legitimately claim to be a Christian living in community if one is not a member of a congregation. Löhe encouraged all people to belong to a congregation even if they lived too far away to regularly attend worship and hear the Word preached and to partake in the Lord's Supper.[117] The sense of belonging to a community, of being part of a community, is central to Christianity.

The second piece of advice addressed to those living in isolated areas by the *Zuruf* concerns education. Löhe emphasizes the importance of education. Obviously many people live in areas too isolated to support a teacher, but education is important enough that these people ought to teach their own children the basics. Children gain nothing if their physical needs are met but their intellectual needs are neglected.[118] To withhold education from children is to condemn them to a life of darkness, a life which cannot be enlightened by reading the Scriptures, by reading the classics of literature, and by the simple skills one needs to function effectively in society.

In this respect Löhe had praise for that Anglo-Saxon innovation—Sunday school. Sunday school, in the nineteenth century, looked different than it does today. Its original intent was to give children a basic education, to teach children to read and to write. The textbook was the Bible, but the goal was to ensure that those children who were unable to receive a formal education received a basic education.[119] Löhe liked the idea and sought to replicate it in his own way.[120] The concept of the Sunday school was an inspiration for Löhe's suggestion to parents that they educate their own children.

For Löhe, no obstacle should be allowed to stand in the way of a basic education. If there were no schools in an area, a group of parents were counseled to form one. If the children were needed to work on the farm, then they ought to be educated in the winter when the work was not onerous. If there were no teachers, parents ought to educate their own children. If parents were uncertain of themselves, if they did not feel self-confident, then perhaps they could hire a teacher to show them how to teach.[121] Whatever the situation, Löhe was convinced that education was critical; any and every barrier to education must be overcome.

The second section of the *Zuruf* is addressed to those who live in larger villages and in cities. Löhe replays most of the themes that he presented in the first section: a warning against compromising on confessional matters and an exhortation to educate children. He warns North American Lutherans not to associate with other denominations in any projects or undertakings. They should avoid schools operated by other denominations, since no teacher has the power to avoid the influence of religion—of confession!—on his or her life and work.[122] Löhe was concerned that children might unwittingly be exposed to false doctrine that would lead them astray. Löhe also repeatedly exhorts his readers to ensure that their children receive a basic education and that they are raised in the apostolic faith.[123] He was clearly alarmed by the reports he had heard of Methodist "New Measures" and of other characteristics of the American church.

One of these other characteristics that alarmed Löhe was the congregational polity of many American churches—including some Lutheran churches. He saw this polity primarily as a threat to confessional integrity and right doctrine; it was also of dubious practical value.[124] Löhe had too much respect for the pastoral office to tolerate an extreme congregationalism. He told his readers that they ought to respect and follow a pastor who adheres to correct doctrine.[125] Good pastors will ensure that their parishioners are properly cared for and will not remain lost in the wilderness of sectarianism.

Löhe addresses the third section to pastors and other church leaders. He offers advice on how pastors can be good pastors, how they might ensure that parishioners do not get lost in the sectarian wilderness. He tells them to live for their flocks, to pour out their time and strength for the salvation of their parishioners. Löhe writes, "Just as the most high Savior gave himself and sacrificed himself for the church, so should every pastor, at the dawn of every day, with every sounding of the bells, again offer himself to the Lord as a sacrifice, ready and willing without hesitation to suffer and do that which is good for the congregation."[126] As parishioners rely on their pastors for their spiritual care, so pastors commit themselves—heart, soul, and mind—to their parishioners (Matt 22:37).

The threat of sectarianism also moved Löhe to make another recommendation to pastors and leaders. He challenged them to be united in the truth.[127] Pastors who were united in doctrine and confession were a powerful contrast to the conflicting claims of sectarian groups. Such a united front would strengthen the faith and love of those who might otherwise be led astray.

CONCLUSION

Next to ecclesiology and liturgics, mission was a central component in Wilhelm Löhe's ministry and theology. On the surface, this statement suggests something of an order or hierarchy to Löhe's theology. Such a conclusion, in fact, is a misunderstanding. Christian Weber has asserted that Löhe's theology of mission has precedence in his theological development.[128] It is possible to quibble with Weber on his assessment, but mission is certainly among the *triad* of Löhe's core theological contributions. The components of this triad—mission, ecclesiology, and liturgics—are not easily separated from one another in his theology.

Löhe's understanding of the relationship between the church and salvation recalls Cyprian's famous statement that there is "no salvation outside the church."[129] Cyprian makes this statement in the context of an argument on the necessity of Baptism. Cyprian writes, "It is essential, therefore, that when they come from heresy to the church, they [heretics] should be baptized."[130] This is exactly the point Löhe makes. One can confess Christ with words and even with actions, but it is Baptism which makes all the difference. Baptism joins one to the community of the saved. Through Baptism one announces one's readiness to participate in the community of the Word.

The centrality of the church in Löhe's theology of mission reveals some affinity to mission as understood in Eastern Orthodox theology. Löhe wrote that "mission is nothing but the one church of God in motion" and that "mission is the life of the catholic church."[131] Mission is not a function of the church; it is the church. The church is not the church if it is not in mission. Eastern Orthodox theologians argue similarly. Ion Bria states that "the church is the aim of mission, not vice versa" and that it is "ecclesiology which determines missiology."[132] Mission begins in the church.

It is not individuals who, on their own initiative and accountable only to themselves, undertake mission. For Löhe, no individual or group of individuals may "embark on a missionary venture without being sent and supported by the church."[133] The Neuendettelsau missionaries were given the explicit instructions to attach themselves to an already established church in North America. Self-initiative in this respect was not encouraged. Löhe's missionaries were missionaries of the church and were to be responsible to the church.

The goal of mission in the Orthodox view is life. Life is found in union with God. The purpose of mission is to bring people into union with

Christ. Clearly this understanding of mission recalls Löhe's opening words of *Three Books about the Church*: "From the very beginning man was so created that he cannot be happy alone."[134] It also echoes one of the important emphases of his understanding of the Lord's Supper: to bring believers into union with Christ.[135] The church is concerned to make its inner life a reality to those who are outside its fellowship.

Community and life in Christ have become important themes in contemporary mission theology. The church is entrusted with the salvation of the world. This responsibility necessarily impels the church to look beyond itself and live for others.[136] This is not to be understood in the sense proposed by Bonhoeffer, that is, the church is a servant church.[137] For Löhe and many today, the church dare not become insular and removed from the everyday reality of those outside its communion. The mission of the church is to make its inner life a reality to those who are not members of it.

David Bosch suggests that there are two basic missiologies operative in the church today. Evangelicals tend to divide the world into the "saved" and the "lost." Liberation theologies (or ecumenical theology) tend to divide the world between the "oppressed" and the "oppressors." Both characterizations are naive in that "they do not maintain the relationship of tension between church and world."[138] One group sees itself as being against the world; the other sees itself as being in the world. The tension of being *in* the world but not *of* the world (cf. 1 John 2:16; John 17:15–19) cannot be circumvented; it has proven difficult to navigate.

Another important development in the theology of mission in the twentieth century is the idea of mission as eschatological event. Mission is not regarded as a prerequisite for the coming of Christ. Nor should the church turn in on itself and isolate itself. Mission as eschatological event reminds the church that its task is never finished. It is called to bear witness to the Gospel of hope in the here and now in all its dimensions (spiritual, physical, psychological, social, political, cultural, etc.) to all those who have not yet experienced it in all its dimensions. This is not to say that the church in its mission is about the task of, for example, political reform. Mission is always primarily about personal conversion.[139] At the same time, mission as eschatological event must be intentionally and consciously wholistic.

The church has experienced something of an identity crisis in the twentieth century. The church can no longer assume the priority of its message and the European (and American) cultures with which it is so

closely entwined. "Mission has to do with the crossing of frontiers."[140]
The frontiers that the church crosses are not only geographic in nature,
they are also cultural and religious. The Christian church seeks to
encounter the Muslim and the Hindu, the African and the Asian, the educated and the illiterate. In these encounters the church seeks not only the
transformation of the other, but the church is open to its own transformation in the interests of proclaiming the Gospel of salvation. The church, to
paraphrase Paul, becomes all things to all people so it might save some
(1 Cor 9:22).

One of the most problematic elements of Löhe's theology of mission
is related to his emphasis—insistence—on German as the preferred language of Lutheran congregations in North America. As Lutherans in later
years were to discover, this had the unhappy effect of isolating people and
congregations. In other contexts it seemed imperialistic. Ion Bria has
pointed out that on Pentecost Day "it was revealed that the Gospel, so as
to be understood by those who are the hearers, must be proclaimed in
their 'own language.' " To insist that converts learn the faith in a foreign
language, Bria plainly states, "is a direct and deliberate contradiction to the
spirit of Pentecost."[141] Although it is true that Löhe did not insist on
German as the language of proclamation but as the language of catechization, this differentiation is too fine. The implicit message from Löhe is
that people can become Christians in another language, but if they want to
be "real" Christians, they have to learn German. In practice, however,
proclamation and catechization are often closely related.

This regrettable component of Löhe's theology of mission should not
be the final word on perspective. Later in his life Löhe softened on this
point.[142] In 1856, Löhe noted that the Lutheran church in North America,
though quite different in many respects from the Lutheran church in
Germany, was nonetheless a genuine Lutheran church.[143] He might have
hoped for a church that was quite different than the one which eventually
developed in North America, but he would have been able to see the
authentic Lutheran life in even those churches which did eventually adopt
English as their worship language.

Löhe had the ability to compromise on matters of penultimate importance. Language was one of these issues. His ability to distinguish between
what was of ultimate and penultimate importance served him well. Of ultimate importance was the church and its actualization or realization in the
world. The church cannot be departmentalized into inner and outer mission. A congregation cannot live in isolation from the catholic church. The

church is a living entity which receives its life from the Spirit of life. These themes, which Löhe developed, anticipated many of the most central and integral elements of mission as it is understood today.

NOTES

1   Stephen Neill, *A History of Christian Missions* (2d ed.; London: Penguin Books, 1986), 35–36.

2   See Neill, *Christian Missions*, 31–52. Neill cites the examples of Thomas in India, Frumentius in Ethiopia, Gregory the Enlightener (or Illuminator) in Armenia, Ulfilas among the Goths, and Patrick in Ireland. This statement and the argument following regarding the development of mission theology is much generalized and simplified. David Bosch, *Transforming Mission: Paradigm Shifts in Theology of Mission* (American Society of Missiology Series; Maryknoll, NY: Orbis Books, 1991), 181–82, 187–78, identifies six periods or "paradigms" of mission theology: primitive Christianity, the patristic period, the Middle Ages, the Reformation, the Enlightenment, and the ecumenical era.

3   Neill, *Christian Missions*, 68.

4   Regarding medieval monasteries as centers of mission, see Neill, *Christian Missions*, 66–67; and Bosch, *Transforming Mission*, 230–36.

5   The efforts of the Roman Catholic Church in Latin America may serve as an example. Neill writes: "The work of the missionaries throughout Latin America followed certain generally accepted lines. A serious attempt was made to learn the local languages, and to provide the beginnings of a Christian literature in them. Schools were founded, though higher education seems to have been limited to those of Spanish or mixed origin. An attempt was made in many regions to gather the Indians into villages, and so to bring them under strict discipline (to be exercised by the priests or their representatives) and under more regular instruction. . . .

"Two grave defects are to be noted in the rapidly developing Christianity of these regions.

"In the first place, the churches of the Indians were almost entirely non-communicating churches . . . it was held that, until [Indians] were better instructed and strengthened in the faith, it would be wise to admit them only to Baptism, matrimony and penance.

"[Second, no] serious attempt was made to build up an indigenous ministry." See *Christian Missions*, 147–48. Regarding the close relationship between the aims of the political and religious "cities," see also Bosch, *Transforming Mission*, 206, 222, 226–30, 302–13, who discusses the cooperation between religious leaders and political leaders in both Eastern and Western Christendom; as well as Lamin Sanneh, "Theology of Mission," in *The Modern Theologians: An Introduction to Christian Theology in the Twentieth Century* (2d. ed.; ed. David F. Ford; Oxford: Blackwell, 1997), 559.

6   Neill, *Christian Missions*, 381; cf. Bosch, *Transforming Mission*, 331. There were exceptions to this. One was Bartholomew Ziegenbalg, a student of August Hermann Francke, who ministered in India. Neill writes about Ziegenbalg's work in India that "it has often been maintained that the missionaries, being

Pietists, were so concerned about rescuing individual brands from the burning as to have little sense of Church and community. This may or may not be true of later missionaries; it is wholly untrue of the pioneers in Tranquebar" (Neill, *Christian Missions*, 196).

7   David Bosch, *Witness to the World: The Christian Mission in Theological Perspective* (Atlanta: John Knox, 1980), 131, notes that Zinzendorf felt that "it was not the *ecclesia* (the formal, established Church) which was important, but the *ecclesiola* (the spontaneous, unorganized group of true believers)."

8   "Aphorismen," *GW* V/1: 261.

9   Ganzert, "Erläuterungen," *GW* IV: 639.

10 Löhe, *Tagebuch des Missionsvereins* (10 November 1827), *GW* IV: 9.

11 Löhe, *Tagebuch des Missionsvereins* (10 November 1827), *GW* IV: 14. The *Kirchliche Mitteilungen* also had the purpose of financially supporting missions. That is to say that by subscribing to the *Kirchliche Mitteilungen* a person supported the mission work described in the periodical. See *Rechenschaftsbericht, GW* IV: 129; as well as Deinzer, III: 15.

12 "Die Mission unter den Heiden," *GW* IV: 34, also 48.

13 See Ganzert, "Erläuterungen," *GW* IV: 622.

14 "Die Mission unter den Heiden," *GW* IV: 50. Beyond that, it is impossible to be outside or beyond confessionalism. One cannot interpret Scripture without a confessional basis ("Die Mission unter den Heiden," *GW* IV: 52). Regarding the importance of right doctrine, see also *GW* IV: 51.

15 See Löhe, "Brief an H. Jos. Schlier" (24 June 1836), *GW* I: 467; and "Brief an Johann Merkel" (27 June 1836), *GW* I: 470.

16 Ganzert, "Erläuterungen," *GW* IV: 21.

17 Indeed, Löhe had been instrumental in establishing a tract society in 1841. See Ganzert, "Erläuterungen," *GW* III/1: 613–14. It could be said that mission also provided Löhe with an outlet for his literary activity. Löhe wrote to Adam Ernst, the first missionary to North America, that he wrote much of the material for *Kirchliche Mitteilungen aus und über Nordamerika*; see "Brief an Adam Ernst" (28 October 1843), *GW* I: 643.

18 Notably, this was after the establishment of the *Lutherischer Verein für weibliche Diakonie* [Lutheran Deaconess Association] and the *Gesellschaft für innere Mission im Sinne der Lutherischen Kirche* [Society for Inner Mission in the Sense of the Lutheran Church].

19 See the discussion on tracts in chapter 5.

20 *Die Heidenmission in Nordamerika: Ein Vortrag in der Generalversammlung des protestantischen Zentralmissionsvereins zu Nürnberg den 2. Juli 1846, GW* IV: 112; hereafter *Die Heidenmission*.

21 *Prediget das Evangelium, GW* IV: 117.

22 "Die Mission unter den Heiden," *GW* IV: 20.

23 Christopher Sugden, s.v. "Mission, Theology of," in *The Blackwell Encyclopedia of Modern Christian Thought* (ed. Alister E. McGrath; Oxford: Blackwell, 1993), 376–77. Sugden identifies the nineteenth century as the time when this notion of mission as expansion was particularly predominant, see 378–79.

24 In *Die Heidenmission*, Löhe writes (*GW* IV: 110) that there is no doubt that nobody

is better situated to lead mission efforts than the church nearest the mission field.

25 "Kirche und Mission," *GW* IV: 627.

26 "Predigt am 2. Pfingstfeiertag 1843 über Apg. 10,42," *GW* IV: 60; hereafter "Predigt am 2. Pfingstfeiertag."

27 "Predigt am 2. Pfingstfeiertag," *GW* IV: 61.

28 *Three Books*, 47. Löhe repeats this point in *Prediget das Evangelium*, *GW* IV: 123.

29 "Die Mission unter den Heiden," *GW* IV: 41.

30 The rest of the sentence is worth citing (though the figures of speech are not so easy to translate). He asks, "Why does not our happiness and the unhappiness of the heathen compel us to open these fountains and to send its waters to the poor soil which is so near to the curse?" (*Prediget das Evangelium*, *GW* IV: 114).

31 "Zum Schelwigschen Aufsatz in Nr. 12 der Mitteilungen von 1851," *GW* IV: 198; hereafter "Zum Schelwigschen Aufsatz." Regarding the assertion that mission is not only the domain of the ordained, see *GW* IV: 199. This assertion is repeated in "Kirche und Amt: Neue Aphorismen," *GW* V/1: 546: " 'Everybody possesses the office [of ministry], since all are spiritual priests.' Now however it is apparent from 1 Peter 2:5 and 9, etc. that all Christians are priests."

32 "Predigt am 2. Pfingstfeiertag," *GW* IV: 64. Löhe emphasized that mission was a divine—and not a human—commandment.

33 Löhe reiterates this often. He calls it the "last commandment": "I do not need to say, dear brothers, what the name of the new covenant is which all children of God should carry out. 'Preach the Gospel to all creatures'—this is the last commandment of the Lord" (*Prediget das Evangelium*, *GW* IV: 114).

34 *Prediget das Evangelium*, *GW* IV: 115.

35 Regarding the qualities of a missionary, see "Predigt am 2. Pfingstfeiertag," *GW* IV: 66.

36 "Die Mission unter den Heiden," *GW* IV: 55.

37 "Die Mission unter den Heiden," *GW* IV: 42.

38 In 1860, Löhe wrote in the *Correspondenzblatt* that candidates for the mission seminary ought to have a zeal for mission. Especially sought after were those who had a good general education and the ability to study. A knowledge of foreign languages was not necessary, but a good knowledge of German, as well as a good rudimentary knowledge of the Bible and the confessions, were essential (Löhe, "Den Abgang mehrerer Zöglinge der hiesigen Missionanstalt im nächsten Frühjahr betreffend," *Correspondenzblatt* 10 [1860]: 40).

39 Friedrich Bauer, "Jahresbericht über die Missionsanstalt in Neuendettelsau für das Winter- und Sommersemester v. 1. Nov. 1858 bis 15. Oct. 1859," *Correspondenzblatt* 10 (1859): 40–42. To these courses can be added "Ethics" (WS 1859/60) and the "Life of Jesus" (SS 1860), which were taught in the next academic year. See "Jahresbericht 1859/60," *Correspondenzblatt* 11 (1861): 16–17. The confessions were an important part of the curriculum as well. The "Bericht über die Missionsanstalt in Neuendettelsau im 21. Jahre ihres Bestehens vom 1. November 1861 bis 1. November 1862," *Kirchliche Mittheilungen aus und über Nord-Amerika* 21 (1863): 27, mentions the confessions individually.

40 *Die Heidenmission*, *GW* IV: 110. Löhe confirms this in *Rechenschaftsbericht*, *GW* IV: 136: "Our experience [in North America] has taught us that mere schoolteachers

are not sufficient to alleviate the need over there; people are needed who can be pastors and schoolteachers at the same time."

41 Translation is mine from the German.

42 "Predigt am 2. Pfingstfeiertag," *GW* IV: 67.

43 Schaaf, *Löhe's Relation to the American Church*, 18–19.

44 *Prediget das Evangelium*, *GW* IV: 120, also 121. See also "Zum Schelwigschen Aufsatz," *GW* IV: 196.

45 See page 145.

46 "Zum Schelwigschen Aufsatz," *GW* IV: 195.

47 Wilhelm Löhe, "Brief an L. A. Petri" (10 July 1842), *GW* I: 606. In the same letter, Löhe says that if trained pastors will not go, then they must send whoever is willing, and if they cannot or will not, then they will send stones. Regarding the sending of whoever will go, see "Brief an Karl von Raumer" (21 February 1843), *GW* I: 626. It is important to note that while Löhe admired the missionary spirit of the Moravians, he was careful to dissociate himself from the Moravian theology; see "Brief an William Sihler" (12 October 1846), *GW* I: 762; as well as *Rechenschaftsbericht*, *GW* IV: 136; and Deinzer, III: 21–22. For more, see Weber, *Missionstheologie*, 204–05, 253.

48 Weber, *Missionstheologie*, 411, rightly points out that theologically trained men were necessary for mission.

49 Löhe was enthusiastic about establishing the seminary in Fort Wayne (*Die Heidenmission*, *GW* IV: 110). The establishment of the Fort Wayne seminary was an accomplishment of which he was proud even after the painful separation from the Missouri Synod; see Löhe, "Die Gesellschaft für innere Mission im Sinne der lutherischen Kirche und ihre Verhältnisse zu Nordamerika," *Kirchliche Mittheilungen aus und über Nord-Amerika* 17 (1859): 58.

50 *Rechenschaftsbericht*, *GW* IV: 129, 145; and "Brief an Friedrich Wucherer" (23 November 1842), *GW* I: 611–12.

51 This seems to have been a concern. Löhe (*Rechenschaftsbericht*, *GW* IV: 128) lamented that the Lutherans in North America did not always welcome advice and suggestions. Regarding the intended relationship between the seminary and the Lutheran church, see "An den Präses," *Kirchliche Mitteilungen* 6 (1848): no. 6, cols. 43–44.

52 Friedrich Bauer, "Jahresbericht über die Missionsanstalt in Neuendettelsau für das Schuljahr vom 1. Nov. 1859 bis 15. Oct. 1860," *Correspondenzblatt* 11 (1861): 15.

53 *Die Heidenmission*, *GW* IV: 102.

54 Regarding reasons for mission, see the discussion on page 141.

55 *Die Heidenmission*, *GW* IV: 102.

56 Löhe, "Brief an L. A. Petri" (5 November 1844), *GW* I: 682.

57 "Brief an L. A. Petri" (5 November 1844), *GW* I: 682–83. For Löhe's assessment of the success of the Frankenmuth colony, see *Die Heidenmission*, *GW* IV: 108.

58 Wilhelm Löhe, "Glück Auf!" *Kirchliche Mittheilungen* 3 (1845): no. 5, cols. 1–2.

59 In *Etwas über die deutsch-lutherischen Niederlassungen in der Grafschaft Saginaw, Staat Michigan*, Löhe spoke about these plans. He added that such a colony would help the poor avoid falling into sin (*GW* IV: 169; see also "Ein Wort," *Kirchliche Mitteilungen* 5 [1847]: no. 1:3).

60 Löhe, "Brief an L. A. Petri" (29 October 1845), *GW* I: 719.

61 *Die Heidenmission*, *GW* IV: 105. The idea that these mission colonies would be witnesses to the Christian faith among the American Indians by virtue of their mere presence is echoed in *Ein Versuch;* see *GW* IV: 149.

62 See *Die Heidenmission*, *GW* IV: 107. This is an example of the monastic model mission mentioned at the outset of this chapter.

63 "Kirche und Mission," *GW* IV: 628.

64 "Brief an L. A. Petri" (29 October 1845), *GW* I: 719. One year later, Löhe could point to the success of the plan. He noted in *Die Heidenmission*, *GW* IV: 109, that the colony had already become a base for mission efforts among American Indians in the area and that the settlers had already done some ministry. Moreover, the colony and the nascent mission showed signs of becoming a synod. The mission colonies were also expected to help German Lutherans retain their faith. In a setting where they were among others like them and under the spiritual care of a pastor, Löhe felt that these settlers were less likely to lose their faith in their new home. Löhe felt that too many German settlers in North America were becoming indifferent to the church and the faith which had nourished them in their youth. See "Wirksamkeit der Gesellschaft durch Kolonisation," *GW* IV: 190.

65 "Die Mission unter den Heiden," *GW* IV: 21.

66 "Die Mission unter den Heiden," *GW* IV: 21.

67 "Die Mission unter den Heiden," *GW* IV: 22–23.

68 "Die Mission unter den Heiden," *GW* IV: 24. A person from the Ziller Valley is a reference to someone firm in their faith. The Ziller Valley in the Austrian Tyrols was populated by Lutheran farmers. In the 1830s, they fell partly under the control of the Salzburg archbishopric and were persecuted and finally driven out in 1837 when they were given a choice: Convert or vacate the land within fourteen days. For more, see Georg Loesche, *Geschichte des Protestantismus im vormaligen und im neuen Österreich* (3d ed.; Leipzig: Julius Klinkhardt, 1930), 567–83, esp. 574–75.

69 *Die Heidenmission*, *GW* IV: 104, Löhe wrote appreciatively about the eagerness of the Oregon Indians.

70 See *Die Heidenmission*, *GW* IV: 103, 106.

71 *Three Books*, 81–82.

72 "Predigt am 2. Pfingstfeiertag," *GW* IV: 61–62.

73 "Die Mission unter den Heiden," *GW* IV: 39. Löhe wrote that the Son was given to the nations to the ends of the earth.

74 "Die Mission unter den Heiden," 39.

75 "Predigt am 2. Pfingstfeiertag," *GW* IV: 62–63.

76 "Predigt am 2. Pfingstfeiertag," *GW* IV: 59.

77 In "Nothstand der Heiden und der deutsch-lutherischen Kirche in Nord-Amerika," *Kirchliche Mittheilungen* 1, no. 3 (1843): col. 3, Löhe wrote that we are blessed by grace and mercy; the entire church is grounded upon grace and mercy.

78 "Predigt am 2. Pfingstfeiertag," *GW* IV: 65.

79 "Predigt am 2. Pfingstfeiertag," *GW* IV: 59.

80 *Three Books*, 81.

81 *Three Books*, 82.

82 "Die Mission unter den Heiden," *GW* IV: 26.

83 *Rechenschaftsbericht, GW* IV: 140–41. In "Schmach für die Deutschen in Nordamerika," *Kirchliche Mittheilungen* 5 (1847): no. 4, cols. 25–30, esp. 25–26, Löhe lamented that Germans in North America quickly became in love with English. They wanted to hear English sermons and send their children to English schools. Even if they wanted to retain their language, it was often difficult. Many of the German immigrants in North America were isolated and scattered. They forgot their mother tongue, they settled in areas where all kinds of sects were to be found, and most important, they lost their love for the church ("Ein Wort," *Kirchliche Mitteilungen* 5 [1847]: no. 1:5).

84 Schaaf, *Löhe's Relation to the American Church*, 86.

85 Löhe, *Zuruf, GW* IV: 85.

86 Löhe, "Die neuen Boten: Georg Wilhelm Hattstädt," *Kirchliche Mittheilungen* 2 (1844): no. 6, col. 2. In *Zuruf, GW* IV: 68, Löhe extolls the clarity of German tongues in praise (see also *Rechenschaftsbericht, GW* IV: 131).

87 See, for example, besides that cited above to Hattstädt, the instructions to Baumgart: "Auszug aus der innern und äußern Mission betreffend," *Kirchliche Mittheilungen* 1 (1843): no. 8, col. 3. Löhe warns that the danger of the Anglicization of Germans is twofold: distancing from the grace of God and uprooting from their nation.

88 *Zuruf, GW* IV: 75.

89 In *Die Heidenmission, GW* IV: 105, Löhe even went so far as to say that words do not lose their effectiveness when spoken with the aid of an interpreter.

90 Löhe, "Über den innern Zustand der lutherischen Kirche Nordamerikas," *Kirchliche Mittheilungen* 4 (1846): nos. 4–5, col. 38. See also col. 40 as well as Wilhelm Löhe, "Die englisch-lutherische Kirche in Nord-Amerika," *Kirchliche Mittheilungen* 1 (1843): no. 7, col. 6.

91 *Prediget das Evangelium, GW* IV: 119–20.

92 Löhe, "Die lutherischen Auswanderer in Nordamerika: Eine Ansprache an die Leser des Sonntagsblattes," *GW* IV: 16; hereafter "Die lutherischen Auswanderer."

93 "Die lutherischen Auswanderer," *GW* IV: 18.

94 "Die lutherischen Auswanderer," *GW* IV: 17.

95 "Die Mission unter den Heiden," *GW* IV: 40.

96 "Die Mission unter den Heiden," *GW* IV: 44. In a sermon on Mark 16:15, Löhe (*Prediget das Evangelium, GW* IV: 114) also suggested that we pray for the confidence to go to the heathen (see also *GW* IV: 123–25).

97 "Predigt am 2. Pfingstfeiertag," *GW* IV: 67. In *Ansprache an die Brüder in Sachen der Judenmission, GW* IV: 251–52, Löhe wrote that many missionaries reported that the prayers of those at home encouraged and strengthened them in their ministry.

98 Johann Friedrich Wucherer, "Jahresbericht des Obermanns der Gesellschaft für innere Mission im Sinn der lutherischen Kirche über deren Bestand und Wirksamkeit im J. 1863," *Correspondenzblatt* 15 (1864): 3–4.

99 The seminary in Fort Wayne was established with this view in mind (*Die Heidenmission, GW* IV: 111).

100 "Jahresbericht 1859/60," *Correspondenzblatt* 11 (1861): 19.

101 In a letter to Karl von Raumer, Löhe mentions that Wyneken and Ernst asked him to produce an agenda for worship (Wilhelm Löhe, "Brief an Karl von Raumer" [9 August 1843], *GW* I: 641). See also Klaus Ganzert's remarks regarding the background of the *Agende* in *GW* VII/2: 684–85.

102 *Rechenschaftsbericht*, *GW* IV: 139.

103 Löhe, "Brief an Adam Ernst" (29 July 1844), *GW* I: 672; see also the introductory remarks by Ganzert, *GW* IV: 630. Interestingly, this integrated understanding of mission does not seem to have always been a feature of Löhe's theology. In the entry for 15 December 1827 of the *Tagebuch des Missionsvereins*, the first mission circle Löhe organized, he lamented that they had spent the evening discussing the contents of a hymn and never did talk about mission and evangelism (*Tagebuch des Missionsvereins* [15 December 1827], *GW* IV: 15). Apparently, Löhe did not see the connection between mission and fellowship as clearly in those early years.

104 "Predigt am 2. Pfingstfeiertag," *GW* IV: 65.

105 "Die Mission unter den Heiden," *GW* IV: 40.

106 In "Aphorismen," *GW* V/1: 307, Löhe writes that all Christians are deacons active in caring for the poor (see also chapter 3).

107 "Aphorismen," *GW* V/1: 299.

108 "Die Mission unter den Heiden," *GW* IV: 40–41.

109 "Die Mission unter den Heiden," *GW* IV: 40.

110 Ganzert, "Erläuterungen," *GW* IV: 631.

111 *Zuruf*, *GW* IV: 69.

112 *Zuruf*, *GW* IV: 69.

113 *Zuruf*, *GW* IV: 70.

114 *Zuruf*, *GW* IV: 70.

115 *Zuruf*, *GW* IV: 70.

116 In *Zuruf*, *GW* IV: 74, Löhe wrote that the forests should ring out with song, that teachers should also be instructors in music.

117 In *Zuruf*, *GW* IV: 74–75, Löhe asserted that in those in whom the idea of the one holy Christian church is important, it would be unbearable to be beyond the pale of a visible congregation.

118 *Zuruf*, *GW* IV: 71.

119 Robert Raikes, an Anglican layperson, is generally acknowledged as the founder of the Sunday school movement. Noticing that many children were a menace on the streets, he spoke to the rector of his parish about these children. The two men together established a Sunday school which quickly expanded and rapidly spread throughout England. For an account, see John H. Overton and Frederic Relton, *The English Church: From the Accession of George I. to the End of the Eighteenth Century (1714–1800)* (vol. 7 of *A History of the English Church*; ed. W. R. W. Stephens and William Hunt; Macmillan, 1906.; repr., New York: AMS Press, n.d.), 300–01; Edwin Wilbur Rice, *The Sunday School Movement (1780–1917) and the American Sunday-School Union (1817–1917)* (Philadelphia: American Sunday-School Union, 1917; repr., New York: Arno Press and the *New York Times*, 1971), 13–17; and Elmer L. Towns,

"Robert Raikes (1735–1811)," in *A History of Religious Educators* (ed. Elmer L. Towns; Grand Rapids: Baker, 1975), 226–35, esp. 228–30.

[120] *Zuruf, GW* IV: 72–73. Löhe was impressed that some of the most important leaders in American politics and society were also Sunday school teachers (*Zuruf, GW* IV: 72).

[121] *Zuruf, GW* IV: 73.

[122] *Zuruf, GW* IV: 76.

[123] In *Zuruf, GW* IV: 77, Löhe wrote that Christians who are true to the Lutheran church would never allow their children to attend Methodist Sunday schools or any other school where their faith might be jeopardized.

[124] Regarding Löhe's misgivings about congregational ecclesiologies, see chapter 2 as well as chapter 3.

[125] A pastor, Löhe said, should be at the center of the congregation (*Zuruf, GW* IV: 78).

[126] *Zuruf, GW* IV: 80.

[127] *Zuruf, GW* IV: 80–82. That the church (and its servants) should be one and united was something Löhe could be passionate about.

[128] Weber, *Missionstheologie*, 193.

[129] Cyprian, "Letter 73.21.2," in *ACW* 47: 66. Interestingly, Joseph Ratzinger seems to suggest that this assertion by Cyprian has been superseded. Following a section in which he sketches the historical context for Cyprian's statement, Ratzinger concludes that it is not an axiom which is independent of its historical setting. For more, see Joseph Ratzinger, *Das neue Volk Gottes: Entwürfe zur Ekklesiologie* (Düsseldorf: Patmos-Verlag, 1969), 339–45.

[130] Cyprian, "Letter 73.21.3," in *ACW* 47: 66.

[131] *Three Books*, 59.

[132] Ion Bria, "Introduction," *Martyria/Mission: The Witness of the Orthodox Churches Today* (Geneva: World Council of Churches, 1980), 8. Incidentally, this idea became an important theme in mission theology in the twentieth century. The idea of "mission is the church in motion" is echoed in Bria's assertion that the church "must continually be in mission, proclaiming, announcing and teaching the good news." See Bria, *Go Forth in Peace: Orthodox Perspectives on Mission* (Geneva: World Council of Churches, 1986), 10. See also Bosch, *Witness to the World*, 82.

[133] Bosch, *Transforming Mission*, 207.

[134] *Three Books*, 47.

[135] See, for example, Löhe, *Schmuck, GW* VII/2: 561. See also the discussion in chapter 4. This emphasis is echoed in the orthodox understanding of mission. Bria writes: Mission aims "at the transmission of the life of the communion that exists in God" (*Go Forth in Peace*, 3).

[136] Bosch, *Witness to the World*, 17; cf. also Paul Vadakumpadan, V.D.B., "Ecclesiological Foundation of Mission," in *Following Christ in Mission: A Foundational Course in Missiology* (ed. S. Karotemprel et al.; Boston: Pauline Books and Media, 1996), 107.

[137] Bonhoeffer wrote that "the church is the church only when it exists for others." Bonhoeffer, *Letters and Papers from Prison*, 382.

138 Bosch, *Witness to the World*, 221. Bosch does not point it out here, but it is implicit on the basis of previous sections that the evangelical emphasis on the "saved" is related to the tendency "to regard Christ as Lord only of the Church and not of the cosmos as well" (202). One might add that the mistake of liberation and ecumenical theology is to neglect Christ's status as head of the church.

139 Carl E. Braaten, *The Flaming Center: A Theology of the Christian Mission* (Philadelphia: Fortress, 1977), 57, makes this clear. He links God, neighbor, and the world together, but all are subsumed to personal conversion. Braaten writes: "Faith in God, love to the neighbor, and hope for the world are links in the divine chain of personal conversion."

140 Bosch, *Witness to the World*, 17. For the following regarding encounter, cf. Bosch, *Witness to the World*, 81.

141 Bria, *Go Forth in Peace*, 16. Georg F. Vicedom, "Mission als Kirche in ihrer Bewegung," in *Wilhelm Löhe—Anstöße für die Zeit*, 92, maintains that Löhe never once mentioned that non-Christians could be helped through the medium of European culture. While this is true, I think that Vicedom overlooks the close relationship between language and culture. To learn a European language is, to some extent, to learn the culture associated with that language.

142 See the discussion on page 153.

143 "Das Verhältnis," *GW* V/2: 706. Löhe wrote that just as the United States reflected English life, so did the Lutheran church reflect a Lutheran life.

6

INNER MISSION

Mission in both its local and global manifestations occupies a primary position in Löhe's theology. Löhe may be a forgotten figure were it not for his contributions to mission within and outside of Germany. He is better known for his efforts on behalf of overseas mission activity, but his contribution to mission and church renewal within Germany ought not be overlooked. He was instrumental in the founding of two organizations dedicated to inner mission. The first, the *Gesellschaft für innere Mission im Sinne der Lutherischen Kirche* [Society for Inner Mission in the Sense of the Lutheran Church], was founded in 1849; and the second, the *Lutherischer Verein für weibliche Diakonie* [Lutheran Association of Deaconesses], was founded in 1853.

What drove Löhe to occupy himself with inner mission? There are many reasons, including, in particular, his understanding of community. He did not understand community to be limited to those who lived in the same neighborhood or village and attended the same church. He did not understand community to be limited to those who lived in the same nation. He did not understand community to be limited to the same culture or race. Community extended to all of humankind. All of humankind is to be considered as our neighbor. Whom should we love? Our neighbor. How should we love? Like the Samaritan.

Löhe went farther than the Lukan parable. He pointed to the example of Christ. Löhe stated that Christ loved our bodies and our souls and has redeemed them and loves them still. He sanctifies them and has designated them to eternal life. In the same way, Christians love and care for the bodies and souls of others.[1] Christians are not merely to love and care for one another, they are to "fuss over" one another. They do good works for one another for the sake of the promised resurrection.

The love of Christ points to a central characteristic of the church which furnishes the impulse for Löhe's understanding of inner mission. The church is a community. It is a community of believers united by their adherence to the apostolic Word and by the regular celebration of the sacraments. It also is a community of love. The logical consequence of this understanding is that "because the church is a community of love, it should exercise love most of all to those who are members of its house."[2] Christians are called to love their fellow believers, *all* those with whom they gather around the Lord's Table.

Inner mission oriented itself to those in the immediate vicinity of a congregation. The deacons of a congregation sought to serve those who lived in the immediate vicinity of that congregation. Löhe wrote that the deaconess houses "had never sought anything more than to do good in the vicinity."[3] Diaconal workers served those in their immediate surroundings, those with whom they might physically stand or kneel at the Table of the Lord.[4] Those whom the diaconal workers served might be of humble or sinful background, they might be impoverished or sick or widowed or orphaned. Most of all, though, they were in need of Christ's love.

The diaconate was established to help Christians live and love *as Christians*. It is, Löhe says, a "helper-office" or "servant-office."[5] *Helping* and *serving* have a twofold meaning. The diaconate helps and serves the church in fulfilling its responsibility to create community; the diaconate also helps and serves others in creating community. It helps local congregations express love for others removed from those congregations. The diaconate arises out of individual congregations; its roots are in the New Testament church as witnessed by Acts 6. The church appointed men to carry out this diaconal service to alleviate the physical needs of people everywhere.

The diaconate functions similarly today. The impulse for diaconal service arises from the congregation, but it serves and works within the entire church. Diaconal service arises out of the church "like a flower from a plant."[6] It belongs to an individual community, but it serves the wider church. The diaconate works in the wider circle of fellowship and community that God has commanded—in the church *catholic*. The diaconate is also evangelical in that it seeks to proclaim the Good News. It is evangelical in that it seeks to express Christ's love for body and soul to all people everywhere.

WHAT IS INNER MISSION?

Inner mission is concerned with the life of the church, the life of the community that gathers to hear the Word and to partake of the body and blood of Christ. It is concerned with extending the fellowship and love of this community, with exercising this love to others. Inner mission seeks to extend and make known the depth and breadth of God's dominion. "The reign of God," Löhe said, "is a reign of mercy."[7] Inner mission is about making God's reign of mercy manifest and present everywhere.

For this reason, Löhe saw inner mission as inseparable from outer mission. He asked:

> Would the Lutheran congregations, which have long existed, not then undertake—if even in intent—to work among the heathen? And would the entire essence of mission not have had to take on a different form, if one had wanted to separate mission to the heathen from compassion for the East Indian congregations which have long existed? One wanted though to serve the heathen most of all, but one does inner mission in order to be able to concern oneself with outer mission.[8]

Clearly mission was unified in Löhe's mind. Inner and outer mission were merely the names by which one indicates the direction or target of missionary efforts.

Inner and outer mission were the labels given to the two spheres of the church's activity. These two spheres are more akin to the different aspects of one task. The task is stated in Mark 16:15–16: "Go into all the world and proclaim the good news to the whole creation. The one who believes and is baptized will be saved; but the one who does not believe will be condemned." Drawing on this command in the Gospel of Mark, Löhe states that mission is nothing other than the task of calling, gathering, inspiring, and preserving the church unto eternal life.[9] To be sure, this task can only be fulfilled by the Spirit of the Lord, but the Spirit accomplishes it through humans.

The means of this task of calling, gathering, and inspiring the church is accomplished by a means unique to the church. It is accomplished through Word and Sacrament. Word and Sacrament are the same means available to the church everywhere. They are common to the church both in its mission to the baptized (inner mission) and to the unbaptized (outer mission). But, Löhe said, "for the sake of the two spheres of mission they should not be separated, but rather internally connected, given the same value and honor, the same love and loyalty."[10] Word and Sacrament bind these two spheres of mission together.

The close relationship between inner and outer mission points to why Löhe can name the mission activity among the German emigrants in North America as *inner mission*. The Germans are, first of all, baptized. Yet by ministering to North American Germans, Germans in the homeland can also support outreach to the native (American Indian) populations. Löhe says that it is totally right that the North American activity belongs to inner mission. The countless Protestant Germans to whom [God] sent preachers and teachers and for whom he established institutes are still members of the church; they are not excluded and do not want to be excluded, but rather seek to be included.[11]

Inner mission has as much to do with spiritual location as with geographic location.

All of this, however, still leaves the question unanswered, "What exactly is inner mission?" What are the distinctive areas of activity of inner mission? Löhe identified four key areas:[12] Preaching and teaching among the brothers and sisters in the faith who have been abandoned; distribution of religious literature; pastoral care for emigrating Christians and the Lutheran colonies; and addressing the state of misery in the immediate vicinity that afflicts spiritual and physical life. These four areas form an organic whole that holds the *proclamation* and the *doing* of the Word together in creative tension.

WHY INNER MISSION?

The situation in Germany in the mid-nineteenth century cried out for a response from the church. The Industrial Revolution was in full swing, and, in many ways, Germany had not yet recovered from the trauma of the Napoleonic campaigns. There was no lack of opportunity for ministry. As Löhe himself wrote:

> We have many young men and women on all sides in our congregations, who, on account of poverty, have no hope of finding a job in their homeland. They are incapable of living unmarried and chaste, so they fall into sin. Their illegitimate children grow up in poverty and, in part, contempt, while the parents themselves, the longer and the more they lose all shame, are driven to stealing and all sorts of other sins because of shameless poverty.[13]

Clearly the situation demanded that the church respond. The church might be able to turn aside from the economic problems, but when these problems drove people into sin, the church was compelled to address them.

Theological reasons always ultimately carried more weight with Löhe. The social situation in Germany was tragic and demanded a response. But pure human sympathy and compassion were not sufficient reasons in themselves to justify inner mission. Whoever was dedicated to inner mission, especially in its diaconal dimensions, may not forget that such service is not purely about improving the lot of one's neighbor. Evil is rooted in sin and unbelief and whoever wants to help, Löhe wrote, "will not forget the best and deepest reaching means—spiritual help."[14] Merely attending to the worldly afflictions will not, in the end, solve the problem. Worldly misery and evil are caused by sin and unbelief—matters of the heart and the spirit. To be truly healed in the body, one must be healed in the heart and in the soul. Ultimately inner mission, like outer mission, is about faith.

It was this crisis in the faith or spiritual life of the church that concerned Löhe. The church had become corrupted with false doctrine.[15] In Bavaria, Pietists, Mystics, Rationalists, the Reformed, and the Lutherans were forced together into one church. No one was happy with this situation. Congregations were compelled to accept whoever was assigned to be pastor, whether they were of a like mind or not. For Löhe, with his high value on confessional integrity and pure doctrine, the situation was intolerable. How could the apostolic Word be properly proclaimed and received when it was lost in this mishmash? Instead of the pure and uncorrupted Word, parishioners were unknowingly partaking of an adulterated fare.[16] The shame was that they did not know any better. They were being led astray by those who were entrusted with their care. Unscrupulous and unbelieving shepherds, Löhe was convinced, were leading congregations away from Zion and into the wilderness; the flock was left to wander aimlessly, prey to all sorts of unspeakable snares and pitfalls.

The consequences were clear: The church had no catechism, liturgy, hymnal, or order for church and worship. When the church has no unified confession and self-identity, it ends up serving two masters.[17] The church must have a clear sense of itself if it is to make an effective witness to the apostolic Word. For Löhe, there was only one solution, only one path to a renewed identity and witness to the Gospel: returning to the apostolic Word.

Yet every group in the Bavarian church had an alternate vision. The confessional Lutherans had one, the Reformed another, and the Rationalists and Pietists still another. The churches within the state church were at the point of destroying one another. They would not let one another live in peace as long as they had to coexist in the same church. In order to survive, they needed to separate.[18] If they were permitted to separate from one another, they could support one another in their ministries.

Out of this nearly intolerable situation of doctrinal and confessional chaos came Löhe's challenge for the Lutheran church to renew itself. His vision of renewal was grounded in the confessions and the apostolic Word. The solution, as Löhe saw it, was to work for the renewal of the *Lutheran* church, that is to say, the solution was inner mission. To this end, he suggested forming an association that would be something of a church alongside the church, a parachurch. The intent was not to form another church, but to reform the existing church. The association which Löhe had in mind was a provisional association.[19] It would only exist as long as the church remains in the wilderness. When the church returns to its apostolic roots, the association would lose its reason for being and, therefore, would disband.

This association, then, functions as yeast in bread. It is the core of the church and will be subsumed by it as the church grows in understanding of and obedience to its mission and ministry. Löhe knew that such an association could divide. This was not his intent. He did not want to divide the church; rather, he wanted to unite the church. He wanted to unite the church around the confessions, around pure doctrine, around the apostolic Word. This association would be a vital part of the life of the church and was intended to awaken it to the recognition and acknowledgment of its mission and ministry;[20] it would function in the center of the already existing church. This association, the Society for Inner Mission in the Sense of the Lutheran Church, existed for the purpose of renewing the church.

INNER MISSION—THE HOW

The distinction between inner and outer mission commonly had to do with the target of mission. Outer mission targeted those who were not yet baptized, inner mission those who were already baptized. A distinction is often made among those who are baptized: those who are loyal to the faith and those who have fallen away from the faith or are in danger of falling away from it. Löhe suggested that there needed to be something of a marriage between "diaconal service" and evangelism.[21] Evangelism, Löhe said, was universally accepted as a legitimate task of inner mission. The legitimacy of diaconal service, on the other hand, was challenged. Löhe argued for balance between diaconal service and evangelism, not only because acts of mercy in the midst of earthly suffering have their rightful place and value in the church, but also because this balance and interrelationship is more universal, broader, richer, and more satisfying to a heart full of love. Above all, it is in accordance with the words of Jesus.[22] An understanding of inner mission that marries evangelism and diaconal service is correct not only because it takes seriously the need for Christian love to express itself, but also—and more important—because it is true to Jesus' message.

This inner connection between evangelism and diaconal service places a double burden on Christians. Not only are they to proclaim the Word, they are to live the Word. At the same time this connection relieves them of a burden. Although Christians are called to actively resist the power of evil and sin in the world, they need not be discouraged when they fail to defeat poverty, hunger, and sickness. Helpless people might be forced into the arms of the evil one through worldly misery, but Christians have a sword greater and more powerful which is "living and active" and penetrates to the soul (Heb 4:12). This sword is, of course, the living word of God. The root causes of earthly misery can only be overcome through the Word of God. The proclaimed and lived-out Word of God are together necessary for effective response to earthly misery:

> The Word of God with its power, its trust, and its saving power is necessary for the unhappy and immoral populace of our Fatherland, for the proletariat and the poor. And inner mission must therefore be concerned, like outer mission, above all with the proclamation and preaching of the Word through speech and writing, through pastoral care and discipline and, through the awakening of the Spirit, with holy discipline.[23]

Inner mission, whether expressed as diaconal service or evangelism, is always about the awakening of faith. The work is fulfilled by the Holy Spirit and is not dependent on human effort.

DISCIPLINE

Discipline is an integral part of inner mission. The church has the right, even the obligation, on the basis of Matt 18:15–19 to exercise discipline over its members. Discipline offered the church the means by which it could prevent its members from neglecting the Word and the sacraments and thus inciting God's wrath.[24] In a word, discipline offered the church the power by which it could effectively disciple its members.

Löhe notes three elements in his discussion of discipline: the instructions found in Matt 18:15–18; the common struggle against sin; and order. The directions given by Jesus in Matthew 18 are, in Löhe's opinion, the chief scriptural exposition for discipline.[25] This passage goes to the heart of Löhe's understanding of discipline in the congregation. Everybody is united in sin, united in the task of repentance, and united in the task of bringing others to repentance. The basis for fellowship is a common set of values and a common means of living out these values. Matthew 18 provides the practical means by which a community can exercise and extend its fellowship; it demonstrates how Christians can express their love for one another.[26] "All have sinned and fall short of the glory of God"; all have offended the offended one. All people are united in this, but they are also united in seeking reconciliation. Löhe explained that the pastor is to be seen as being like Jesus Christ.[27] Just as Christ Jesus is the offended one, so should the pastor be seen as the one offended and all humans are the ones who have offended. The pastor then calls all those in the congregation to account for the wrongs they have committed against Christ, and he seeks to reconcile each of them to Christ in accordance with Matthew 18. The pastor is Christ's representative in the church. This is not a license to judge and punish; rather, it carries the weight of compassionately seeking out those who have offended and gently but firmly bringing them into the community of faith after they have repented of their wrongdoing.

The pastor is not alone in this task. The entire community is called to join together in disciplining those who have offended. The entire fellowship is given the responsibility to discipline one another. This is the second element of Löhe's understanding of discipline. The task of discipline is a common undertaking; it is a common struggle against sin.[28] The implications of this struggle against sin are seen clearly in how a community rallies around the task of saving even one sinner. Like the shepherd who left ninety-nine sheep to find the lost one (Luke 15:3–7) or the woman who seeks a lost coin in her house (Luke 15:8–10), so does the community seek to find those who are lost. The community of faith gathers to seek and to find the lost and does everything in its power to bring that person into the fellowship that surpasses all understanding.

It might seem that in speaking of the offended one and the offender that Löhe missed the obvious meaning of the text. In fact, Löhe points out that the passage begins not with "if a member of the church offends you," but with "if a member of the church sins against you" (Matt 18:15). Sin is a much broader concept than offense. A pure heart full of love will consider every offense to be a sin and every sin to be an offense. If you are motivated by love, you will recognize the sin of your every offense against your sisters and brothers in Christ.[29] Out of love for others, you would want someone whom you have offended to come to you and point out your sin so you could make amends.

In this light, discipline is not about the raw exercise of abusive or authoritarian power; it is about love: "The church of God and the communion of saints is a community of love, a body for which others are responsible for individual members and their prosperity."[30] Love draws members of a community together and motivates them to exhort and encourage one another to a common vision. The motivation is not power or dominion over others; it is, instead, the desire to work together in fostering a community in which the members can trust one another.

By entrusting the power to discipline in the hands of pastors, the church attains the strength to do effective diaconal service. Pastors who are gifted in this way and parishioners who are able and willing should join together and exercise mutual discipline.

The clergy play a central role in Löhe's conception of discipline. He combined the commandment of Matthew 18 to reconcile with one who has sinned against you with the office of the keys as instituted in Matthew 16 in a unique way. In Matthew 18, everybody in the church is called to provide peace in the congregation, but only the pastor has the authority and the responsibility to grant forgiveness publicly.[31] The power that belongs to Christians in the broader sense according to Matthew 18 belongs to the clergy in the narrower sense according to Matthew 16. The pastor grants absolution to the sinner with the agreement of the congregation. The congregation and the pastor work together in confronting sin in their midst and addressing the needs of the sinner in overcoming the sin, but finally it is the pastor who grants absolution.

Discipline can be harsh and severe and oppressive, but this is not the intent of Christian discipline as Löhe envisioned it. Just as a coach might be harsh or severe with an athlete that the athlete might excel, so Christians sometimes admonish one another and hold one another accountable for their sins that they might attain a "more excellent way" (1 Cor 12:31). The intent is to provide an atmosphere of love, an ethos where people do not merely guard their neighbor but, in accordance with Luther's explanation of the Fifth Commandment, actively care and provide for their neighbor.[32] In this sense discipline is closely connected to the doctrine of the communion of saints as described in Acts 2, ("all who believed were together and had all things in common"), in 1 Corinthians 12 ("the body does not consist of one member but of many"), and in Ephesians 4 ("one Lord, one faith, one Baptism"). The point of discipline is to "equip the saints for the work of ministry, for building up the body of Christ" (Eph 4:12). Everyone is obligated to exercise the gift which he or she has received. Discipline is about honing these gifts for the benefit of one's neighbor, for the benefit of the church.

The third element (or goal) of discipline is that of establishing and maintaining good order in a church. Already at the first Pentecost good order was established. When the apostles and disciples spoke in tongues, it could very well have happened that no one understood the others and that chaos prevailed. But God has already proven to be a God of order: Those who were present at the first Pentecost understood one another and order prevailed. Paul commanded the church in Corinth that it was to maintain good order even when speaking in tongues. Matthew 18 gives a prescribed procedure for handling potentially explosive and injurious cases within the church. It gives to those who have been offended a means, an established and just procedure, to confront the offender. Cases can be handled either by individuals or by a group of two or three. A predetermined procedure has been given.[33] The offended party goes to the offending person and presents the grievance. If this does not work, then some others who are gifted in speech and wisdom are included so as to give a proper admonition or witness according to the Scriptures. If this fails, finally the entire congregation can judge whether the accusations are just and, if they are, what is the next step. The pastor plays an important role in all this. The pastor is, at the same time, a judge, a representative of the congregation, and an advocate for the one offended. All members of the congregation are entrusted with the task of disciplining one another, but the pastor is entrusted with the keys that either bind or loose the decisions of the church.

Church discipline (*Kirchenzucht*) is an integral part of pastoral care. It is the congregation's exercise of pastoral care. If souls are to be saved, then for the sake of souls, individuals may, from time to time, need to be excluded from the life of the congregation. Such an individual who is excluded has already in fact excluded himself or herself from the congregation by either confession or action. The congregation is merely acknowledging this individual's decision to turn away. But the congregation's ministry only begins here because it must regularly pray for that individual and leave open the door for return into the fellowship centered in the apostolic Word. There is always hope: "many a man has lived his life in such a way that only on his deathbed did salvation come to him through the grace offered in pastoral care."[34] The door is always open; one need merely to walk through it into the fellowship of those who have responded to the call, to those who have received God's Word of grace.

Church discipline is like a breath of fresh air. It purifies, brings unity, and strengthens the poor to do the works of Jesus.[35] The exercise of discipline makes diaconal service possible. A congregation or cluster of congregations could then work together in unity, knowing that they have a common moral base and—more important—a common doctrinal base.[36] Each person knows that the others believe and live essentially the same.

DIACONAL SERVICE

Diaconal service is one of the enduring legacies of Wilhelm Löhe. In diaconal service, according to Schoenauer, Löhe's inner mission finds its meaning.[37] This is perhaps a debatable point, but it is clear that diaconal service was integral to Löhe's understanding of the life of the congregation. Deacons and their work enriched the life of the church.

Mission and diaconal service are expressions of faith and love. Faith and love belong together if that faith is faith in the Gospel proclaimed in and by love. Löhe used a typically vivid illustration in describing faith: "Faith is the herald, who trumpeting with a loud sound so that one can hear it in the distance, even to the ends of the earth, announces the great acts of salvation in Christ Jesus, which he himself has experienced."[38] Love is never far from faith: "Serving love, no less than faith, proclaims the fame of the Lord Jesus. It accompanies faith which preaches [*predigenden Glauben*] with the quiet works of mercy and the flask of oil, which endeavors to alleviate all human pain and suffering of this time, like the holy women who accompanied the Lord and his disciples."[39] Faith might be equated to words and love equated to deeds. Both words and deeds are necessary if the saving Gospel is to be effectively communicated and heard.

This mention of the Gospel points to the mission dimension of diaconal service. Diaconal service is about ministering to humans in their suffering, but it is ultimately about mission. Christians seek to make manifest the works of the Lord. The key element of mission is mercy; it is, Löhe said, the virtue that comes from heaven and moves the earth. It is the service of mercifulness to which deacons are called. We wanted, Löhe wrote, nothing other "than that the mercy of the Lord is praised and made known in various good works."[40] Diaconal service is about proclaiming the Gospel of Christ in deeds. Christians love their neighbor as the good Samaritan loved his neighbor; in this way, they make Christ manifest.

To love one's neighbor is to concretely participate in the expansion of God's reign, a reign characterized by mercy. This is mission, both in its inner and outer expressions. God seeks to make mercy and love manifest to the ends of the earth. Humans are called to participate in this mission: "God effects all his works through his servants. His works are therefore at one and the same time divine and human, and wherever he works, there he immediately opens up to his saints a wide road of mercy. They may only—

as they should—be co-workers of the divine worker."[41] The Spirit works in and through human beings to make God's reign of mercy and love manifest.

Service is the primary characteristic of the diaconate, service to those who suffer, to those who need the Gospel to salve and to save their souls. Diaconal service is about serving as Christ served.[42] Christ served all those who were in need. He served all regardless of their position in society, regardless of their wealth, regardless of his own needs. Deacons seek to serve as Christ served so the Gospel of Christ might be proclaimed.

Inner mission is about exercising mercy. Mercy, Löhe says, "is goodness and love, but goodness and love in a special relationship, namely in the relationship to the unfortunate and impoverished."[43] Out of mercy, one preaches the Gospel to those who have fallen away from the faith. Out of mercy, one cares for those neighbors who are spiritually and physically afflicted.

Löhe is emphatic that mission and diaconal service are not directed to people of one's own choosing. Just as individuals do not initiate mission efforts on their own, so is mission—both inner and outer—directed to large groups of people, to whole groups of people.[44] Mission does not selectively seek out certain individuals; rather, it seeks to serve and heal *all* who suffer.

One ministers and evangelizes to the glory of the Lord.[45] If Christians were to minister to certain individuals, they risk ministering merely to gain personal honor or a good reputation. More important than human reputation, Löhe notes often, is the glory of the Lord. Paraphrasing the Sermon on the Mount, Löhe might say, "Let the light of the gospel shine in your works of mission and diaconal service" (Matt 5:16).

Diaconal service is most authentically diaconal service when it is *person to person*. Löhe exhorted his listeners, "Dedicate yourself, as much as you can, to the ministry of the suffering personally."[46] Diaconal service occurs between individuals. Christians, as individuals, share the love and mercy of Christ.

Diaconal service, like Jesus' ministry, seeks to serve others without establishing whether that person is an enemy or a friend, a member of the same nation or a foreigner. Service in the name of the Gospel is service to all apart from social standing:

> If we look to the person to whom divine compassion extends, then we find that neither the citizen nor the alien is forgotten, neither the Levite nor the priest nor the simple member of the congregation, neither the elderly nor the young, neither the free nor the slave, neither the widow nor the orphan, neither the healthy nor the sick, neither

the blind nor the deaf, not even the murderer or the manslaughterer. The law of mercy does not even find its limit within the boundaries of humankind since it does not forget the animals and the birds in the nests. If we look not to the person, but rather to the opportunity in which mercy should be manifested, we find God's will to be merciful is expressed.[47]

In serving as Jesus served, there is neither Jew nor Greek, neither slave nor free, neither male nor female; all are one in Christ Jesus (Gal 3:28). Diaconal service is blind to everything and everybody; it sees only the opportunity to serve and to proclaim the Gospel.

The motivation for diaconal service is mercy born out of love. This motivation, this love, comes from the desire to bring the Word to the baptized who are falling into misery. The desire is that the body and spirit of a brother or sister may delight in the living God. The *primary* goal is not that the misery of another may be alleviated, but that the soul receives the Spirit:

> The body remains second, not first—earthly mercy follows first from the spiritual—just as love and works proceed from faith. It is more important to proclaim the faith than the transient seedgrains of earthly assistance which, despite one's high valuation of them against the expansion of the Word and the faith, are far removed from one another, just as body is from spirit, and heaven from earth. If mercy must lose some popularity on account of this understanding and the right consequences of its activity, then that does no harm to its true effects. A little disgrace is good for it so that it does not conform to the world and is not contaminated by the world's approval which sees Christ's mission not in inner mission but only as a means to a temporal end.[48]

Inner mission is ultimately about Christ and the Spirit, not about eradicating misery in the world. The end of inner mission is finally that sinners come to faith and experience the joy of community in Christ.

For this reason, Löhe could praise spiritual care as an important gift. A deacon may show compassion, teach well, and serve tirelessly, but these qualities paled in comparison to spiritual care.[49] A deacon so gifted could bring people to an awareness of their sin, an awareness of God's grace, and to God's calling to live in the power of this grace. Inner mission, while it did not ignore the pervasive reality of misery, was ultimately about bringing those who lived in misery to the Gospel of Christ.

Diaconal workers participated in the church's mission and ministry as integral components to the church's work. Diaconal workers existed to support pastors in their ministry.[50] Deacons were never intended to replace ordained pastors but to supplement and complement them in their ministry.

Diaconal workers and pastors are as closely related to each other as mission is to diaconal service or outer mission is to inner mission. Inner mission cannot be separated from outer mission, diaconal service from foreign mission. Löhe wrote that

> according to the correct understanding of the nature of a deaconess, mission is very close to the task of a deaconess. The diaconate was assigned to the preaching ministry from the beginning like Eve was to Adam. A church which carries out God's work among the heathen without diaconal ministry seems to me to be like a person with only one leg.[51]

A church without a wholistic understanding of mission was severely impaired in its ability to effectively proclaim the Gospel. A church without a diaconal service was similarly impaired. Its proclamation of the Gospel might be incomplete and partial.

For Löhe, the diaconate is a legitimate ministry of the church. Following the example of the apostles, the church should call and set aside those who possess the gift of diaconal service. When a person becomes a deacon, some type of ordination or consecration recognizes and confirms that calling.[52] An important task of the Lutheran church was to reinstate this important ministry that had been founded by the apostles but since the Reformation had fallen into neglect. To this end Löhe and his colleagues established the Lutheran Association of Deaconesses in 1853.

LUTHERAN ASSOCIATION OF DEACONESSES

One of the most important or most lasting achievements of Löhe was the founding of the *Lutherischer Verein für weibliche Diakonie*. The motivations for its establishment were many.[53] In some areas women had taken on diaconal service but did not have any training in caring for the sick and shut-in. They were not organized, and their efforts were uncoordinated. Consequently, in some parts of the country there were more "diaconal workers" than were needed, and in other areas there were not enough. In rural areas, families with daughters often had no means of employment. The diaconate offered such women an opportunity to be meaningfully engaged in diaconal service. The gifts and resources for diaconal service were waiting to be used. Many women, however, lacked the formal training to serve.[54] Löhe was convinced that women for a diaconate could be found; the real challenge was to provide opportunities in and through congregations.

One motivation was to provide the church a means by which it could exercise its diaconal service. The church is called to care for the poor and the sick. All members of the church have a share in diaconal service; they are to care for their neighbors. Löhe and his colleagues who founded the *Lutherischer Verein für weibliche Diakonie* hoped for "the awakening and formation of a sense of service to suffering humanity in the Lutheran population of Bavaria."[55] They wanted to reestablish the diaconate of the early church and to reawaken the sense of ministry and love for one's immediate neighbor.

Alongside this dream of reestablishing the diaconate was the desire to use the deaconess houses to model Christian congregational life. Löhe thought that the houses could provide a visible model of congregational life as envisioned by the apostles. Löhe sought to establish an "apostolic-episcopal" church with its center in "the sacrament [of the Altar] and the doctrine of justification by faith."[56] The deaconess houses were to embody this vision.

This desire to reestablish the diaconate is important in another respect. Although the establishment of a deaconess institute was important, it was not the primary goal. In 1853 when Löhe and his colleagues were in the midst of founding the Lutheran Association of Deaconesses, the intent was exactly that: to establish an *association* of Lutheran deaconesses.[57] The intent was not to establish yet another institution or organization. The church had enough of those. The goal was to establish and reawaken interest in a ministry of the church which had lain dormant for hundreds of years.

The basic strategy was to establish an institute for deaconesses. At this institute women would be trained as nurses and caregivers. The training would not only take place in the classrooms in the institute located in Neuendettelsau, but also in the homes, the missions, and the schools where the women would later serve as consecrated deaconesses. Once trained they would be commissioned to serve in homes but chiefly in hospices and hospitals. In this way the institute "would sow blessings throughout the entire land."[58]

The goal of the deaconess association was determined by the service of the diaconate: to "awaken and form the desire for ministry to those suffering in the Lutheran populace of Bavaria."[59] The objective was not merely to do this work, but to awaken interest among all Bavarian Lutherans for this important service.

Two important or noticeable elements of life in the deaconess house stand out: caring for the sick, for children, and for the handicapped; and worship. In the chronicles of the deaconess house, much of the reported activity has to do with caring. On October 14, 1856, the diaconal students were examined for their medical knowledge; on October 29, 1856, Gertrud Köhler went to Nuremberg to take over the administration of a home for young children; on November 15, 1856, Eleonore Reichold took the care of a young boy; and on November 18, 1856, Pauline Haag and Anna Näpfel departed for Fürth to oversee the care of the female patients in the Protestant hospital there. In late November of the same year, Deaconess Marie Böttinger was sent to Elpersdorf to care for a couple suffering from a nervous fever, and in December this same Marie Böttinger was sent to the hospital in Fürth.[60] One entry dated November 27, 1856, contains the sad news that one of the mentally ill patients died. The patient suffered terribly until her death, but she did experience some alleviation of her illness during her residency in the house.[61] The chronicles witness to the service of care that the deaconesses carried out.[62]

Although the service of the deaconesses was chiefly one of caring for the sick and infirm, it was not exclusively so. The curriculum of the deaconess institute in Neuendettelsau included medical instruction, religious instruction, and instruction in the basic school subjects (reading, writing, literature, and arithmetic). The practicums would take place according to their calling or vocation in an industrial school (the pupils would be instructed in sewing and knitting), in a home for troubled children, or in a home for mentally handicapped children.[63] Diaconal service took on many forms. To care for the neighbor does not mean to only care for her when she is sick and infirm, but to care for her well-being. Luther's explanation to the Fifth Commandment was relevant: Christians are commanded, "You shall not kill." Luther notes that this means that "we should fear and love God, and so we should not endanger our neighbor's life, nor cause him any harm, but help and befriend him in every necessity of life."[64] Löhe, following Luther, understood that all Christians are called—obligated—to care for their neighbors. To care for the neighbor, Löhe asserts, means to care for those at the fringes of society: Christians care for those for whom nobody else will care.

This wholistic understanding of service to the physical and the spiritual was always at the center of the mission of the deaconess house. Its training program stated that the house would teach first of all, "everything, which is necessary and useful for the spiritual care of minors and the suffering."[65] To adequately serve the earthly needs, one must attend to the spiritual needs of those who suffer.

WORSHIP

Diaconal service takes on many forms, but even at a specific time and place diaconal service has a unifying center: worship. For Löhe, worship was always front and center of diaconal service. Worship is the "alpha and omega" of Christian life. In worship the Christian is renewed for service to the world. In worship the Christian is united with Christ. Worship unites the ministries of the church. Deaconesses gathered for daily worship wherever they served. The 1858 annual report notes, "this year the different parts of the house have found their unifying point in daily worship, namely in Vespers."[66] In the simple act of worship, the deaconesses, despite their manifold means of service and their differing experiences, are united with Christ and with one another. In worship their common humanity and common faith in the risen Christ bonds them together. Opportunities for worship were offered so the women at the deaconess house could be strengthened in their daily work.

Diaconal service was not simply about serving others in their physical needs. Worship was central to the life of those who served in the diaconate. Löhe always saw the ministry of the church as a unified whole; ministry is organic. A deacon was engaged in one facet of a unified ministry. Löhe once wrote that if he were a singer or a painter, he would describe the life of a deacon in a series of songs or paintings which depicted the various aspects and tasks of diaconal life: "I would paint the young woman in a stable and at the altar and in the laundry,—and how she clothes the naked in the pure linen of mercy—in the kitchen and in the sick rooms, in the fields and singing both the Sanctus in the choir as well as the Nunc Dimittis solo."[67] Worship and ministry are one.

Since Löhe closely connected the spiritual and the physical in the task of inner mission or diaconal service, he also believed that diaconal workers are called to pray. They pray for those who suffer: "Let your prayers, your morning and evening offerings, rise over and over like clouds of smoke to thoughts of those who live in misery and suffering."[68] Simple acts of mercy were not enough to overcome suffering. The physical act of caring for the one in need of diaconal service needs to be supplemented with the spiritual discipline of prayer.

While the deaconess house in Neuendettelsau was well known for its service to the sick and to the poor, this was not its only work. In 1864, Löhe reminded the deaconesses that their service also served the worship life of the church.

> We remember also that the [deaconess] house attends to the production
> of paraments. In this way the women's work attains a holy end. . . . Altar
> clothing and other church decorations for the congregation are pro-
> duced, which until now without exception have been to the satisfaction
> of both pastors and congregations. Additionally there is instruction on
> paraments which instructs on both the old and the new and which seeks
> to teach and establish the aesthetics of church form and color.[69]

The diaconal service of supporting the festive worship life of the church
was equally as important as its mundane work of caring for the sick, the
poor, and the needy.

This "altar guild" service was intended not only to support the church
in its worship life, it also had the purpose of educating those who wanted
to enter into the diaconal service about the church's worship. This education in the liturgical life of the church had the purpose of enabling and
equipping those who cared for the sick and needy to properly decorate the
prayer chapels so they reflected the church year.[70] Knowing when to use
the different paraments enabled diaconal ministers to communicate the
richness of the church year as well as life in the Word and the Sacraments.
Diaconal workers in this way communicated the Gospel as received
through the apostles not only through their service to the body, but also to
the soul.

INNER MISSION AND NORTH AMERICA

Löhe linked inner mission closely with outer mission and inner mission
with mission to North America. One of his goals in North America was the
establishment of mission colonies. At least one of these colonies was to be
settled by those who because of economic circumstances had few opportunities in Germany. This is where inner mission came in. These unfortunate
souls who faced a bleak future in Germany and were susceptible to falling
into all kinds of evil (e.g., thievery or prostitution) could perhaps be saved.
Löhe suggested that one of the tasks of inner mission was to direct emigrants
to already established settlements with churches and pastors.[71] This was true
of not only those who faced an uncertain future in Germany. Those who
emigrated to North America often ended up settling in isolated areas, far
removed from a German Lutheran church. Why not direct those who were
emigrating to already established colonies with churches and pastors? In this
way their spiritual and physical needs would be attended to.

Löhe was further aroused to action by his knowledge that the problem
of isolation was compounded by the American immigrants' amnesia of

their life in Germany. Many of the German Lutherans in North America had apparently forgotten about the faith that sustained them in their homeland; they were going to other churches whose doctrine was not nearly as pure as that of the Lutheran church. These settlers should have been homesick and ordinarily would have eagerly sought out the familiar, especially in matters of faith. Evidently they were not and did not.[72] Many went to more attractive denominations—in his writings Löhe singled out the Methodists. The situation was a serious challenge to the Lutheran church in North America and to Lutherans in Germany who wanted to prevent the German immigrants from falling away from the faith.

This threat was one reason Löhe was inclined to name inner mission as more important than outer mission. Support for the German emigrants in North America was critical; these fellow Christians should not be ignored in favor of the heathen.[73] The Germans in North America, nourished in their faith, could witness to the Gospel among the American Indians there. It was, therefore, self-defeating to neglect inner mission. Outer mission could be successful only with the strong support of the already baptized; that is to say, strong inner mission made successful outer mission possible.[74] Inner mission had to do with the inner life of the already baptized. By supporting and nurturing the spiritual lives of the already baptized, Löhe felt that these could be effective "ambassadors for Christ" (2 Cor 5:20).

The mission seminary in Neuendettelsau, dependent on the support of the *Gesellschaft für innere Mission im Sinne der Lutherischen Kirche*, reflects this connection between inner and outer mission. The goal of the mission seminary was to help Germans in the United States who were in danger of neglecting religious instruction or who were thinking about changing denominations.[75] Löhe wanted to "make the Gospel" accessible to these Germans. The mission seminary also sought to prepare men so they could be immediately ordained upon arrival in North America. By working in Bavaria, the Bavarian church could support and encourage mission in North America.

TRACTS AND POSTILLES

The writing, publication, and distribution of tracts was an interest of Löhe's at an early age. As a young student at Erlangen, he organized a Mission Circle (*Missionskränzchen*) that met weekly on Saturday evenings. The participants gathered to study, then afterward enjoyed tea together.[76] At the age of nineteen, Löhe wrote Pastor Brand in Roth and "thanked him for his efforts to promote Christ" and asked for permission to redistribute some tracts.[77] Soon after, Löhe joined the tract society which Brand headed, as well as another society based in northern Germany. For the duration of his university and vicarage years (1830s), Löhe was actively involved in the writing, publication, and distribution of tracts.

What was the appeal of tracts? They were brief, written in simple, clear language. Tracts responded to everyday questions of everyday people. The reformers, especially Luther, made effective use of tracts. Mark Edwards notes that the tracts and pamphlets of the reformers

> were handy, relatively cheap, readily concealed and transported, and accordingly well suited for delivering their message to a large popular audience. They could be easily transported by itinerant peddlers, hawked on street corners and in taverns, advertised with jingles and intriguing title pages, and swiftly hidden in a pack or under clothing when the authorities made an appearance.[78]

Tracts were specially suitable for evangelism. They sought to present the Christian Gospel succinctly. Because they were small they could be quickly printed and distributed at minimal cost. Tracts could be pressed into somebody's hand who could then fold it and read it at his or her leisure. Yet this advantage, Löhe saw, turned out to be its disadvantage when a *personal* witness was lacking.

Around the time Löhe went to Neuendettelsau (1837), he began to lose interest in tracts, or perhaps he simply became more realistic about the benefits of tracts. He still published tracts, but now he recognized that their effectiveness was limited. Löhe wrote in 1842

> that it is not so long ago that one set one's hopes too high for the distribution of tracts for the expansion of the Reign of God. One distributed them in large quantities, gave them to the willing and the unwilling, one even left them behind in houses or scattered them on walkways. Today one is cool [to the practice]. The extreme of overvaluing is over and many have gone to the extreme of contempt [for tracts].[79]

Tracts had their place . . . if they were correctly used.

Tracts need not be left to extremists. They could be used to good purpose. "Most of Luther's writings were tracts," Löhe noted.[80] In 1841, with a new appreciation and understanding of tracts, he founded a new tract society. He was clear about how the society ought to go about its work. He wanted to "avoid all subjectivity."[81] They should not be Methodist or pietistic in their doctrine. The form should be different than that of other tracts. The print and paper should be of good quality. Most important,

"Löhe was clear that the distribution of tracts may not occur for any length of time without the living, personal Word and witness."[82] Tracts should not be carelessly and randomly left in public (or private) places. They should only be distributed with a personal witness to the apostolic Word.

The idea that tracts should witness to the apostolic Word is borne out by a small section Löhe included in *Three Books about the Church*. He noted that Bible societies' methods are sometimes marked by extravagance and caricature. At the same time, Löhe wrote, "one thing remains quite clear. These Bible societies . . . are powerful witnesses to the clarity of the Holy Scriptures."[83] Löhe understood that the Word is paramount and is not obscured by the questionable methods by which the tracts are distributed.

The message is primary, not the messenger. Since the apostolic Word takes primacy, Löhe suggested that Lutheran preachers in North America be peddlars (*Kolporteure*). These preachers "should be provided with Bibles, catechisms, books of sermons, prayer books, calendars, etc. to sell and to give away—they should be able to give away small things in large quantities. The Methodists win many in this way."[84] Tracts did have a place in mission as long as their content and purpose were centered in the apostolic Word and not in the extravagant claims of miracles and other questionable tactics.

Luther's writings tended to be occasional and contextual. They were written for the purpose of addressing a specific pastoral need. Löhe had a similar view. Because of his parish experience, he particularly saw a need for tracts in support of pastoral care. Often he wished that he had an appropriate tract to place in the hands of his parishioners to reinforce advice he had given and to provide parishioners with something to read and reflect on. Löhe wanted deeply to be "supported in his pastoral care by suitable tracts."[85] To this end he began to write tracts which could be used in the course of everyday pastoral ministry. Examples of such tracts would be "*Vom christlichen Hausgottesdienste*" ["On Christian Worship for the Home"] and "*Hülfsmittel zum täglichen Bibellesen: Eine Neujahrsgabe für fleißige Leser des göttlichen Wortes*" ["Helps for Daily Bible-Reading: A New Year's Gift for Industrious Readers of the Divine Word"].[86] These were the first of many tracts that could be used by pastors, teachers, elders, and other congregational leaders in everyday parish ministry, addressing ordinary needs of Christians.

Certainly by the 1850s, Löhe's interest in tracts had reawakened and he encouraged their publication and distribution with renewed enthusiasm. In 1866 he reported that the women of the deaconess houses had used them to great effect:

> How many hundreds of prayer books and other suitable writings, how many hundreds of biblical drawings have been distributed gratis and without remuneration in the districts! And how much all of this work has contributed to the ordained ministry! Recently some discouraged pastors have expressed the opinion that the time of distributing tracts, Bibles and religious literature is over. Our sisters have found the situation to be entirely otherwise. Nearly everywhere their literary gifts have been joyfully and thankfully received. Many men, who have defiantly refused gifts for the sick, have buried their hands deep in their pockets with embarrassment when their wives received edifying literature, when their sons received the *Daily Seedgrains* [*Tageslauf*], when their children received an attractive biblical drawing.[87]

Tracts and religious literature could work, one might say, subversively in those who might not otherwise be reached. They could also work through those who might not otherwise be capable or equipped to verbally communicate the Gospel.

CONCLUSION

Inner mission is the area of Löhe's thought most profoundly influenced by Pietism, especially the early Pietism as characterized by August Hermann Francke at Halle. Francke spoke not only of attending to a person's religious needs, but also to a person's physical needs.[88] Clearly this parallels Löhe's insistence that the Christian's love for the neighbor extends not only to the neighbor's earthly needs, but to the neighbor's religious needs as well. At the same time, Löhe was influenced by the Roman Catholic religious orders. He himself admitted that the deaconesses are a Protestant imitation of Roman Catholic nuns.[89] He was ecumenically minded enough to look beyond the boundaries of his own theological background and influences for models.

Models is the key word. Both Pietist and Roman Catholic models had their weaknesses. Löhe sought to build on the strengths of both, using classical Lutheran theology as his source.[90] More than that, he recognized that what worked in the first century, in the Middle Ages, or even in the previous century might not necessarily work in the nineteenth century. Times change and ministry that is most effective must change too. Consequently, diaconal service must change to meet the challenges of the present.[91] Doctrine was not a matter of the times; it was not adiaphora.

The form of ministry, on the other hand, is a matter of adiaphora. It is not central to the faith, though it does convey and communicate it.

Löhe's concern was always the church and its mission and ministry. His understanding of inner mission cannot be separated from his understanding of mission as a whole.[92] In many respects, mission is inner mission. Mission is the activity of the church. And the church is always the concrete gathering of people in a concrete place. It is these people, these Christians, who are the church and who consequently carry out the church's mission and ministry. Mission is the concrete, visible activity of the people of God. It is the concrete, visible ministry of mercy and evangelism in immediate surroundings. They cannot do mission at a location removed from their own lives. They can only support the efforts of others who live at that location. Outer mission is always the fruit of inner mission.

The church was at the center of Löhe's understanding of mission. Mission was about bringing people into community—into community with Christ and with other Christians. Mission begins with its own, the baptized, so redeemed people might draw the unbaptized into their community. Because mission was closely linked to the life of the church, Löhe suggested that reports of missionary activity should be included in church periodicals as supplements and not as independent periodicals.[93] He was careful to always place the church at the center.

Löhe's wholistic understanding of mission, his vision of inner and outer mission as a unified whole, anticipates twentieth-century conceptions. Mission, Löhe said, is about making God's reign of mercy manifest. In like manner, Carl Braaten defines mission as "the activity of the church by which it works for the transformation of its own latency into its self-manifestation all over the world."[94] Mission is about the church's effort to make its identity and mission—its very self—manifest. It is about mercy, about love, about salvation, and most of all, about Christ and life in Christ. The life and ministry of Jesus cannot be separated from the meaning of his life and ministry. In the same way the church cannot be separated from its own activity. Christ's words and his deeds belong together. The church's word and its deed belong together. Löhe implicitly understood this when he argued that mission must, first of all, be about the conversion of the heart. Mission must be grounded in right thought as well as right deed. Löhe's wholistic understanding of mission correctly linked word with deed and humanization with evangelization.

·   NOTES

1   "Vorschlag," *GW* V/1: 245. The example of Christ is central for Löhe. Just as Christ alleviates physical misery, so shall we alleviate physical misery; just as Christ gives us the promise of the resurrection, so should we attend to [literally: fuss over] our neighbor's body for the sake of the resurrection.

2   Löhe, "Etwas über die deutsch-lutherischen Niederlassungen in der Grafschaft Saginaw, Staat Michigan," *GW* IV: 163.

3   Löhe, "Das Krankenwesen der Diakonissenanstalt," *GW* IV: 435; hereafter "Das Krankenwesen."

4   In "Von der Barmherzigkeit," *GW* IV: 485, Löhe commented that there can be no greater mercy than to share Word and Sacrament to all who are lost.

5   "Vorschlag," *GW* V/1: 247. Löhe translates διακονία [diakonia] with the German words *Diakonie* [diaconal ministry], *Helferamt* [helping ministry], and *Dieneramt* [servant ministry].

6   "Vorschlag," *GW* V/1: 248

7   "Von der Barmherzigkeit," *GW* IV: 481.

8   "Das Verhältnis," *GW* V/2: 702. In the same lecture, Löhe asserted that one can do inner mission and outer mission independently of each other (*GW* V/2: 704).

9   *Innere Mission im allgemeinen*, *GW* IV: 179.

10 *Innere Mission im allgemeinen*, *GW* IV: 180. Along these lines, in "Die Gesellschaft für innere Mission," 62–63 (also 66), Löhe defined the task of a mission society as developing a mission field, then handing it over to local congregations. Inner and outer mission are not separate from each other, neither do they operate in isolation from congregations.

11 "Hervorgerufene Erklärung über die Tätigkeit der Neuendettelsauer Missionschule für Heidenmission und über die Verbindung unserer Thätigkeit in Nord-Amerika mit der Heidenmission," *Kirchliche Mittheilungen* 13 (1855): no. 5: col. 37; hereafter "Erklärung."

12 *Innere Mission im allgemeinen*, *GW* IV: 185.

13 "Die deutsch-lutherischen Niederlassungen," *GW* IV: 176.

14 *Innere Mission im allgemeinen*, *GW* IV: 181. Löhe was clear in "Von der Barmherzigkeit," *GW* IV: 468, that the source and root of misery is sin. To overcome sin is the biggest task and the most difficult.

15 "Aphorismen," *GW* V/1: 321.

16 "Vorschlag," *GW* V/1: 214–15. Löhe pointed out that trusting parishioners would assume that their pastor would preach God's Word.

17 In "Vorschlag," *GW* V/1: 215, Löhe even suggested that the church has been at odds with itself.

18 In "Vorschlag," *GW* V/1: 216, Löhe used a descriptive metaphor of a family which can no longer live under one roof and must separate so its members can continue to support and uphold one another.

19 "Vorschlag," *GW* V/1: 219.

20 "Vorschlag," *GW* V/1: 220. Löhe spoke of this Lutheran association for apostolic life as a focus point for the church.

21 I will use these two terms to signify the church's activity of serving the physical

worldly needs of people (diaconal service) and to the evangelistic activity of proclaiming God's saving Word to those who have fallen away or are in danger of doing so (evangelism).

22 *Innere Mission im allgemeinen, GW* IV: 180.

23 *Innere Mission im allgemeinen, GW* IV: 181.

24 *Innere Mission im allgemeinen, GW* IV: 182.

25 "Vorschlag," *GW* V/1: 229.

26 "Vorschlag," *GW* V/1: 229–30. Löhe explained that discipline allows the holy love and fellowship of the Lord to be unveiled. Nobody ought to suffer under the bondage of sin; everybody ought to wish fulfillment for one another. Löhe wrote ("Vorschlag," *GW* V/1: 230) that such love is the diametric opposite of Cain's question of whether he ought to be his brother's keeper.

27 "Vorschlag," *GW* V/1: 229.

28 "Vorschlag," *GW* V/1: 229, 230.

29 "Vorschlag," *GW* V/1: 230. Löhe goes further in explaining that those who are not motivated by love do not concern themselves with the welfare of their neighbors.

30 Löhe, "Von der züchtigenden Liebe," *GW* IV: 465.

31 "Vorschlag," *GW* V/1: 233. Werner Ost describes the event of absolution as it occurred at regular services at Neuendettelsau: Löhe stood at the altar alongside a council member. If the council member had no objections, then Löhe would grant forgiveness of sins to that Christian. But if the council member named something that was yet uncleansed, then that sin must first be cleansed and purified. See Ost, *Löhe*, 85; see also Schattauer, "Announcement, Confession, and Lord's Supper," 84, 88–93.

32 "Vorschlag," *GW* V/1: 234.

33 "Vorschlag," *GW* V/1: 231. Löhe accounted for those who are not gifted in speech and may not be able to adequately present their case to those who have sinned against them. He said that somebody else (perhaps the pastor) could handle the case. See "Vorschlag," *GW* V/1: 231–32, for an explanation of the procedure for handling cases where somebody has sinned against another.

34 *Three Books*, 100.

35 *Innere Mission im allgemeinen, GW* IV: 185.

36 In "Warum bekenne ich mich?" *GW* IV: 225, Löhe wrote, "To be united in the Spirit means to be united in thought and principles."

37 Schoenauer, *Kirche lebt vor Ort*, 32.

38 "Ansprache, betreffend die Sammlung von Natural- und anderen freien Gaben für die Neuendettelsauer Anstalten," *GW* IV: 351; hereafter "Ansprache."

39 "Ansprache," *GW* IV: 351.

40 *Etwas aus der Geschichte des Diakonissenhauses Neuendettelsau, GW* IV: 271; hereafter *Etwas aus der Geschichte.*

41 "Von der Barmherzigkeit," *GW* IV: 482. Löhe's phrase, "co-workers of the divine worker" is evocative of Philip Hefner's concept of humans as "created co-creators." See Hefner, "The Creation," in *CD* 1: 325–28.

42 "Mercy," Löhe said, "is the reason and intention of Christ's work" ("Von der

Barmherzigkeit," *GW* IV: 484). Regarding the obligation of Christians to be merciful, see "Von der seligen Übung der Barmherzigkeit," *GW* IV: 463. At the funeral of Karoline Rheineck, one of the first women to join the deaconess association, Löhe noted that she served her family; the sick in Augsburg, Kaiserswerth, and Neuendettelsau; children in Memmingen; as well as all others whom she encountered. "Her path," Löhe said, "was the path of Jesus" ("Lebenslauf der Jungfrau Karoline Rheineck, 1. Vorsteherin des Diakonissenhauses zu Neuendettelsau: Gelesen bei der Beerdigung am 23. August 1855," *GW* IV: 359).

43 Von der Barmherzigkeit," *GW* IV: 467. On the following page (*GW* IV: 468), Löhe defines mercy as love for those in misery; it enters into their misery.

44 Regarding the fact that mission is not to be individually initiated, see the discussion on page 164. Regarding the social focus of mission, see "Ansprache," *GW* IV: 351.

45 In "Ansprache," *GW* IV: 352, Löhe wrote that Christians ought to let the light of their faith shine so the Lord is honored.

46 Löhe, "Von der seligen Übung der Barmherzigkeit," *GW* IV: 464.

47 "Von der Barmherzigkeit," *GW* IV: 483. In "An die Schwestern und Probeschwestern," *GW* IV: 528–29, Löhe told the deaconesses that they do not serve their families, but the alien. Their service is one among the abandoned, the weak, and the helpless.

48 *Innere Mission im allgemeinen, GW* IV: 183.

49 Löhe lifted up the gifts of spiritual care in the case of at least one deacon. Although Sister Pauline Haag was gifted in practical matters and was a good teacher, Löhe pointed to her spiritual care for others as especially noteworthy. See Löhe, "Schwester Pauline Christine Friederike Haag, geb. zu Feuerbach, Badischen Bezirksamts Lörrach, am 24. Juni 1834, gestorben im fürstlichen Schloß zu Budingen am 20. Dezember 1863," *GW* IV: 372.

50 In "Schwester Cäcilie ruhe im Frieden und das ewige Licht leuchte ihr! Amen," *GW* IV: 387, Löhe cited the example of Sister Cäcilie von Zeschau who, he reported, knew that the ordained ministry could not by itself attend to the tasks of the church's ministry and mission. Regarding Löhe's understanding of the relationship of the *Amt* to the diaconate (as well as to laity), see Ganzert, *Vom Heiligtum her*, 20.

51 Löhe, "Das zehnte Jahr der Diakonissenanstalt Neuendettelsau," *GW* IV: 419; quote also cited in Deinzer, III: 279.

52 Löhe, "Von den Diakonissen," *GW* IV: 450. This consecration or ordination is grounded in apostolic teaching, Löhe said. However, it does not have the same weight or value as the ordination of a presbyter or pastor ("Die Einsegnung der in ihren Wirkungskreis abgehenden Diakonissen in Neuendettelsau," *GW* IV: 347).

53 See "Bedenken über weibliche Diakonie innerhalb der protestantischen Kirche Bayerns, insonderheit über zu errichtende Diakonissenanstalten," *GW* IV: 272–73, for the motivations for the establishment of the *Lutherischer Verein für weibliche Diakonie*.

54 Training women for the diaconate was a pressing need for the church; see "Bedenken über weibliche Diakonie," *GW* IV: 272. In "Rede bei einer Schwestern-Einsegnung," *GW* IV: 550, Löhe mentioned that the deaconess association provided a means for unmarried women to become established in a vocation.

55 "Statuten: Lutherischer Verein für weibliche Diakonie," *Correspondenzblatt* 5 (1854): 15.

56 Deinzer, III: 327–28. Löhe contrasted this vision with that of the Missourians and the "Old Lutherans": "If one wants to know, what we really want (with our ecclesial efforts) then one must look at the deaconess houses, only one must not think only of the sisters. We want an apostolic-episcopal church. Lutheranism is not partisan. We are, to the depths of our souls, Lutheran in the sacraments and the doctrine of justification. . . . What we want is a continuation of Lutheranism to a apostolic-episcopal church."

57 *Etwas aus der Geschichte*, *GW* IV: 260.

58 "Bedenken über weibliche Diakonie," *GW* IV: 273; also "Statuten," *Correspondenzblatt* 5 (1854): 15.

59 *Etwas aus der Geschichte*, *GW* IV: 262. In "Die bisherigen Satzungen der Diakonissenanstalt Neuendettelsau," *GW* IV: 342, the stated goal is the education of women for service to minors and suffering humanity, especially of teachers for primary schools and of nurses in families and hospices. Löhe also mentioned this goal in "An die ausgesegneten Diakonissen," *GW* IV: 443.

60 *Correspondenzblatt* 8 (1857): 3–4.

61 *Correspondenzblatt* 8 (1857): 3–4.

62 The chronicles contained in the *Correspondenzblatt* are full of such reports. For more, see the sections titled "Aus der Chronik des Diakonissenhauses in Neuendettelsau" scattered throughout the issues of *Correspondenzblatt*.

63 "Die Diakonissenanstalt in Neuendettelsau," *Correspondenzblatt* 5 (1854): 22. Education seems to have taken on an increasingly important role for the deaconesses: "The school for the education of school teachers serves . . . to be able to provide German schoolteachers." See "Vierter Bericht über den Bestand und Fortgang der Diakonissenanstalt zu Neuendettelsau," *Correspondenzblatt* 9 (1858): 8.

64 "Small Catechism," in *BC*, 343. Luther expands on this in his explanation to the Fifth Commandment in the Large Catechism by referring to Matt 5:20–26 and Matt 25:31–46: "This commandment is violated not only when a person actually does evil, but also when he fails to do good to his neighbor, or, though he has the opportunity, fails to prevent, protect, and save him from suffering bodily harm or injury. If you send a person away naked when you could clothe him, you have let him freeze to death. If you see anyone suffer hunger and do not feed him, you have let him starve. Likewise, if you see anyone condemned to death or in similar peril and do not save him although you know ways and means to do so, you have killed him. It will do you no good to plead that you did not contribute to his death by word or deed, for you have withheld your love from him and robbed him of the service by which his life might have been saved.

"Therefore God rightly calls all persons murderers who do not offer counsel and aid to men in need and in peril of body and life" ("Large Catechism," in *BC*, 390–91; see also "Lectures on Galatians (1535)," *LW* 27: 58–59).

65 "Die bisherigen Satzungen," *GW* IV: 342.

66 "Vierter Bericht," *Correspondenzblatt* 9 (1858): 9. In *Etwas aus der Geschichte*, *GW* IV: 326, it was reported that the worship life in the deaconess house in Neuendettelsau consisted of Sunday morning worship, daily worship services, Matins worship on Thursdays, and evening devotions.

67 "Dettelsauer Leben," *GW* IV: 401.

68 "Von der seligen Übung der Barmherzigkeit," *GW* IV: 464.

69 "Die Wohltätigkeitsanstalten von Dettelsau," *GW* IV: 417.

70 "Die Wohltätigkeitsanstalten von Dettelsau," *GW* IV: 417.

71 "Niederlassungen," *GW* IV: 176.

72 Löhe was clearly disturbed that hundreds (more likely thousands) of German Lutherans fell away from the Lutheran faith in North America. He never ceased to puzzle over the situation ("Wirksamkeit der Gesellschaft durch Kolonisation," *GW* IV: 190).

73 In "Brief an Hornung" (13 March 1843), *GW* IV: 624, Löhe wrote that the North Americans' need for help was what moved him most.

74 In *Die Heidenmission*, *GW* IV: 111, Löhe suggested that the unity of inner and outer mission has to do with strong inner mission at the core which makes the outer known.

75 Bauer, "Die Missionsanstalt in Neuendettelsau im Jahre 1855/56," *Kirchliche Mittheilungen* 14 (1856): nos. 1 and 2: 2–3.

76 Deinzer, I: 58.

77 Löhe, "Brief an Ch. Ph. H. Brandt" (12 July 1827), *GW* I: 258. His brief letter is revealing for his enthusiasm and eagerness for mission.

78 Mark U. Edwards Jr., *Printing, Propaganda, and Martin Luther* (Berkeley: University of California Press, 1994), 15.

79 Wilhelm Löhe, "Religiöse Schriften zur Unterstützung der Seelsorge: Ein Bericht," *GW* III/1: 136; hereafter "Religiöse Schriften."

80 "Religiöse Schriften," *GW* III/1: 136. Löhe goes on to exclaim how effective they were.

81 Wilhelm Löhe, "Brief an Cph. K. Hornung" (23 July 1842), *GW* I: 607.

82 Ganzert, "Erläuterungen," *GW* III/1: 612–13.

83 *Three Books*, 71.

84 *Rechenschaftsbericht*, *GW* IV: 146.

85 "Religiöse Schriften," *GW* III/1: 137; see also Ganzert, *Vom Heiligtum her*, 9–10, and for a fuller discussion, Dietrich Blaufuß, "Wilhelm Löhe und die 'Alten Tröster': Zur Wirkung barocker Erbauungsliteratur im 19. Jahrhundert," *Zeitschrift für bayerische Kirchengeschichte* 59 (1990): 153–58.

86 Wilhelm Löhe, "Vom christlichen Hausgottesdienste," *GW* III/1: 42–57. Regarding "Hülfsmittel zum täglichen Bibellesen," see "Religiöse Schriften," *GW* III/1: 137; and Ganzert, "Erläuterungen," *GW* III/1: 615.

87 "Das Krankenwesen," *GW* IV: 439.

88 August Hermann Francke, "Projekt zu einem Seminario universali, 1701," in *August Hermann Francke: Werke in Auswahl* (ed. Erhard Peschke; Berlin: Luther-Verlag, 1969), 108, spoke of a "real improvement in all social classes both inside and outside Germany, indeed in Europe and all parts of the world." Löhe spoke admiringly of the contributions of Francke and Philipp Jakob Spener. The influence of Francke, Löhe ("Von der Barmherzigkeit," *GW* IV: 517) said, could still be felt in the nineteenth century.

89 "Von der Barmherzigkeit," *GW* IV: 519.

90 For example, Löhe was unwilling to make admission into the deaconess association binding (deaconesses were unmarried). A deaconess could leave the associa-

tion at any time if she wanted to marry or for any other reason. See Löhe, "An die Schwestern und Probeschwestern," *GW* IV: 531; and Löhe, "Rede bei einer Schwestern-Einsegnung," *GW* IV: 552–53.

91 *Von der Barmherzigkeit*, *GW* IV: 519.

92 "Erklärung," *Kirchliche Mittheilung* 12 (1855): no. 5: 39.

93 Löhe, "Brief an Jakob Schmidt" (22 October 1845), *GW* I: 714.

94 Braaten, *The Flaming Center*, 33.

7

SIGNIFICANCE AND ASSESSMENT

The past decades have witnessed numerous attempts to assess the significance of Wilhelm Löhe from a *historical* perspective. Fewer are the attempts to assess the *theological* significance of Löhe and his thought. Moreover, these efforts have all been focused on the sphere of practical theology—pastoral care, diaconal service, and liturgical studies—or mission. I believe that Löhe's accomplishments as a church leader and practical theologian are important and ought not to be overlooked. At the same time I am convinced that Löhe's life and writings are of theological import as well, that he ought not to be simply dismissed as one who merely repristinated and replicated other ideas and traditions. To be sure, he relied on the theological traditions that he received, but this is the task of every theologian and pastor. Yet Löhe shaped these ideas in new, creative, and innovative ways. The preceding pages represent my attempt to systematize his rich and complex thought.

Löhe's theology, I argue, reveals a marked similarity to the so-called "evangelical catholic" movement which in recent years has come to some prominence in North America. As with many labels, "evangelical catholic" is difficult to define completely. The movement has neither an acknowledged leader nor a manifesto; no single individual defines and embodies the vision of what it means to be evangelical catholic. No one person has established the evangelical catholic agenda or written the charter document.

Nonetheless, some broad contours are apparent. The evangelical catholic movement is a broadly ecumenical movement, that is, its principles and theology are espoused by theologians of many Protestant stripes.[1] In many respects evangelical catholicism is most apparent and strongest within Lutheranism. While an exhaustive description of evangelical catholicism is not possible, I suggest that among its main themes and goals are three overarching motifs: liturgy and the sacraments; continuity and communion; and ecumenism and catholicity.

Catholicity is perhaps the most important motif. Catholicity has to do with unity and universality—the unity and universality of the church. How is the church one and universal? Oliver Olson maintains that it means "what has always been taught."[2] Unity and universality is to be found "in Word and Sacrament, that is to say in fundamental doctrine and practice."[3] Catholicity is attained in two spheres: liturgy and doctrine.

Regarding liturgy, liturgical *unity* is a primary goal here. Leonard Klein has written, "Whatever else it is, evangelical catholicism is a liturgical movement."[4] It is a movement that seeks a common worship among all Christians. Closely linked to this desire for common worship is a desire for worship centered in the sacraments. The regular—weekly—celebration of the Lord's Supper is often seen as a visible sign of a common liturgical life.

The third of the triad of evangelical catholic themes is communion and continuity. *Communion* may refer to the fellowship experienced in the Lord's Supper, to the communion of the church, or to both. In other words, communion is a *liturgical* communion, a *doctrinal* communion, or both. In the first case communion is about unity in worship; in the second, it is about unity in doctrine. Thus evangelical catholics can speak of "continuity with the church throughout the ages manifested in commitment to the apostolic Scriptures, creeds, sacraments, and ministries."[5] Communion is seen as an organic whole.

Continuity is necessary for communion. Evangelical catholicism "points to a church that wants to remain faithful to the Reformation and at the same time affirm immense riches of the catholic tradition both East and West."[6] It wants to be in continuity with the entire tradition of the Christian church.

This desire to be in continuity leads one to the partner of catholicity: ecumenism. To be in continuity and communion with the catholic church is to seek partnerships with those who adhere to the same doctrine and with those whose worship life is also centered in the sacraments. Thus Klaus Penzel speaks of an "ecumenical Lutheran confessionalism."[7] The confessions seek to root the Lutheran church in the broader catholic church. Evangelical catholics endeavor to realize this catholicity in worship and doctrine.

Hardly any of those who call themselves "evangelical catholics" express an obvious concern for order. Yet I submit that they do. Leonard Klein speaks about a ministry that is "ordered."[8] Within a church that seeks a common witness in worship and doctrine, order is necessarily in the background.

These broad themes are readily apparent in Löhe's theology and life.[9] In the following pages, I want to briefly reflect on three themes in Löhe's thought which, I believe, he shares with the modern evangelical catholic movement: order, catholicity, and ecumenism. Löhe anticipated the twentieth century in his thinking on these three themes.

ORDER

The idea of order (*Ordnung*) represents a strong undercurrent in Löhe's theology. In the midst of a chaotic and turbulent time, Löhe seeks order. In his words, "God is a God of order: he has ordered the stars and everything else according to his divine ideas. And this God, who has created such great things, who has founded an order of salvation [*Heilsordnung*], who looks upon the small, rejoices; and the heavens shine when you do what you ought to do."[10] Two issues are apparent: first, God is a God of order; second, Christians are called to do that which contributes to the divine order.

A central feature of this divine order is peace. With order comes peace; with disorder there is no peace. If Christians want peace, they must maintain order.[11] The community that Löhe envisioned, the community gathered around the Table of the Lord in peace and harmony, must be characterized by order. This order recognizes the different gifts that each member brings but also seeks to channel these gifts so disorder—and, therefore, strife—is held at bay.

Löhe's desire for order links him to Romanticism and to a social philosophy espoused by many Romantic thinkers. Walter Conser notes that "confessional social philosophy recognized the existence and importance of the individual, but placed that individual within a framework of duties, expectations, specific times, places, and persons."[12] Löhe's ecclesiology is clearly situated within this worldview; he centered the church in the community of those gathered at the eucharistic table.

CATHOLICITY

A recurring theme throughout Löhe's theology, especially after 1848, is *catholicity*. This catholicity was not affiliation with Rome, but a sense of the larger church that traced its doctrine and life to the apostles. In the concluding comments to his 1856 lecture "*Das Verhältnis der Gesellschaft für innere Mission im Sinne der lutherischen Kirche zum Zentralmissionverein in Bayern*" ["The Relationship of the Society for Inner Mission in the Sense of the Lutheran Church to the Central Mission Association in Bavaria"], Löhe said:

> If we [the two organizations] were to go together, then our blessings would be doubled, our work on this side and on the other side of the ocean would bloom more mightily. And with true loyalty to God and his holy Word, nobody would seriously make the accusation against us on account of our heartfelt local amalgamation [in Bavaria] that we have denied the catholicity of the Lutheran church.[13]

A catholic Lutheran church, that is to say a Lutheran church united in doctrine and ministry, was an integral part of Löhe's ecclesiology and vision.

Catholicity—unity—is an important theme in Löhe's theology. Although he never addressed the question of catholicity in an essay or article, it was always present in his thinking. To be catholic is to have a view of the whole church. It is not to be set over and against "Lutheran." In a short essay titled *"Warum bekenne ich mich zur lutherischen Kirche?"* ["Why Do I Confess the Lutheran Church?"], Löhe wrote, "I will not be ashamed of [Luther's] name so long as I can call myself—without being misunderstood—what I truly am: a catholic Christian in the true and correct understanding of the word."[14] A true and correct understanding of *catholic* did not confuse the word with the pope and his church but identified "the catholic church" as the one church of Christ united in the apostolic Word.

Löhe was *not* an ecumenist in the contemporary sense of the word. He was an ecumenist who was quite aware of the tradition in which he stood. He understood himself as a Lutheran. His self-understanding was, in many ways, very narrow. But it is from this particular understanding, this unshakable certainty of the pureness of the Lutheran confessions and doctrine, that he could claim to be catholic: "What is more beautiful, more delightful, more powerful and lively than Luther's catechisms? What is more catholic than the Augsburg Confession and its Apology? What is more thoughtful and steadfast than the Smalcald Articles?"[15] There is no doubting Löhe's confessionalism, yet at the same time his confessional moorings provided the foundation for his catholicity.

ECUMENISM

Löhe is commonly portrayed as a hardheaded confessional Lutheran. This characterization is only partly true. Certainly Löhe insisted on adherence to the Lutheran confessions, but the Scriptures and the writings of the early church were of equal—even greater—importance. His personal and professional life suggest that he was more open to the possibility of ecumenical dialogue than might be initially supposed.[16] In the nineteenth century there was nothing like the ecumenical dialogues that occur today between the Lutheran and Roman Catholic churches and between the Lutheran and Reformed churches. Löhe's personal contacts with those in other confessions was a particularly innovative step on his part. Löhe named Christian Krafft, a professor of Reformed theology at Erlangen, as the professor who had the greatest impact on him as a student. Moreover, Löhe maintained relationships with neighboring Roman Catholic priests and was willing to borrow the best of their tradition.[17] Much of his liturgical thinking was influenced by his reading of Roman Catholic thinkers, and his desire to observe the commemorations of the saints and of Mary points to his willingness to learn from other Christian traditions.[18] He could reach out to other traditions and borrow from them even as he remained firmly Lutheran.

Löhe also encouraged deacons to explore other traditions. Such exploration, he was convinced, could only strengthen the Lutheran church. He wrote to the students of the deaconess house at Neuendettelsau that "the deaconess cannot avoid exploring the writings of other denominations in detail, this is why she should be so fast in the divine truth: so that she can recognize the good of all denominations and so that she and her church can learn something [from them] without being drawn to the errors of others."[19] Simply because something did not originate in Luther and his followers did not mean that it could not be used to great effect in the Lutheran church. An important theme in ecumenism is "the perception that in exploring together the shared foundations which make Christians one, we learn from each other and find new ways of expressing the fullness of Christian faith and life."[20] Löhe was not afraid to mine other denominations for nuggets that illuminate the apostolic faith.

It was Löhe's strict confessionalism that enabled him to look beyond the parochialism of Lutheranism. The Lutheran churches are one, he said, because "they have universally accepted and valid confessions."[21] This unity allows the Lutheran church to speak with one voice. The various Lutheran congregations had a common doctrine to which they appealed. They had a common vision that allowed them to establish clear boundaries in their relationships with other denominations.

Löhe was persuaded that this common confession enabled the Lutheran church to positively influence other denominations. He contended that the Lutheran church in North American had an impact on other churches there. They could be called "Lutheranizing churches." Lutheran doctrine had also penetrated the Reformed churches in Germany;

even the Roman church was indebted to the Reformation.[22] The Lutheran church in being Lutheran was ecumenical. It contributed to the growth and progress in other denominations in their understanding of the truth.

Löhe was not against ecumenical conversations or pulpit and altar fellowship. To suggest this is to misrepresent his position. He was, however, against a soft ecumenism, an ecumenism that set aside doctrine or interpreted a doctrine such that it was palatable to the other party. In the confessional struggles of the 1830s to the early 1850s, especially in matters of unionism in Prussia, of enforced reception of Reformed Christians at Lutheran communion rails, or of the meddling of a Roman Catholic prince in the affairs of a Lutheran church, Löhe maintained the Lutheran position on the basis of the confessions. In 1852, Löhe reported in the *Correspondenzblatt* that "two worthy brothers" had asked him if Lutherans could not agree to a union with the Reformed on the basis of the "truth and the pure doctrine of the Lutheran church." His reply was that such a union was indeed possible "but only on the basis of the truth by loyal Lutherans."[23] Löhe saw no reason to depart from the example established by Luther and the other sixteenth-century reformers.

Ecumenism was not something to be attained by negotiation. It was, rather, something to be attained on the basis of the truth of the apostolic Word. This reliance on the apostolic Word as revealed and contained in the Scriptures was an integral component of Löhe's ecumenism. Löhe did not seek out relationships with other churches, at least not in the sense of doing common ministry and mission. At the same time, his reliance on the Scriptures mirrors the method of contemporary ecumenical theology. The confessions were important, but they served to illuminate Scripture, and Löhe, as often as possible, always referred first to the scriptural witness.[24]

For Löhe, an ecumenism based on the principle that two churches could yield on a doctrine (for example, the real presence of Christ in the Lord's Supper) was not a unity worth having. It was a unity based on a falsehood and, therefore, could not endure. Only a unity founded on truth endures. The apostles showed that unity must be based not only on faith and knowledge, but also on Word and confession.[25] Only the truth of the apostolic Word can serve as an adequate basis for ecumenical unity.

Lutheranism, as Löhe saw it, was clear and definite. The Lutheran church and its doctrine was defined by the confessions contained in the *Book of Concord*. He knew what Lutheranism was and he could communicate it to others. More problematic was what the Reformed church was. Which confessional statement—or statements—defines and shapes the doctrine of the Reformed church? The Westminster Confession? The Heidelberg Catechism? The Dordrecht Confession? There was no single confessional statement or collection of statements that any Reformed church could point to as binding upon *all* Reformed churches. In this respect, the Lutheran church was comprehensible and the Reformed church was *in*comprehensible. To enter into any kind of union or pulpit and altar fellowship with the Reformed would be to enter into a relationship with an unknown partner. Löhe expressed his reluctance to such a relationship, noting that "we Lutherans all over the world have common symbols [confessions]. Everybody can see in the symbols what we must teach and do in the life of the church now and through the ages. The Reformed, on the other hand, have never had a common confession of faith."[26] If any kind of ecumenical partnership is to occur, then the two churches must know who the other is. For Löhe, it is impossible to know the Reformed and their doctrine.

The type of ecumenism that minimizes or ignores doctrine so churches might worship together is equally impotent. To worship God is to confess corporately a certain vision and understanding of God. Luther understood God to be ultimately a God of grace, a God who forgives sinners and names them righteous in the face of their unrighteousness. Human beings are justified by faith. Luther's confession stood opposed to the Roman Catholic assertion that one could work out one's salvation by being righteous. These things matter, said Löhe. Do we worship because by worshiping we gain a seat in heaven? Or do we worship simply to give thanks to a merciful God? If Lutherans are to worship with the Reformed, then they must agree about the nature and purpose of worship and especially the sacraments. To agree to worship in common without settling these doctrinal questions is to overlook them; it is to forge and declare a partnership without genuine agreement.[27] Löhe warned against this kind of ecumenism that was indifferent to history and doctrine.

A partnership of any kind is a relationship of love. Inseparable from love is truth. In this indifferent type of ecumenism, truth is lacking. As Löhe said, "Truth in love, love in truth—this is lacking here. But it is not missing there where one—with a hand on the Word, under the sunshine of truth, with fervent love—wants to lead the soul from error to truth."[28] An outer or superficial ecumenism will not lead to the community that possesses the peace "which surpasses all understanding" (Phil 4:7). To be sure, this is a tough kind of ecumenism, a "hard" ecumenism. It is an ecumenism that seeks partnership only on its own terms.[29] One does not (or ought not) enter into a partnership without determining who the parties are and what they stand for.

In this connection Löhe repeatedly called for Lutherans to rediscover their roots. In the *Correspondenzblatt* he wrote that "pastors and laity . . . learned anew what is Lutheran and what is Reformed."[30] This is also an important motivation for his "Vorschlag zu einem Lutherischen Verein für apostolisches Leben" ["Proposal for a Lutheran Association for Apostolic Life"].[31] Congregations and pastors need to call the church back to its Lutheran roots so it can be genuinely Christian and apostolic. Identity is important. Identity makes community and partnership in ministry—ecumenism—possible.

CONCLUSION

Löhe cannot be dismissed as a simple country pastor who repristinated the theology of Lutheran Orthodoxy. His theology, as reflected in his thinking on mission and ministry, was certainly unique in the nineteenth century and anticipated the concerns of the evangelical catholicism in our day. While his ecumenism was nothing like the ecumenical vision of twentieth-century Lutheran evangelical catholics, his vision was nonetheless ecumenical. More than that, he had a vision of the universal church, a church that extended to all peoples, to all corners of the earth. Löhe was both evangelical and catholic.

Löhe, as Georg Merz correctly writes, was "a promoter of missionary activity, a path breaker of liturgical renewal, and one of the fathers of diaconal ministry in the nineteenth century."[32] His vision was as broad and encompassing as the new Jerusalem depicted in Revelation 21. He was evangelical in that he was truly concerned to preach the Gospel of grace; he was catholic in that he sought to proclaim this Gospel to the ends of the earth, to make it the center of the church.

Löhe's vision was ecclesial. He was less concerned with evangelization in and of itself, with diaconal service in and of itself, or even with churches and congregations in and of themselves. He envisioned a community bound together in faith and love. In a word, he envisioned the church in its fullness. As Hans Lauerer noted in a booklet published on the occasion of the centennial anniversary of the deaconess house in Neuendettelsau, Löhe sought "to build the Lutheran Church, to preserve and create church unity and customs [*Gewöhnung*]."[33] In this Löhe succeeded far beyond his original vision. Löhe once described a priestly person, that is a person who lived out the Christian faith, as "a holy witness to the world and before the brethren."[34] Löhe was—and is—such a witness.

NOTES

1   I consciously say "Protestant" because the Roman Catholic Church (and the Eastern Orthodox Church) already understand themselves as "catholic" or universal. The evangelical catholic movement is largely about reclaiming catholicity. As such, it is strongest in those churches nearest the Roman Catholic Church, those churches that did not emerge out of the radical Reformation or are otherwise radical or extreme breakaway factions. In using the words "radical" and "extreme," I do not intend in any way to denigrate these churches, but only to point out that these churches were often sectarian in nature and sought a complete break with a predominant church which they saw as beyond reform.

2   Oliver K. Olson, "How to Be Evangelical and Catholic," *Lutheran Forum* 26 (Pentecost 1992): 58.

3   Leonard R. Klein, "An Unbearable Lightness of Being," *Lutheran Forum* 28 (Reformation 1994): 5.

4   Leonard R. Klein, "Evangelical Catholic: 'Why Are You Guys So Negative?' II," *Lutheran Forum* 28 (Advent 1994): 5; see also Leonard R. Klein, "If the Ministry Is Catholic: A View from Inside the Parish," *Dialog* 27 (1988): 34.

5   Frank C. Senn, "Lutheran Movement, but Evangelical, Catholic Church," *Dialog* 30 (1991): 249; see also Carl A. Volz, "Evangelical Catholics," *Dialog* 30 (1991): 183.

6   Richard Koenig, "The New Lutheran Church: The Gift of Augustana," *Christian Century* 104 (1987): 558.

7   Klaus Penzel, "Philip Schaff's Mercersburg Program of 'Evangelical Catholicism,' " *Lutheran Forum* 26 (Pentecost 1992): 38.

8   Klein, "If the Ministry Is Catholic," 37. Klein may well take issue with how I have equated his use of "order" with that of Löhe; nonetheless, I believe the parallels exist.

9   Consider, for example, the place of liturgy and the sacraments in the life of the church. In addition, one could name the importance of the ordained ministry as another shared concern, but this has been addressed adequately in the main body of this work.

10   "Rede des Herrn Pfarrer Löhe bei einer Schwestern-Einsegnung i.J. 1859," *GW* IV: 526.

11   Löhe writes, "An die Schwestern und Probeschwestern," *GW* IV: 532, that "disorder stands in opposition to peace, but peace is mixed with order. There is never true peace where there is no order. Order consists in order over, under and with. Whoever wants peace must maintain order, and whoever wants order must be able and willing to submit one's self to an order above, below and with. All of that is interconnected with joyful obedience."

12   Conser, *Church and Confession*, 315.

13   "Das Verhältnis," *GW* V/2: 706–07.

14   "Warum bekenne ich mich?" *GW* IV: 221.

15   "Warum bekenne ich mich?" *GW* IV: 223. Although he believed the central doc-
     trines of the Christian faith are better understood than in the Reformation era,
     Löhe maintained that the divisions could not be overcome so simply; see Löhe,
     "An meine Freunde in Neuendettelsau," *GW* V/2: 748–49.

16   See Sihvonen, "Wer sein will, der muß werden," 456; and Merz, *Das bayerische
     Luthertum*, 25. As early as 1825, Löhe reported that he visited a Roman Catholic
     Mass. On September 8, 1825, the Feast of the Birth of Mary, Löhe went to Mass
     in the Bamberg cathedral. He wrote in his diary, *GW* II: 550, that "the sermon—
     what I understood—seemed good to me."

17   Already in 1838, at the beginning of his ministry in Neuendettelsau, Löhe could
     claim a "friendly relationship" with the neighboring Roman Catholic priest and
     indicated that he had been present at some services of that priest. See "Brief an
     das Königliche Dekanat" (16 May 1838), *GW* V/1: 63; as well as Friedrich
     Wilhelm Kantzenbach, *Zwischen Erweckung und Restauration* (Gladbeck:
     Schriftenmissions-Verlag, 1967), 44.

18   Löhe thought it was important to commemorate all the saints of the church and
     read Roman Catholic literature in his endeavor to learn more about the saints. See
     "Von Benutzung des Heiligenkalenders für das eigene Leben," *GW* IV: 425–28,
     esp. 427. The foreword to the second edition of the *Agende* is also instructive in
     this respect, *GW* VII/1: 21–22.

19   "Von der Barmherzigkeit," *GW* IV: 520.

20   Michael Root, "Ecumenical Theology," in *The Modern Theologians: An Introduction
     to Christian Theology in the Twentieth Century* (2d ed.; ed. David F. Ford; Oxford:
     Blackwell, 1997), 538; see also Ted Peters, *God—the World's Future*, ix.
     Kantzenbach, *Zwischen Erweckung und Restauration*, 45, wrote in this respect that
     "the willingness to learn from others who think differently is certainly the basic
     presupposition for every ecumenical effort."

21   "Warum bekenne ich mich?" *GW* IV: 225.

22   "Warum bekenne ich mich?" *GW* IV: 226.

23   Löhe, "Von Vereinigung der Lutheraner und Reformierten auf Grund der
     Wahrheit," *GW* V/1: 614; hereafter "Vereinigung."

24   On this point, The Lutheran Church—Missouri Synod notes that because biblical
     language is subject to interpretation, theologians have turned to dogmatic formu-
     lations to handle the misunderstandings or lack of agreement regarding biblical
     language. See "Lutheran Church—Missouri Synod," in *Churches Respond to BEM:
     Official Responses to the "Baptism, Eucharist and Ministry Text*, vol. 3 (ed. Max
     Thurian; Geneva: World Council of Churches, 1987), 132.

25   This assertion, *GW* V/2: 985, is in a revised edition of "Vorschlag."

26   "Vereinigung," *GW* V/1: 616.

27   "Vereinigung," *GW* V/1: 619.

28   "Vereinigung," *GW* V/1: 619.

29   In "Vereinigung," *GW* V/1: 619–20, Löhe stated that he was ready to receive the
     Reformed into shared ministry if they agreed to subscribe to the Lutheran confes-
     sions. It was union on Lutheran confessional terms.

30   "Vereinigung," *GW* V/1: 621.

31   See "Vorschlag," *GW* V/1: 213–25 passim, esp. 220.

32 Merz, *Das bayerische Luthertum*, 26.

33 Hans Lauerer, *Die Diakonissenanstalt Neuendettelsau aus Geschichte und Gegenwart* (Neuendettelsau: Verlag der Buchhandlung der Diakonissenanstalt, 1924), 8.

34 "Unsere Lage," *GW* V/1: 462.

BIBLIOGRAPHY

PRIMARY LITERATURE

The following literature which has no author indicated can probably be assumed to be from the hand of Löhe. The literature which lists Löhe or somebody else as the author can be assumed to be from the hand of the author indicated.

"An den Präses der deutschen evangelisch-lutherischen Synode von Missouri, Ohio und andern Staaten, Herrn Karl Ferdinand Wilhelm Walther zu St. Louis, Mo." *Kirchliche Mittheilungen aus und über Nord-Amerika* 6 no. 6 (1848): cols. 43–45.

"Aus der von Pfarrer Löhe am Jubiläum der amerikanischen Mission gehaltenen Festpredigt." *Correspondenzblatt der Gesellschaft für innere Mission nach dem Sinne der lutherische Kirche* 17 (1866): 40–44.

Bauer, Friedrich. "Jahresbericht über die Missionsanstalt in Neuendettelsau für das Schuljahr vom 1. Nov. 1859 bis 15. Oct. 1860." *Correspondenzblatt der Gesellschaft für innere Mission nach dem Sinne der lutherischen Kirche* 11 (1861): 15–17; 19–20.

Bauer, Friedrich. "Jahresbericht über die Missionsanstalt in Neuendettelsau für das Winter- und Sommersemester v. 1. Nov. 1858 bis 15. Oct. 1859." *Correspondenzblatt der Gesellschaft für innere Mission nach dem Sinne der lutherischen Kirche* 10 (1859): 39–42.

Bauer, Friedrich. "Die Missionsanstalt in Neuendettelsau im Jahre 1855/56." *Kirchliche Mittheilungen aus und über Nord-Amerika* 14 nos. 1 and 2 (1856): cols. 2–3.

"Bedenken über weibliche Diakonie innerhalb der protestantischen Kirche Bayerns, insonderheit über zu errichtende Diakonissenanstalten." In *GW* IV: 272–76.

"*Bericht über die Missionsanstalt in Neuendettelsau im 21.* Jahre ihres Bestehens vom 1. November 1861 bis 1. November 1862." *Kirchliche Mittheilungen aus und über Nord-Amerika* 21 (1863): 25–29.

"Die bisherige Satzungen der Diakonissenanstalt Neuendettelsau." In *GW* IV: 342–47.

Deinzer, Johannes. *Wilhelm Löhes Leben: Aus seinem schriftlichen Nachlaß zusammengestellt.* 4th ed. 3 vols. Neuendettelsau: Freimund-Verlag, 1935.

"Die Diakonissenanstalt in Neuendettelsau." *Correspondenzblatt der Gesellschaft für innere Mission nach dem Sinne der lutherischen Kirche* 5 (1854): 21–22.

"Die Einsegnung der in ihren Wirkungskreis abgehenden Diakonissen in Neuendettelsau." In *GW* IV: 347–50.

"Die Gesellschaft für innere Mission im Sinne der lutherischen Kirche am Anfang des Jahres 1855." *Correspondenzblatt der Gesellschaft für innere Mission nach dem Sinne der lutherische Kirche* 6 (1855): 2–5.

"Hervorgerufene Erklärung über die Tätigkeit der Neuendettelsauer Missionschule für Heidenmission und über die Verbindung unserer Thätigkeit in Nord-Amerika mit der Heidenmission." *Kirchliche Mittheilungen aus und über Nord-Amerika* 13 no. 5 (1855): cols. 37–41.

Löhe, Wilhelm. *Agende für christliche Gemeinden des lutherischen Bekenntnisses.* In *GW* VII/1: 5–487.

Löhe, Wilhelm. "An die ausgesegneten Diakonissen." In *GW* IV: 443–46.

Löhe, Wilhelm. "An die Schwestern und Probeschwestern." In *GW* IV: 527–36.

Löhe, Wilhelm. *An meine Freunde in Neuendettelsau.* In *GW* V/2: 747–57.

Löhe, Wilhelm. "Den Abgang mehrerer Zöglinge der hiesigen Missionanstalt im nächsten Frühjahr betreffend." *Correspondenzblatt der Gesellschaft für innere Mission nach dem Sinne der lutherische Kirche* 10 (1860): 40.

Löhe, Wilhelm. *Ansprache an die Brüder in Sachen der Judenmission.* In *GW* IV: 250–56.

Löhe, Wilhelm. "Ansprache, betreffend die Sammlung von Natural- und anderen freien Gaben für die Neuendettelsauer Anstalten." In *GW* IV: 351–53.

Löhe, Wilhelm. *Aphorismen über die neutestamentlichen Ämter und ihr Verhältnis zur Gemeinde: Zur Verfassungsfrage der Kirche.* In *GW* V/1: 253–330.

Löhe, Wilhelm. "Auszug aus der Instruction des für Columbus bestimmten deutschen Schullehrers P. J. Baumgart." *Kirchliche Mittheilungen aus und über Nord-Amerika* 1 no. 8 (1843): cols. 1–8.

Löhe, Wilhelm. "Die bayerische Generalsynode vom Frühjahr 1849 und das lutherische Bekenntnis: Eine Beleuchtung der Synodalbeschlüsse in Betreff der Petition Wahrung des Bekenntnisses und Einführung desselben in seine Rechte usw." In *GW* V/1: 333–68.

Löhe, Wilhelm. "Brief an das Dekanat (24. Februar 1840)." In *GW* V/1: 70–74.

Löhe, Wilhelm. "Brief an das Königliche Dekanat (16. Mai 1838)." In *GW* V/1: 61–65.

Löhe, Wilhelm. "Dettelsauer Leben." In *GW* IV: 400–03.

Löhe, Wilhelm. "Einige Worte über Herrn Prof. Delitzsch's neueste Schrift betreffend die 'bayerische Abendmahlsgemeinschaftsfrage.'" In *GW* V/1: 632–36.

Löhe, Wilhelm. "Die englisch-lutherische Kirche in Nord-Amerika." *Kirchliche Mittheilungen aus und über Nord-Amerika* 1 no. 7 (1843): cols. 6–8.

Löhe, Wilhelm. *Erinnerungen aus der Reformationsgeschichte von Franken, insonderheit der Stadt und dem Burggraftum Nürnberg ober- und unterhalb des Gebirgs.* In *GW* III/2: 523–681.

Löhe, Wilhelm. *Etwas aus der Geschichte des Diakonissenhauses Neuendettelsau.* In *GW* IV: 259–341.

Löhe, Wilhelm. *Etwas über die deutsch-lutherischen Niederlassungen in der Grafschaft Saginaw, Staat Michigan.* In *GW* IV: 162–78.

Löhe, Wilhelm. *Gesammelte Werke.* 7 vols. Edited by Klaus Ganzert. Neuendettelsau: Freimund-Verlag, 1951–86.

Löhe, Wilhelm. "Die Gesellschaft für innere Mission im Sinne der lutherischen Kirche und ihre Verhältnisse zu Nordamerika." *Kirchliche Mittheilungen aus und über Nord-Amerika* 17 (1859): cols. 57–63, 65–67.

Löhe, Wilhelm. "Glück Auf!" *Kirchliche Mittheilungen aus und über Nord-Amerika* 3 no. 5 (1845): cols. 1–5.

Löhe, Wilhelm. *Gutachten in Sachen der Abendmahlsgemeinschaft: Vor einigen Freunden gelesen.* In *GW* V/2: 882–908.

Löhe, Wilhelm. *Hausbedarf christlicher Gebete für Augsburgische Konfessionsverwandte.* In *GW* VII/2: 9–164.

Löhe, Wilhelm. *Die Heidenmission in Nordamerika: Ein Vortrag in der General-versammlung des protestantischen Zentralmissionsvereins zu Nürnberg den 2. Juli 1846*. In *GW* IV: 102–12.

Löhe, Wilhelm. *Innere Mission im allgemeinen*. In *GW* IV: 178–88.

Löhe, Wilhelm. *Kirche und Amt: Neue Aphorismen*. In *GW* V/1: 523–88.

Löhe, Wilhelm. "Kirche und Mission." In *GW* IV: 626–28.

Löhe, Wilhelm. "Kirchliche Briefe." In *GW* V/2: 843–65.

Löhe, Wilhelm. "Das Krankenwesen der Diakonissenanstalt." In *GW* IV: 434–40.

Löhe, Wilhelm. "Lebenslauf der Jungfrau Karoline Rheineck, 1. Vorsteherin des Diakonissenhauses zu Neuendettelsau: Gelesen bei der Beerdigung am 23. August 1855." In *GW* IV: 355–60.

Löhe, Wilhelm. "Die lutherischen Auswanderer in Nordamerika: Eine Ansprache an die Leser des Sonntagsblattes." In *GW* IV: 16–19.

Löhe, Wilhelm. *Die Mission unter den Heiden: Zwei Gespräche zur Belehrung des Volks geschrieben*. In *GW* IV: 20–58.

Löhe, Wilhelm. "Mitteilung der Windsbacher Predigerkonferenz (am 7. November 1837): Vom Abendmahlsgenuß." In *GW* V/1: 47–60.

Löhe, Wilhelm "Nach Bekanntwerden der Krankenölung (Ende 1857–Frühjahr 1859)." In *GW* V/2: 719–43.

Löhe, Wilhelm. "Die neuen Boten: Georg Wilhelm Hattstädt." *Kirchliche Mittheilungen aus und über Nord-Amerika* 2 no. 6 (1844): cols. 1–5.

Löhe, Wilhelm. "Der Nothstand der Heiden und der deutsch-lutherischen Kirche in Nord-Amerika." *Kirchliche Mittheilungen aus und über Nord-Amerika* 1 no. 3 (1843): cols. 1–5.

Löhe, Wilhelm. *Prediget das Evangelium Aller Kreatur: Predigt, am Missionsfest 1847 gehalten über Mark. 16,15*. In *GW* IV: 112–25.

Löhe, Wilhelm. "Predigt am 2. Pfingstfeiertag 1843 über Apg. 10,42." In *GW* IV: 58–68.

Löhe, Wilhelm. "Predigt am 7. Dezember 1. Korinther 11,28ff." In *GWE* I: 164–70.

Löhe, Wilhelm. "Predigt am 17. August 1. Korinther 10,15 bis 17." In *GWE* I: 55–63.

Löhe, Wilhelm. "Predigt über 2 Chron. 7:3, D.D.F. Pentecostes. 1834 (18. Mai)." In *GW* VI/1: 117–22.

Löhe, Wilhelm. "Predigt über Jer. 3,12, D.D.p. Trin. XXIII. 1834. Reformationsfest (2. Nov.)." In *GW* VI/1: 179–86.

Löhe, Wilhelm. *Prüfungstafel und Gebete für Beicht- und Abendmahlstage: Beicht- und Kommunionbüchlein für evangelische Christen (Zum Gebrauch sowohl im als außerhalb des Gotteshauses)*. In *GW* VII/2: 232–317.

Loehe, Wilhelm. *Questions and Answers to the Six Parts of the "Small Catechism" of Dr. Martin Luther*. 2d ed. Edited and translated by Edward T. Horn. Columbia, SC: W. J. Duffie, 1893; reprint, Fort Wayne, IN: Repristination Press, 1993.

Löhe, Wilhelm. *Rauchopfer für Kranke und Sterbende und deren Freunde*. In *GW* VII/2: 406–88.

Löhe, Wilhelm. *Rechenschaftsbericht der Redaktoren der kirchlichen Mitteilungen aus und über Nordamerika über das, was seit 1841 geschehen ist, samt Angabe dessen, was sofort geschehen sollte*. In *GW* IV: 126–47.

Löhe, Wilhelm. "Rede bei einer Schwestern-Einsegnung." In *GW* IV: 548–54.

Löhe, Wilhelm. "Rede des Herrn Pfarrer Löhe bei einer Schwestern-Einsegnung i.J. 1859." In *GW* IV: 524–27.

Löhe, Wilhelm. "Religiöse Schriften zur Unterstützung der Seelsorge: Ein Bericht." In *GW* III/1: 136–40.

Löhe, Wilhelm. "Schmach für die Deutschen in Nordamerika." *Kirchliche Mittheilungen aus und über Nord-Amerika* 5 no. 4 (1847): cols. 25–30.

Löhe, Wilhelm. "Schwester Cäcilie ruhe im Frieden und das ewige Licht leuchte ihr! Amen." In *GW* IV: 382–89.

Löhe, Wilhelm. "Schwester Pauline Christine Friederike Haag, geb. zu Feuerbach, Badischen Bezirksamts Lörrach, am 24. Juni 1834, gestorben im fürstlichen Schloß zu Budingen am 20. Dezember 1863." In *GW* IV: 369–73.

Löhe, Wilhelm. *Tagebuch des Missionsverein.* In *GW* IV: 9–16.

Löhe, Wilhelm. *Three Books about the Church.* Translated, edited, and with an introduction by James L. Schaaf. Philadelphia: Fortress, 1969.

Löhe, Wilhelm. "Über Betstunden." In *GW* VII/2: 521–30.

Löhe, Wilhelm. "Ueber den innern Zustand der lutherischen Kirche Nordamerikas." *Kirchliche Mittheilungen aus und über Nord-Amerika* 4 nos. 4–5 (1846): cols. 25–40.

Löhe, Wilhelm. *Unsere kirchliche Lage.* In *GW* V/1: 369–492.

Löhe, Wilhelm. "Verbindung der innern und äußern Mission betreffend." *Kirchliche Mittheilungen aus und über Nord-Amerika* 2 no. 1 (1844): cols. 1–5.

Löhe, Wilhelm. "Das Verhältnis der Gesellschaft für innere Mission im Sinne der lutherischen Kirche zum Zentralmissionsverein in Bayern." In *GW* V/2: 690–707.

Löhe, Wilhelm. *Ein Versuch, auf die deutschen Auswanderer nach Nordamerika und auf die dortige Kolonisation kirchlich einzuwirken.* In *GW* IV: 148–61.

Löhe, Wilhelm. "Eine Verteidigung." In *GW* IV: 229–35.

Löhe, Wilhlem. "Vom Schmuck der heiligen Orte." In *GW* VII/2: 557–78.

Löhe, Wilhelm. "Von Benützung des Heiligenkalenders für das eigene Leben." In *GW* IV: 425–28.

Löhe, Wilhelm. "Von den Diakonissen." In *GW* IV: 447–53.

Löhe, Wilhelm. *Von der Barmherzigkeit: Sechs Kapitel für jedermann, zuletzt ein siebentes für Dienerinnen der Barmherzigkeit.* In *GW* IV: 467–523.

Löhe, Wilhelm. *Vom christlichen Hausgottesdienst.* In *GW* III/1: 42–57.

Löhe, Wilhelm. "Von der seligen Übung der Barmherzigkeit." In *GW* IV: 462–65.

Löhe, Wilhelm. "Von der züchtigenden Liebe." In *GW* IV: 465–66.

Löhe, Wilhelm. "Von Vereinigung der Lutheraner und Reformierten auf Grund der Wahrheit." In *GW* V/1: 614–22.

Löhe, Wilhelm. *Vorschlag zu einem Lutherischen Verein für apostolisches Leben samt Entwurf eines Katechismus des apostolischen Lebens.* In *GW* V/1: 213–52.

Löhe, Wilhelm. "Warum bekenne ich mich zur lutherischen Kirche?" In *GW* IV: 221–26.

Löhe, Wilhelm. "Wirksamkeit der Gesellschaft durch Kolonisation." In *GW* IV: 188–93.

Löhe, Wilhelm. "Die Wohltätigkeitsanstalten von Dettelsau." In *GW* IV: 408–17.

Löhe, Wilhelm. "Ein Wort vom Auswandern." *Kirchliche Mittheilungen aus und über Nord-Amerika* 5 no. 1 (1847): 1–7.

Löhe, Wilhelm. "Das zehnte Jahr der Diakonissenanstalt Neuendettelsau." In *GW* IV: 417–21.

Löhe, Wilhelm. "Zum Schelwigschen Aufsatz in Nr. 12 der Mitteilungen von 1851." In *GW* IV: 193–99.

Löhe, Wilhelm. "Zur Amtsfrage." *Kirchliche Mittheilungen aus und über Nord-Amerika* 11 no. 7–8 (1853): cols. 49–60; reprinted in *GW* V/2: 1239–44.

Löhe, Wilhelm. *Zuruf aus der Heimat an die deutsch-lutherische Kirche Nordamerikas.* In *GW* IV: 68–102.

Loehe, William. *Liturgy for Christian Congregations of the Lutheran Faith.* 3d ed. Edited by J. Deinzer. Translated by F. C. Longaker with an introduction by Edward T. Horn. Newport, KY: n.p., 1902; reprint, Fort Wayne, IN: Repristination Press, 1995.

"Statuten: Lutherischer Verein für weibliche Diakonie." *Correspondenzblatt der Gesellschaft für innere Mission nach dem Sinne der lutherische Kirche* 5 (1854): 15–19.

"Der Tod zu Dettelsau." In *GW* IV: 440–42.

"Vierter Bericht über den Bestand und Fortgang der Diakonissenanstalt zu Neuendettelsau." *Correspondenzblatt der Gesellschaft für innere Mission nach dem Sinne der lutherischen Kirche* 9 (1858): 1–11, 15–16.

Wucherer, Johann Friedrich. "Jahresbericht des Obermanns der Gesellschaft für innere Mission im Sinn der lutherischen Kirche über deren Bestand und Wirksamkeit im J. 1863." *Correspondenzblatt der Gesellschaft für innere Mission nach dem Sinne der lutherischen Kirche* 15 (1864): 2–6.

Secondary Literature

Althaus, Paul. *Forschungen zur evangelischen Gebetsliteratur.* Gütersloh: Verlagshaus Gerd Mohn, 1927; reprint, Hildesheim: Georg Olms Verlagsbuchhandlung, 1966.

Althaus, Paul. *The Theology of Martin Luther.* Translated by Robert C. Schultz. Philadelphia: Fortress, 1966.

Andersen, Wilhelm, et al. eds. *Dem Wort Gehorsam: Landesbischof D. Hermann Dietzfelbinger DD. zum 65. Geburtstag.* München: Claudius Verlag, 1973.

Balthasar, Hans Urs von. *Herrlichkeit.* 3 vols. Einsiedeln: Johannes Verlag, 1961–69.

Barth, Karl. *Dogmatics in Outline.* New York: Harper & Row, 1959.

Bauer, Herbert. "*Gedanken über die Bildung.*" Pages 167–77 in *Wilhelm Löhe—Anstöße für die Zeit.* Edited by Friedrich Wilhelm Kantzenbach. Neuendettelsau: Freimund-Verlag, 1972.

Beinert, Wolfgang, and Francis Schüssler Fiorenza, eds. *Handbook of Catholic Theology.* New York: Crossroad, 1995.

Bigler, Robert M. *The Politics of German Protestantism: The Rise of the Protestant Church Elite in Prussia, 1815–1848.* Berkeley: University of California Press, 1972.

Blaufuß, Dietrich. "Wilhelm Löhe und die 'Alten Tröster': Zur Wirkung barocker Erbauungsliteratur im 19. Jahrhundert." *Zeitschrift für bayerische Kirchengeschichte* 59 (1990): 149–62.

Bonhoeffer, Dietrich. *Letters and Papers from Prison.* Enl. ed. Edited by Eberhard Bethge. New York: Macmillan, 1972; Collier Books.

Bonhoeffer, Dietrich. *Life Together.* Translated and with an introduction by John W.

Doberstein. San Francisco: Harper & Row, 1954.

Bonhoeffer, Dietrich. *The Cost of Discipleship.* New York: Macmillan, 1959; Touchstone, 1995.

Boon, Rudolf. "Child and Church, Communion and Culture." Pages 218–33 in *Omnes Circumadstantes: Contributions Towards a History of the Role of the People in the Liturgy Presented to Herman Wegman.* Edited by Charles Caspers and Marc Schneiders. Kampen, Netherlands: J. H. Kok, 1990.

Bosch, David. *Transforming Mission: Paradigm Shifts in Theology of Mission.* American Society of Missiology Series. Maryknoll, NY: Orbis Books, 1991.

Bosch, David. *Witness to the World: The Christian Mission in Theological Perspective.* Atlanta: John Knox Press, 1980.

Bosinski, Gerhard. "Wilhelm Löhe (1808–1872)." Pages 193–210 in *Wer mir dienen will.* Edited by Karl H. Neukamm. Moers: Brendow Verlag, 1985.

Braaten, Carl E. *The Apostolic Imperative: Nature and Aim of the Church's Mission and Ministry.* Minneapolis: Augsburg, 1985.

Braaten, Carl E. *The Flaming Center: A Theology of the Christian Mission.* Philadelphia: Fortress, 1977.

Braaten, Carl E. *Principles of Lutheran Theology.* Philadelphia: Fortress, 1983.

Braaten, Carl E. "Prologomena to Christian Dogmatics." Pages 5–78 in volume 1 of *Christian Dogmatics.* 2 vols. Edited by Carl E. Braaten and Robert W. Jenson. Philadelphia: Fortress, 1984.

Bria, Ion. *Go Forth in Peace: Orthodox Perspectives on Mission.* Geneva: World Council of Churches, 1986.

Bria, Ion, ed. *Martyria/Mission: The Witness of the Orthodox Churches Today.* Geneva: World Council of Churches, 1980.

Briese, Russell John. *Foundations of a Lutheran Theology of Evangelism.* Frankfurt am Main: Peter Lang, 1994.

Briese, Russell John. "Wilhelm Löhe and the Rediscovery of the Sacrament of the Altar in Nineteenth-Century Lutheranism." *Lutheran Forum* 30 (1996): 31–34.

Brueggemann, Walter. *Hopeful Imagination: Prophetic Voices in Exile.* Philadelphia: Fortress, 1986.

Brueggemann, Walter. *The Prophetic Imagination.* Philadelphia: Fortress, 1978.

Calvin, John. *Institutes of the Christian Religion.* 2 vols. Edited by John T. McNeill. Translated and indexed by Ford Lewis Battles. Philadelphia: Westminster, 1960.

Conser, Walter H., Jr. *Church and Confession: Conservative Theologians in Germany, England, and America 1815–1866.* Macon, GA: Mercer University Press, 1984.

Conser, Walter H., Jr. "A Conservative Critique of Church and State: The Case of the Tractarians and Neo-Lutherans." *Journal of Church and State* 25 (1983): 323–41.

"The Constitution on the Sacred Liturgy" (*Sacrosanctum Concilium*). Pages 1–282 in *Vatican Council II: The Conciliar and Post Conciliar Documents.* Rev. ed. Vatican Collection Series. Edited by Austin Flannery, O.P. Northport, NY: Costello Publishing, 1988.

Cooke, Bernard. *Ministry to Word and Sacraments: History and Theology.* Philadelphia: Fortress, 1976.

Cyprian of Carthage. *The Letters of St. Cyprian of Carthage: Volume IV* (Letters 67–82).

In vol. 47 of Ancient Christian Writers. Translated and annotated by G. W. Clarke. New York: Newman Press, 1989.

"Dogmatic Constitution on the Church" (*Lumen Gentium*). Pages 350–426 in *Vatican Council II: The Conciliar and Post Conciliar Documents*. Rev. ed. Vatican Collection Series. Edited by Austin Flannery, O.P. Northport, NY: Costello Publishing, 1988.

Dulles, Avery. *Models of the Church*. Garden City, NY: Doubleday, 1974.

Edwards, Mark U. Jr. *Printing, Propaganda, and Martin Luther*. Berkeley: University of California Press, 1994.

Empie, Paul C., and T. Austin Murphy, eds. *Eucharist and Ministry: Lutherans and Catholics in Dialogue IV*. Minneapolis: Augsburg, 1979.

Erb, Jörg. "Wilhelm Löhe." In *Die Wolke der Zeugen: Lesebuch zu einem evangelischen Namenkalender*. Volume 2. 2d ed. Kassel: Johannes Stauda-Verlag, 1957.

Erb, Peter C., ed. *Pietists: Selected Writings*. The Classics of Western Spirituality. Introduction by Peter C. Erb. Preface by F. Ernest Stoeffler. New York: Paulist Press, 1983.

Fagerberg, Holsten. *Bekenntnis, Kirche und Amt in der deutschen konfessionellen Theologie des 19. Jahrhunderts*. Uppsala: Almqvist & Wiksells Boktryckeri, 1952.

Fagerberg, Holsten. "Amt/Ämter/Amtverständnis VII." Pages 574–93 in volume 2 of *Theologische Realenzyklopädie*. Edited by Gerhard Krause and Gerhard Müller. Berlin and New York: Walter de Gruyter, 1977– .

Fahey, Michael A. "Church." Pages 3–74 in volume 2 of *Systematic Theology: Roman Catholic Perspectives*. 2 vols. Edited by Francis Schüssler Fiorenza and John P. Galvin. Minneapolis: Fortress, 1991.

Fiorenza, Francis Schüssler, and John P. Galvin, eds. *Systematic Theology: Roman Catholic Perspectives*. 2 vols. Minneapolis: Fortress, 1991.

Flannery, Austin O.P., ed. *Vatican Council II: The Conciliar and Post Conciliar Documents*. Rev. ed. Vatican Collection Series. Northport, NY: Costello Publishing, 1988.

Ford, David F., ed. *The Modern Theologians: An Introduction to Christian Theology in the Twentieth Century*. 2d ed. Oxford: Blackwell, 1997.

Forde, Gerhard. "The Christian Life." Pages 391–469 in volume 2 of *Christian Dogmatics*. 2 vols. Edited by Carl E. Braaten and Robert W. Jenson. Philadelphia: Fortress, 1984.

Francke, August Hermann. "Projekt zu einem Seminario universali, 1701." Pages 108–15 in *August Hermann Francke: Werke in Auswahl*. Edited by Erhard Peschke. Berlin: Luther-Verlag, 1969.

Ganzert, Klaus. "Einleitung." In *GW* I: 15–240.

Ganzert, Klaus, ed. "Erläuterungen." In *Gesammelte Werke*. 7 vols. Neuendettelsau: Freimund-Verlag, 1951–86.

Ganzert, Klaus. *Vom Heiligtum her*. Neuendettelsau: Freimund-Verlag, 1950.

Ganzert, Klaus. *Zucht aus Liebe: Kirchenzucht bei Wilhelm Löhe*. Neuendettelsau: Freimund-Verlag, 1949.

Garrett, James Leo, Jr. *Systematic Theology: Biblical, Historical, and Evangelical*. 2 vols. Grand Rapids: Eerdmans, 1990–95.

George, Martin. "In der Kirche leben: Eine Gegenüberstellung der Ekklesiologie

Wilhelm Löhes und Aleksej Chomjakovs." *Kerygma und Dogma* 31 (1985): 212–48.
Goeser, Robert. "Whither Lutheranism?" *Lutheran Quarterly* n.s., 1 (1987): 40–53.
Grane, Leif. *The Augsburg Confession: A Commentary.* Translated by John H. Rasmussen. Minneapolis: Augsburg, 1987.
Gritsch, Eric W. *Fortress Introduction to Lutheranism.* Minneapolis: Fortress, 1994.
Hall, Fred Perry. "The Lutheran Doctrine of the Holy Spirit in the Sixteenth Century: Developments to the 'Formula of Concord.'" Ph.D. diss., Fuller Theological Seminary, 1993.
Harrisville, Roy A. *Ministry in Crisis: Changing Perspectives on Ordination and the Priesthood of All Believers.* Minneapolis: Augsburg, 1987.
Hebart, Siegfried. *Wilhelm Löhe's Lehre von der Kirche, ihrem Amt und Regiment: Ein Beitrag zur Geschichte der Theologie im 19. Jahrhundert.* Neuendettelsau: Freimund-Verlag, 1939.
Hefner, Philip. "The Church." Pages 179–247 in volume 2 of *Christian Dogmatics.* 2 vols. Edited by Carl E. Braaten and Robert W. Jenson. Philadelphia: Fortress, 1984.
Hefner, Philip. "The Creation." Pages 265–357 in volume 1 of *Christian Dogmatics.* 2 vols. Edited by Carl E. Braaten and Robert W. Jenson. Philadelphia: Fortress, 1984.
Heintzen, Erich Hugo. "Wilhelm Loehe and the Missouri Synod, 1841–1853." Ph.D. diss., University of Illinois (Urbana), 1964.
Heubach, Joachim. "Das Verständnis des Schlüsselamtes bei Löhe, Kliefoth, und Vilmar." Pages 313–24 in *Bekenntnis zur Kirche: Festgabe für Ernst Sommerlath zum 70. Geburtstag.* Edited by Ernst-Heinz Amberg and Ulrich Kühn. Berlin: Evangelische Verlagsanstalt, [1960].
Heuer, Ansgar. "Function der Kirche: Widerstände bayerischer Lutheraner gegen Wicherns Konzept." Pages 165–69 in *Reform von Kirche und Gesellschaft.* Edited by Hans Christoph von Hase and Peter Meinhold. Stuttgart: Evangelisches Verlagswerk, 1973.
Hodgson, Peter C., and Robert C. Williams. "The Church." Pages 223–47 in *Christian Theology: An Introduction to Its Traditions and Tasks.* 2d. ed., rev. and enl. Edited by Peter C. Hodgson and Robert H. King. Philadelphia: Fortress, 1985.
Hodgson, Peter C., and Robert H. King, eds. *Christian Theology: An Introduction to Its Traditions and Tasks.* 2d. ed., rev. and enl. Philadelphia: Fortress, 1985.
Hodgson, Peter C. *Winds of the Spirit: A Constructive Christian Theology.* Louisville: Westminster John Knox, 1994.
Hollaz, David. *Examen theologicum acroamaticum.* 2 vols. Stargard, 1707; reprint, Darmstadt: Wissenschaftliche Buchgesellschaft, 1971.
Holm, Bernard. "The Work of the Spirit: The Reformation to the Present." Pages 99–135 in *The Holy Spirit in the Life of the Church: From Biblical Times to the Present.* Edited by Paul D. Opsahl. Minneapolis: Augsburg, 1978.
Hommel, Hildebrecht. "Die Tagebücher von Friderich Hommel (geb. 1813) 1828–1892: Aus dem Kreis der 'Erweckten' um Wilhelm Löhe." Pages 245–85 in *Pietismus in Gestalten und Wirkungen.* Edited by Heinrich Bornkamm, Friedrich Heyer, and Alfred Schindler. Bielefeld: Luther-Verlag, 1975.
Jeanrond, Werner G. "Hans Küng." Pages 162–78 in *The Modern Theologians: An*

Introduction to Christian Theology in the Twentieth Century. 2d ed. Edited by David F. Ford. Oxford: Blackwell, 1997.

Jenson, Robert W. "The Means of Grace—Part 2: The Sacraments." Pages 289–389 in volume 2 of *Christian Dogmatics.* 2 vols. Edited by Carl E. Braaten and Robert W. Jenson. Philadelphia: Fortress, 1984.

Kantzenbach, Friedrich Wilhelm. "Die 'befreundeten Gegner': Ekklesiologische Konzepte rund um Wilhelm Löhe." *Zeitschrift für bayerische Kirchengeschichte* 44 (1975): 114–42.

Kantzenbach, Friedrich Wilhelm. "Persönlichkeit und Zeitgenosse." Pages 39–68 in *Wilhelm Löhe —Anstöße für die Zeit.* Edited by Friedrich Wilhelm Kantzenbach. Neuendettelsau: Freimund-Verlag, 1972.

Kantzenbach, Friedrich Wilhelm. "Wilhelm Löhe (1808–1872)." Pages 174–89 in volume 2 of *Klassiker der Theologie.* 2 vols. Edited by Heinrich Fries and Georg Kretschmar. Munich: Verlag C. H. Beck, 1983.

Kantzenbach, Friedrich Wilhelm. "Wilhelm Löhe, Frankens Grosser Lutheraner." In *Evangelischer Geist und Glaube im neuzeitlichen Bayern.* Munich: C. H. Beck'sche Verlagsbuchhandlung, 1980.

Kantzenbach, Friedrich Wilhelm. *Gestalten und Typen des Neuluthertums: Beiträge zur Erforschung des Neokonfessionalismus im 19. Jahrhundert.* Gütersloh: Verlagshaus Gerd Mohn, 1968.

Kantzenbach, Friedrich Wilhelm. "Wilhelm Löhe als organischer Denker (Zum Verständnis seiner theologischen Entwicklung)." *Zeitschrift für bayerische Kirchengeschichte* 31 (1961): 80–104.

Kantzenbach, Friedrich Wilhelm. "Wilhelm Löhes Stellung in der Frömmigkeitsgeschichte." *Zeitschrift für bayerische Kirchengeschichte* 41 (1972): 38–62.

Kantzenbach, Friedrich Wilhelm. "Zwei unbekannte Löhe-Briefe als Dokumente seiner kirchlichen Einstellung 1835." *Zeitschrift für bayerische Kirchengeschichte* 41 (1972): 63–67.

Kantzenbach, Friedrich Wilhelm. *Zwischen Erweckung und Restauration.* Gladbeck: Schriftenmissions-Verlag, 1967.

Kantzenbach, Friedrich Wilhelm, ed. *Wilhelm Löhe—Anstöße für die Zeit.* Neuendettelsau: Freimund-Verlag, 1972.

Karotemprel, S. et al., eds. *Following Christ in Mission: A Foundational Course in Missiology.* Boston: Pauline Books and Media, 1996.

Keller, Rudolf. "August Vilmar und Wilhelm Löhe: Historische Distanz und Nähe der Zeitgenossen im Blick auf ihr Amtsverständnis." *Kerygma und Dogma* 39 (1993): 202–23.

Keller, Rudolf. "Reformatorische Wurzeln der Amtslehre von Wilhelm Löhe." Pages 106–24 in *Unter einem Christus sein und streiten: Festschrift zum 70. Geburtstag von Friedrich Wilhelm Hopf, D.D.* Edited by Jobst Schöne and Volker Stolle. Erlangen: Verlag der Evangelisch-Lutherischen Mission, 1980.

Keller, Rudolf. "Wilhelm Löhe im Spiegel seiner Briefe: Zum Abschluß von Löhes Gesammelten Werken." *Zeitschrift für bayerische Kirchengeschichte* 56 (1987): 261–83.

Keller, Rudolf. "Wilhelm Löhe und Carl Eichhorn: Ein unbekannter Brief aus dem Jahr 1851." *Zeitschrift für bayerische Kirchengeschichte* 58 (1989): 199–208.

Klein, Leonard R. "Evangelical Catholic: 'Why Are You Guys So Negative?' II." *Lutheran Forum* 28 (Advent 1994): 5–7.

Klein, Leonard R. "If the Ministry Is Catholic: A View from Inside the Parish." *Dialog* 27 (1988): 34–39.

Klein, Leonard R. "An Unbearable Lightness of Being." *Lutheran Forum* 28 (Reformation 1994): 4–6.

Koenig, Richard. "The New Lutheran Church: The Gift of Augustana." *Christian Century* 104 (1987): 555–58.

Kolden, Marc. "Luther on Vocation." *Word and World* 3 (1983): 382–90.

Korby, Kenneth Frederick. "The Theology of Pastoral Care in Wilhelm Löhe with Special Attention to the Function of the Liturgy and the Laity." Th.D. diss., Chicago: Lutheran School of Theology, 1976.

Korby, Kenneth F. "Theoretiker und Praktiker der Seelsorge." Pages 137–47 in *Wilhelm Löhe—Anstöße für die Zeit*. Edited by Friedrich Wilhelm Kantzenbach. Neuendettelsau: Freimund-Verlag, 1972.

Kressel, Hans. *Wilhelm Löhe als Katechet und als Seelsorger*. Neuendettelsau: Freimund-Verlag, 1955.

Kreßel, Hans. *Wilhelm Löhe als Prediger*. Gütersloh: C. Bertelsmann Verlag, 1929.

Kreßel, Hans. *Wilhelm Löhe, der lutherische Christenmensch: ein Charakterbild*. Berlin: Lutherisches Verlagshaus, 1960.

Kreßel, Hans. *Wilhelm Löhe: Ein Lebensbild*. Erlangen: Martin Luther-Verlag, 1954.

Krimm, Herbert. "Wilhelm Löhe und Johann Hinrich Wichern: Vergleichende Betrachtung anläßlich der 150. Wiederkehr ihrer Geburtstage." Pages 14–24 in *Diakonie der Kirche*. Edited by Herbert Krimm, Walter Künneth, and B. Dyroff. Nürnberg: Landesverband der inneren Mission in Bayern, 1958.

Krodel, Gerhard. *Acts*. Augsburg Commentary on the New Testament. Minneapolis: Augsburg, 1986.

Küng, Hans. *The Church*. Garden City, NY: Image Books, 1976.

Kuhr, Georg. "Briefwechsel des Bürgermeister Johann Merkel in Nürnberg mit Wilhelm Löhe 1835–1837." *Zeitschrift für bayerische Kirchengeschichte* 41 (1972): 68–121.

Lathrop, Gordon W. *Holy Things: A Liturgical Theology*. Minneapolis: Fortress, 1993.

Lauerer, Hans. *Die Diakonissenanstalt Neuendettelsau aus Geschichte und Gegenwart*. Neuendettelsau: Verlag der Buchhandlung der Diakonissenanstalt, 1924.

Loesche, Georg. *Geschichte des Protestantismus im vormaligen und im neuen Österreich*. 3d ed. Leipzig: Julius Klinkhardt, 1930.

Löser, Werner. "Church." Pages 99–101 in *Handbook of Catholic Theology*. Edited by Wolfgang Beinert and Francis Schüssler Fiorenza. New York: Crossroad, 1995.

Lotze, D. Ernst. *Erinnerungen an Wilhelm Löhe*. Neuendettelsau: Verlag der Diakonissenanstalt Neuendettelsau, 1956.

Luther, Martin. "The Blessed Sacrament of the Holy and True Body of Christ, and the Brotherhoods." In LW 35: 45–73.

Luther, Martin. *Confession Concerning Christ's Supper*. In LW 37: 151–372.

Luther, Martin. *Lectures on Galatians (1535)*. In LW 26–27.

Luther, Martin. *On the Councils and the Church*. In LW 41: 3–178.

Luther, Martin. *The Private Mass and the Consecration of Priests*. In LW 38: 139–214.

Luther, Martin. *The Sermon on the Mount.* In LW 21: 1–294.

"Lutheran Church—Missouri Synod." Pages 131–41 in *Churches Respond to BEM: Official Responses to the "Baptism, Eucharist and Ministry" Text.* Vol. 3. Edited by Max Thurian. Geneva: World Council of Churches, 1987.

Marshall, Bruce D. "Why Bother with the Church?" *Christian Century* 113 (24 January 1996): 74–76.

Maurer, Wilhelm. *Historical Commentary on the Augsburg Confession.* Translated by H. George Anderson. Philadelphia: Fortress, 1986.

Maurer, Wilhelm. "Wilhelm Löhe und der römische Katholizismus." Pages 69–88 in *Wilhelm Löhe—Anstöße für die Zeit.* Edited by Friedrich Wilhelm Kantzenbach. Neuendettelsau: Freimund-Verlag, 1972.

McGrath, Alister E., ed. *The Blackwell Encyclopedia of Modern Christian Thought.* Oxford: Blackwell, 1993.

McNeill, John T. "The Church in Sixteenth-Century Reformed Theology." Pages 169–79 in *Major Themes in the Reformed Tradition.* Edited by Donald K. McKim. Grand Rapids: Eerdmans, 1992. First published in *Journal of Religion* 22 (1942): 251–69.

Meister, Johannes. "Ein Beispiel kirchlicher Gemeinschaft." Pages 119–33 in *Wilhelm Löhe—Anstöße für die Zeit.* Edited by Friedrich Wilhelm Kantzenbach. Neuendettelsau: Freimund-Verlag, 1972.

Merz, Georg. *Das bayerische Luthertum.* München: Verlag des Evangelischen Presse-verbandes für Bayern, 1955.

Messer, Donald E. *Contemporary Images of Christian Ministry.* Nashville: Abingdon, 1989.

Müller, Gerhard. "Die Erlanger Theologische Fakultät und Wilhelm Löhe im Jahr 1849." Pages 242–54 in *Dem Wort Gehorsam: Landesbischof D. Hermann Dietzfelbinger DD. zum 65. Geburtstag.* Edited by Wilhelm Andersen et al. München: Claudius Verlag, 1973.

Müller, Gerhard. "Der Student Wilhelm Löhe und das Amt: Eine Äußerung aus dem Jahr 1829." *Jahrbuch für fränkische Landesforschung* 34–35 (1975): 593–601.

Müller, Gerhard. "Wilhelm Löhe." Pages 71–86 in *Die neueste Zeit* II. Vol. 9 of *Gestalten der Kirchengeschichte.* Edited by Martin Greschat. Stuttgart: Verlag W. Kohlhammer, 1985.

Müller, Gerhard. "Wilhelm Löhes missionarisch-diakonisches Denken und Wirken." Pages 44–52 in *Sichtbare Kirche: Für Heinrich Laag zu seinem 80. Geburtstag.* Edited by Ulrich Fabricius und Rainer Volp. Gütersloh: Verlagshaus Gerd Mohn, 1973.

Müller, Gerhard. "Wilhelm Löhes Theologie zwischen Erweckungsbewegung und Konfessionalismus." *Neue Zeitschrift für Systematische Theologie und Religionsphilosphie* 15 (1973): 1–37.

Neill, Stephen. *A History of Christian Missions.* 2d ed. London: Penguin Books, 1986.

Nelson, E. Clifford "The Doctrine of the Church among American Lutherans in the Nineteenth Century." Pages 202–11 in *Ich glaube eine heilige Kirche: Festschrift für D. Hans Asmussen zum 65. Geburtstag am 21. August 1963.* Edited by Walter Bauer et al. Stuttgart: Evangelisches Verlagswerk and Berlin & Hamburg: Lutherisches Verlagshaus, 1963.

Nichol, Todd W. *All These Lutherans: Three Paths toward a New Lutheran Church*. Minneapolis: Augsburg, [1986].

Nichol, Todd, and Marc Kolden, eds. *Called and Ordained: Lutheran Perspectives on the Office of the Ministry*. Minneapolis: Fortress, 1990.

Nichol, Todd. "Wilhelm Lohe, the Iowa Synod and the Ordained Ministry." *Lutheran Quarterly* n.s., 4 (1990): 11–29.

Niebergall, Alfred. "Abendmahlsfeier III." Pages 287–310 in volume 1 of *Theologische Realenzyklopädie*. Edited by Gerhard Krause and Gerhard Müller. Berlin: Walter de Gruyter, 1977– .

Olson, Oliver K. "How to Be Evangelical and Catholic." *Lutheran Forum* 26 (Pentecost 1992): 56–62.

O'Meara, Thomas Franklin O.P. *Theology of Ministry*. New York: Paulist Press, 1983.

Opsahl, Paul D., ed. *The Holy Spirit in the Life of the Church: From Biblical Times to the Present*. Minneapolis: Augsburg, 1978.

Overton, John H., and Frederic Relton. *The English Church: From the Accession of George I to the End of the Eighteenth Century (1714–1800)*. Volume 7 of A History of the English Church. Edited by W. R.W. Stephens and William Hunt. n.p.: Macmillan, 1906.; reprint, New York: AMS Press, n.d.

Ost, Werner. "Das Bild Luthers und der Reformation bei Wilhelm Löhe (1808–1872)." *Luther 68* (1997): 127–43.

Ost, Werner. "Begegnung im Amt der Kirche." In *Wilhelm Löhe—Anstöße für die Zeit*. Edited by Friedrich Wilhelm Kantzenbach, 151–63. Neuendettelsau: Freimund-Verlag, 1972.

Ost, Werner. *Wilhelm Löhe: Sein Leben und sein Ringen um eine apostolische Kirche*. Neuendettelsau: Freimund-Verlag, 1992.

Ottersberg, Gerhard. "Wilhelm Loehe." *Lutheran Quarterly* 4 (1952): 170–90.

Pannenberg, Wolfhart. *The Apostles' Creed in Light of Today's Questions*. Translated by Margaret Kohl. Philadelphia: Westminster Press, 1972.

"Pastoral Constitution on the Church in the Modern World" (*Gaudium et Spes*). Pages 903–1014 in *Vatican Council II: The Conciliar and Post Conciliar Documents*. Rev. ed. Vatican Collection Series. Ed. Austin Flannery, O.P. Northport, NY: Costello Publishing, 1988.

Penzel, Klaus. "Philip Schaff's Mercersburg Program of 'Evangelical Catholicism.' " *Lutheran Forum* 26 (Pentecost 1992): 34–38.

Peters, Albrecht. "Abendmahl III/4." Pages 131–45 in volume 1 of *Theologische Realenzyklopädie*. Edited by Gerhard Krause and Gerhard Müller. Berlin: Walter de Gruyter, 1977– .

Peters, Ted. *God—The World's Future: Systematic Theology for a Postmodern Era*. Minneapolis: Fortress, 1992.

Pieper, Francis. *Christian Dogmatics*. 3 vols. St. Louis: Concordia, 1950–53.

Piepkorn, Arthur Carl. "What the Symbols Have to Say about the Church." In *The Church: Selected Writings of Arthur Carl Piepkorn*. Edited and introduced by Michael P. Plekon and William S. Wiecher. Afterword by Richard John Neuhaus. Delhi, NY: ALPB Books, 1993.

Pragman, James H. "Ministry in Lutheran Orthodoxy and Pietism." Pages 67–76 in *Called and Ordained: Lutheran Perspectives on the Office of the Ministry*. Edited by

Todd Nichol and Marc Kolden. Minneapolis: Fortress, 1990.

Pragman, James H. *Traditions of Ministry: A History of the Doctrine of the Ministry in Lutheran Theology*. St. Louis: Concordia, 1983.

Prenter, Regin. *Spiritus Creator*. Translated by John M. Jensen. Philadelphia: Muhlenberg Press, 1953.

Rahner, Karl. *Foundations of Christian Faith: An Introduction to the Idea of Christianity*. Translated by William V. Dych. New York: Crossroad, 1989.

Rau, Gerhard. *Pastoraltheologie: Untersuchungen zur Geschichte und Struktur einer Gattung praktischer Theologie*. Munich: Christian Kaiser Verlag, 1970.

Reumann, John. "Ordained Minister and Layman in Lutheranism." Pages 227–82 in *Eucharist and Ministry: Lutherans and Catholics in Dialogue IV*. Edited by Paul C. Empie and T. Austin Murphy. Minneapolis: Augsburg, 1979.

Rice, Edwin Wilbur. *The Sunday School Movement (1780–1917) and the American Sunday-School Union (1817–1917)*. Philadelphia: American Sunday-School Union, 1917; reprint, New York: Arno Press and the *New York Times*, 1971.

Root, Michael. "Ecumenical Theology." Pages 538–54 in *The Modern Theologians: An Introduction to Christian Theology in the Twentieth Century*. 2d. ed. Edited by David F. Ford. Oxford: Blackwell, 1997.

Rusch, William G. "The Doctrine of The Holy Spirit in the Patristic and Medieval Church." Pages 66–98 in *The Holy Spirit in the Life of the Church: From Biblical Times to the Present*. Edited by Paul D. Opsahl. Minneapolis: Augsburg, 1978.

Saarinen, Risto. "The Word of God in Luther's Theology." *Lutheran Quarterly* n.s., 4 (1990): 31–44.

Sanneh, Lamin. "Theology of Mission." Pages 555–74 in *The Modern Theologians: An Introduction to Christian Theology in the Twentieth Century*. 2d. ed. Edited by David F. Ford. Oxford: Blackwell, 1997.

Sasse, Herman. "Zur Frage nach dem Verhältnis von Amt und Gemeinde." Pages 121–30 in *In statu confessionis: Gesammelte Aufsätze*. Edited by Friedrich Wilhelm Hopf. Berlin: Lutherisches Verlagshaus, 1966.

Schaaf, James L. "The Genesis of a Worldwide Mission Thrust." *Lutheran Theological Journal* 22 (1988): 129–34.

Schaaf, James L. "Wilhelm Loehe and the Missouri Synod." *Concordia Historical Institute Quarterly* 45 (1972): 53–67.

Schaaf, James L. "Wilhelm Loehe and the Ohio Synod." *Essays and Reports of the Lutheran Historical Conference* 5 (1974): 85–101.

Schaaf, James L. "Wilhelm Löhe's Relation to the American Church: A Study in the History of Lutheran Mission." D.Theol. diss., Heidelberg, 1961.

Schaaf, James L., ed. and trans. "Introduction" to *Three Books about the Church*, by Wilhelm Löhe. Philadelphia: Fortress, 1969.

Schattauer, Thomas. "Announcement, Confession, and Lord's Supper in the Pastoral-Liturgical Work of Wilhelm Löhe: A Study of Worship and Church Life in the Lutheran Parish at Neuendettelsau, Bavaria, 1837–1872." Ph.D. diss., University of Notre Dame, 1990.

Schattauer, Thomas H. "Sunday Worship at Neuendettelsau under Wilhelm Löhe." *Worship* 59 (1985): 370–84.

Schillebeeckx, Edward. *Ministry: Leadership in the Community of Jesus Christ*. New

York: Crossroad, 1981.

Schlichting, Wolfhart. "Löhe, Johann Konrad Wilhelm (1808–1872)." Pages 421–25 in volume 23 of *Theologische Realenzyklopädie*. Edited by Gerhard Krause and Gerhard Müller. Berlin and New York: Walter de Gruyter, 1977– .

Schmid, Heinrich. *The Doctrinal Theology of the Evangelical Lutheran Church.* Translated by Charles A. Hay and Henry E. Jacobs. Philadelphia: Lutheran Publication Society, 1899.

Schmidt, Martin. *Wort Gottes und Fremdlingschaft: Die Kirche vor dem Auswanderungsproblem des neunzehnten Jahrhunderts.* Erlangen: Martin Luther Verlag, 1953.

Schober, Theodor. "Die Gemeindediakonie." Pages 105–15 in *Wilhelm Löhe—Anstöße für die Zeit.* Edited by Friedrich Wilhelm Kantzenbach. Neuendettelsau: Freimund-Verlag, 1972.

Schober, Theodor. "Wilhelm Löhe 1808–1872: Gestalter der Inneren Mission im Sinne der Lutherischen Kirche." Pages 45–69 in *Helfen in Gottes Namen.* Edited by Karl Leipziger. München: Claudius Verlag, 1986.

Schoenauer, Gerhard. *Kirche lebt vor Ort: Wilhelm Löhes Gemeindeprinzip als Widerspruch gegen kirchlichen Großorganisation.* Stuttgart: Calwer, 1990.

Schulz, Frieder. "Der Beitrag Wilhelm Löhes zur Ausbildung eines evangelischen Eucharistiegebetes." Pages 457–67 in *Gratias Agamus: Studien zum eucharistischen Hochgebet.* Edited by Andreas Heinz und Heinrich Rennings. Freiburg: Herder, 1992.

Schumann, Frank. "Löhe, Johann Konrad Wilhelm." Pages 163–67 in volume 5 of *Biographisch-Bibliographisches Kirchenlexikon.* Edited by Friedrich Wilhelm Bautz and Traugott Bautz. Herzberg: Verlag Traugott Bautz, 1975– .

Schwammberger, Adolf. "Der junge Löhe." Pages 13–36 in *Wilhelm Löhe—Anstöße für die Zeit.* Edited by Friedrich Wilhelm Kantzenbach. Neuendettelsau: Freimund-Verlag, 1972.

Schwarz, Hans. *The Christian Church: Biblical Origin, Historical Transformation, and Potential for the Future.* Minneapolis: Augsburg, 1982.

Schwarz, Hans. *Divine Communication: Word and Sacrament in Biblical, Historical, and Contemporary Perspective.* Philadelphia: Fortress, 1985.

Schwarz, Hans. *True Faith in the True God: An Introduction to Luther's Life and Thought.* Translated by Mark W. Worthing. Minneapolis: Augsburg, 1996.

Senn, Frank C. "Lutheran Movement, but Evangelical, Catholic Church." *Dialog* 30 (1991): 248–50.

Sihvonen, Matti. *Jumalan Kaunein Kukka: Wilhelm Löhen kirkkokäsitys.* Zusammenfassung: "Die schönste Blume Gottes: Wilhelm Löhes Auffassung von der Kirche." Helsinki: n.p., 1980.

Sihvonen, Matti. "Wer sein will, der muß werden." *Homiletisch-Liturgisches Korrespondenzblatt* n.s. 13 (1995–96): 453–58.

Spener, Philip Jacob. *Pia Desideria.* Translated, edited, and with an introduction by Theodore G. Tappert. Philadelphia: Fortress, 1964.

Spener, Philipp Jakob. "From the Spiritual Priesthood: Briefly Described According to the Word of God in Seventy Questions and Answers." Pages 50–64 in *Pietists: Selected Writings.* The Classics of Western Spirituality. Edited with an introduction by Peter C. Erb. Preface by F. Ernest Stoeffler. New

York: Paulist Press, 1983.

Stählin, Adolf. "Löhe, Wilhelm." Pages 576–86 in volume 11 of *Realencyklopädie für protestantische Theologie und Kirche*. 3d ed. 24 vols. Edited by Albert Hauck and Johann J. Herzog. Leipzig: Hinrichs, 1896–1913.

Steck, K. G. "Krafft, Christian." Page 30 in volume 4 of *Religion in Geschichte und Gegenwart*. 3d ed. 7 vols. Edited by K. Galling. Tubingen: J. C. B. Mohr (Paul Siebeck), 1957–65.

Stempel-de Fallois, Anne. "Die Anfänge von Wilhelm Löhes missionarisch-diakonischem Wirken im Bannkreis von Erweckungsbewegung und Konfessionalisierung (1826–1837)." *Pietismus und Neuzeit* 23 (1997): 39–52.

Sugden, Christopher. S.v. "Mission, Theology of." Pages 376–83 in *The Blackwell Encyclopedia of Modern Christian Thought*. Edited by Alister E. McGrath. Oxford: Blackwell, 1993.

Tappert, Theodore G., trans. and ed. *The Book of Concord: The Confessions of the Evangelical Lutheran Church*. Philadelphia: Fortress, 1959.

Thielicke, Helmut. *The Evangelical Faith*. 3 vols. Translated and edited by Geoffrey W. Bromiley. Grand Rapids: Eerdmans, 1974.

Threinen, Norman J. *Like a Mustard Seed: A Centennial History of the Ontario District of Lutheran Church—Canada*. Kitchener, Ontario: Ontario District, 1989.

Thurian, Max, ed. *Churches Respond to BEM: Official Responses to the "Baptism, Eucharist and Ministry" Text*. Vol. 3. Geneva: World Council of Churches, 1987.

Thurneysen, Eduard. *Die Lehre von der Seelsorge*. München: Christian Kaiser Verlag, 1948.

Tietjen, John H. "The Ecclesiology of Wilhelm Loehe." S.T.M. Thesis, Union Theological Seminary, New York, 1954.

Torrance, T. F. *Royal Priesthood*. London: Oliver & Boyd, 1955.

Towns, Elmer L. "Robert Raikes (1735–1811)." Pages 226–35 in *A History of Religious Educators*. Edited by Elmer L. Towns. Grand Rapids: Baker Book House, 1975.

Trillhaas, Wolfgang. "Wilhelm Löhe—ein unbürgerlicher Christ." Pages 144–50 in *Perspektiven und Gestalten des neuzeitlichen Christentums*. Göttingen: Vandenhoeck & Rupprecht, 1975. First published in *Zeitwende* (Hamburg) 25 (1954): 378–84.

Vadakumpadan, Paul, V.D.B., "Ecclesiological Foundation of Mission." Pages 99–117 in *Following Christ in Mission: A Foundational Course in Missiology*. Edited by S. Karotemprel et al. Boston: Pauline Books and Media, 1996.

Vicedom, Georg F. "Mission als Kirche in ihrer Bewegung." Pages 91–102 in *Wilhelm Löhe—Anstöße für die Zeit*. Edited by Friedrich Wilhelm Kantzenbach. Neuendettelsau: Freimund-Verlag, 1972.

Volz, Carl A. "Evangelical Catholics." *Dialog* 30 (1991): 183–84.

Wainwright, Geoffrey. *Doxology: The Praise of God in Worship, Doctrine, and Life*. London: Epworth Press, 1980.

Watson, Philip, "Luther's Doctrine of Vocation." *Scottish Journal of Theology* 2 (1949): 364–77.

Weber, Christian. *Missionstheologie bei Wilhelm Löhe: Aufbruch zur Kirche der Zukunft*. Gütersloh: Gütersloher Verlagshaus, 1996.

Wendel, François. *Calvin: The Origins and Development of His Religious Thought*. Translated by Philip Mairet. London: William Collins & Sons; Fontana Library

Edition, 1965.

Willimon, William. *Acts*. Interpretation: A Bible Commentary for Teaching and Preaching. Atlanta: John Knox, 1988.

Wingren, Gustav. *Luther on Vocation*. Translated by Carl C. Rasmussen. Philadelphia: Muhlenberg Press, 1959.

Wittenberg, Martin. "Geistliches Leben nach Martin Luther und Wilhelm Löhe." *Lutherische Kirche in der Welt* 24 (1977): 37–81.

Wittenberg, Martin. *Wilhelm Löhe und die Juden*. Neuendettelsau: Freimund-Verlag, 1954.

Wittenberg, Martin. "Wilhelm Löhe und die lutherische Kirche." *Lutherische Kirche in der Welt* 19 (1972): 11–35.

Wittenberg, Martin, ed. *Gesammelte Werke: Ergänzungsreihe*. Vol. 1, *Abendmahlspredigten* (1866), by Wilhelm Löhe. Neuendettelsau: Freimund-Verlag, 1991.